PRIVATIZATION

INITIATIVE FOR POLICY DIALOGUE AT COLUMBIA

PRIVATIZATION

Successes and Failures

——

EDITED BY GÉRARD ROLAND

Foreword by Joseph E. Stiglitz

Columbia University Press
NEW YORK

Columbia University Press
Publishers Since 1893
New York   Chichester, West Sussex

Copyright © 2008 Columbia University Press

Library of Congress Cataloging-in-Publication Data

Privatization : successes and failures / edited by
Gérard Roland ; foreword by Joseph E. Stiglitz.
p.   cm.
Includes bibliographical references and index.
ISBN 978-0-231-14160-4 (cloth : alk. paper)—
ISBN 978-0-231-51828-4 (e-book)
1. Privatization.   I. Roland, Gérard, 1954–   II. Title.
HD3580.P737   2008
338.9'25—dc22
2008002449

Columbia University Press books are printed
on permanent and durable acid-free paper.
This book is printed on paper with recycled content.

Printed in the United States of America
c 10 9 8 7 6 5 4 3 2 1

THE INITIATIVE FOR POLICY DIALOGUE AT COLUMBIA

JOSE ANTONIO OCAMPO, JOSEPH E. STIGLITZ, AND SHARI SPIEGEL, SERIES EDITORS

The Initiative for Policy Dialogue (IPD) at Columbia University brings together academics, policy makers, and practitioners from developed and developing countries to address the most pressing issues in economic policy today. IPD is an important part of Columbia's broad program on development and globalization. The Initiative for Policy Dialogue at Columbia: Challenges in Development and Globalization presents the latest academic thinking on a wide range of development topics and lays out alternative policy options and trade-offs. Written in a language accessible to policy makers and students alike, this series is unique in that it both shapes the academic research agenda and furthers the economic policy debate, facilitating a more democratic discussion of development policies.

Privatization—the conversion of state-owned enterprises into privately managed assets—has been one of the most radical and controversial economic policies of the last quarter century. Set in motion in the 1980s as a response to the disappointing performance of publicly owned companies, the privatization wave that began in the West became part of policy prescriptions for developing countries in Asia, Latin America, and Africa and the transition economies in Central and Eastern Europe. But while there have been some successful cases of privatization, it has often turned out to be more disappointing than some of its advocates originally expected, and in some places it has generated great social unrest.

This volume brings together some of the world's foremost experts on the subject of privatization, presenting a comprehensive overview of the issues as well as coverage of specific privatization projects undertaken in different continents, with a sophisticated analysis of the trade-offs involved. It is written not just for academics but also for a far wider audience of policy makers and for all those who want to understand all sides of the privatization debate and want to participate in the search for ways to manage the privatization process to maximize the likelihood of success and enhance sustainable economic growth in developing countries.

For more information about IPD's activities and its upcoming books, visit www.policydialogue.org.

CONTENTS

Foreword   ix
Joseph E. Stiglitz

Acknowledgments   xxi

Joseph E. Stiglitz

This book brings together a set of essays on recent experiences and current thinking in the debate over privatization, the conversion of state-owned assets into privately managed assets. Especially after Ronald Reagan and Margaret Thatcher assumed office in the United States and the United Kingdom, a conventional wisdom developed that private management and ownership was better, in some sense, than public ownership and management: enterprises would be run more efficiently and there would be less opportunity for corruption. The World Bank and the International Monetary Fund (IMF) pushed countries to privatize as much as they could and as fast as they could. Privatization became not only one of the pillars of the "Washington Consensus" but also a condition imposed on countries seeking assistance.

The experiences of the last 15 years have cast a pallor over this unbridled enthusiasm for privatization. As these essays illustrate, a new, more pragmatic consensus is developing—more consistent with economists' normal two-handed stance, "it depends." Privatization has had some successes, but it has also been marked by dramatic failures and disappointments. There are dramatic successes, and failures, in state ownership. The questions being posed today are: When will privatization be successful? And how can the privatization process be managed to maximize the likelihood of success?

Perhaps no subject in development arouses more passions—on both sides—than privatization. The privatization process has been marked by enormous abuses: in many countries a few individuals managed to grab hold of previously state-owned resources for a pittance and become millionaires—or billionaires. In a few years, Russia became a country marked by great inequality, with a Gini coefficient as bad as many in Latin

America. By some estimates, $1.5 trillion in assets were stolen. While Russian became a language commonly spoken in the most fashionable resorts around the world, Russia's pensioners were becoming increasingly impoverished, its educational system, once one of the finest in the world, was decaying, and the Russian economy was declining. Life expectancy was decreasing, while elsewhere (outside of those African countries afflicted with AIDS) it was on the rise.[1]

Elsewhere, I have explained why these results should not have been unexpected.[2] Critics of state-owned enterprises (SOEs) argued that they were subject to corruption; that is, that government officials responsible for managing them often did not act in the interests of those they were supposed to be serving (i.e., the public). This is an example of a classic principal-agent problem. But there is an even more serious principal-agent problem in the privatization process itself. What is at stake is not just the current flow of profits (rents), but the present discounted value of these rents, which is much larger. It follows that incentives for abuse are all the greater. Moreover, there are a variety of ways by which the extent of abuse in the running of SOEs can be monitored and controlled (e.g., by benchmarking), but experience suggests that it may be more difficult to control abuses within the privatization process. Standard remedies have focused on the use of auction processes, but in Russia and elsewhere it became clear that there is ample scope for auctions to be rigged by setting the rules (including "qualifying" bidders).

Other failures of privatization arose when monopolies (especially natural monopolies) were privatized before regulatory and antitrust systems were put into place. The private sector was better at exploiting monopoly power than the government: overall economic efficiency was not enhanced. Monopoly in Mexico's telecommunications sector, the result of a poorly designed privatization, has helped create one of the richest men in the world. High telephone prices, however—a multiple of those in India— have not helped Mexico's development.

But while privatization has deservedly had its critics, so have SOEs. Many have not been run efficiently, and many have created losses that have been a burden on the state—money that could have been used for education or to pursue other developmental objectives. There are instances of corruption. Even advocates of state ownership, like Greece's socialist prime minister, Andrea Papandreou, talked of the challenges of "socializing" the SOEs,[3] making them act in ways that were consistent with social objectives, not just the interests of their managers and workers.

It would be easy to suggest that, after all, it was these abuses that motivated the privatization agenda; but that would be incorrect. Privatization has been pushed even when state-run enterprises have been highly efficient. The IMF pushed Korea to privatize its state-run steel company, which was markedly more efficient than many of the privately run steel companies in the United States. U.S. Republicans pushed for privatization of the social security (pension) program, even though its transaction costs were far lower than those in any private sector firm.[4] In Europe, there was a push for privatization of France's state-run electricity company, even though there was little prospect that a privately run firm would lower costs or increase quality (reliability).

One of the reasons for the drive for privatization is simple-minded ideology—and one of the objectives of the Initiative for Policy Dialogue (IPD) at Columbia University is to expose these ideological biases, ungrounded in theory or empirical evidence. But another of the motivations for the drive for privatization is special interests (greed): even an inefficient privatization process can generate large wealth for a few. Financial markets in the United States looked with hopeful anticipation at the commissions that they would earn from managing the trillions of dollars in the social security system. While pensioners may lose from increased transactions costs, Wall Street would gain.

ECONOMIC THEORY

Simpleminded economic theory suggested that private ownership should be better than state-run enterprises. After all, private ownership provided incentives that were missing under state ownership. Many years ago, Nobel Prize winner Herbert Simon explained what was wrong with this reasoning:[5] few large modern firms are run by owners;[6] there is, in modern parlance, a principal-agent problem. But there is little difference between this principal-agent problem and that facing the government, trying to motivate those entrusted to manage SOEs.[7]

Actually, the flaws in the simplistic reasoning go deeper. The simplistic reasoning is predicated on three hypotheses: (1) profit maximizing (stock market value maximizing) behavior on the part of the firm leads to Pareto efficiency; (2) all shareholders will want the firm to maximize market value; and (3) competitive markets ensure that firms act in a profit-maximizing way; if a firm does not maximize profits, it will be taken over. Someone will buy the firm and change the firm's strategy, and will thereby reap a capital gain. None of these hypotheses is, in fact, correct under general conditions (e.g., when there is imperfect information or incomplete risk markets).

The first hypothesis is, of course, simply Adam Smith's invisible hand conjecture; Arrow and Debreu (1954) showed that it was correct, but only under highly restrictive conditions. Subsequently, Greenwald and Stiglitz (1986) showed that whenever information is imperfect or markets are incomplete, markets are not in general constrained Pareto efficient (i.e., even taking into account that information is costly and that there are transaction costs). Shareholder maximization in particular did not result in (Pareto) efficiency.[8] Grossman and Stiglitz (1980) showed that in the absence of a complete set of securities (markets), different shareholders might want the firm to pursue different objectives. For instance, some might want the firm to maximize stock market value today, but others (especially shareholders who are planning to hold onto the shares for a long time) might argue that most stock market investors are shortsighted and that the firm should focus on long-run profits.

Finally, the takeover mechanism is far from perfect[9]—and it is in managers' interest to keep it that way. They can create information asymmetries and other barriers to takeover.[10] There is ample evidence that firms can and do pursue policies (over extended periods of time) that are not value maximizing.[11]

As an almost immediate corollary of these results, Sappington and Stiglitz (1987) showed that the only conditions under which privatization could be guaranteed to be an effective way of implementing social objectives are precisely the same conditions under which markets are Pareto efficient: there can be no market failures—including no information asymmetries or other market imperfections of the kind discussed by Greenwald and Stiglitz.

In short, the theoretical case for privatization is, at best, weak or nonexistent. It is strongest in the areas in which there is by now a broad consensus—areas like steel or textiles, conventional commodities in which market failures may be more limited. But by the same token, these are precisely the sectors in which abuses can most easily be controlled, appropriate incentives can best be designed, and benchmarks against other firms can most easily be set.

EXAMPLES

In other areas, there are many examples illustrating the difficulties in designing appropriate incentives for private sector owners to act in society's interests. For instance, America's partial privatization of the army—the use of contractors—has not only been extraordinarily expensive, but in many ways it has also proven counterproductive. The contractors have focused on minimizing costs, not on "winning the hearts and minds" of the Iraqis, an objective that was impossible to translate into financial incentives. At the early stages of the Iraq war, when Iraqi unemployment hit 60%, it was important to create employment, but cost minimization by the contractors induced them to bring in workers from Nepal and the Philippines.

Or consider the problems of managing airports. The private owners' profits are derived today largely from commissions on sales at airport stores. The longer individuals spend at the airport, the more the profits are increased. Randomness in security checks—making it necessary for individuals to arrive early to ensure that they catch their planes—is, to the owners, a benefit, even if to both passengers and the airlines it is a huge cost. Their incentives are not well aligned.

Recent anxiety over sovereign funds (funds owned by foreign governments) highlights the view even in liberal advanced industrial countries that ownership matters. These critics have explained why we should be worried about foreign owners, but not about domestic owners. For instance, the United States privatized the United States Enrichment Corporation (USEC), which is responsible for enriching uranium. Low-enriched uranium is used in nuclear power plants, highly enriched uranium is used in atomic bombs, and the same plant can produce either. A private owner's incentive to sell the enriched uranium to the highest bidder is obviously not in the national interest of limiting nuclear proliferation. It would clearly be a concern to sell USEC to Iran or a foreign government interested in obtaining highly enriched uranium. But should it not equally be a concern to sell it to a private domestic firm?[12]

Not only are there many examples, like these, where private management has not worked well, but there are also many examples where public management has. I have already cited several (Korean steel, French electricity). There are others: Malaysia claims that its state-run oil company is able to deliver to its citizens a larger fraction of the value of that country's natural resource than any private company could or would have. The incentive of a private oil company is to minimize what it pays the country from which it takes the resource. There is a natural conflict of interest: the objective of the country should be to maximize the amount the oil company pays. And unfortunately, it is difficult to design and enforce contracts and competitive auction processes that minimize the rents paid to private oil companies. Oil companies have repeatedly tried to get advantageous contracts and, even after signing a contract, to cheat on what they pay—even with seemingly sophisticated governments like that of the state of Alaska.[13]

COMPARING PRIVATE AND PUBLIC MANAGEMENT

The fact that, on average, private firms seem more profitable than public firms does not necessarily mean that private firms are more efficient. The public firms may, for instance, face constraints that the private firms do not; the solution to the problem may not be privatization but changing the constraints. Most importantly, many public firms face tight investment constraints. This comes because many developing countries face tight budget constraints in which the IMF has artificially consolidated state-run enterprises with the rest of the government budget. (It does not do this, at least in the same way, for advanced industrial countries.) These budget constraints mean that there is underinvestment in state-run enterprises; the poor performance is a result of this underinvestment.

Moreover, many public firms are entrusted with distributional objectives. Everyone, no matter how poor, should have access to clean water. This may entail delivering water at below average cost—and even below marginal cost. There is a cross subsidy, but the "water tax" imposed on higher-income individuals may not be enough to offset the losses on the low-income individuals. By contrast, a private profit-maximizing water company will focus on those able to pay more. If there is a limit on the amount of treated water, it may not even supply water to the poor, and in any case, it will not deliver water to anyone at below marginal cost.

It is thus no surprise that water privatizations have been the subject of such controversy. While they have often been justified as providing the resources necessary for the investment to expand service to all, they have not been perceived as doing this.

LEGAL DISPUTES

Some governments, of course, have been worried about these distributional consequences of privatizations and have tried to mitigate the adverse reactions by imposing service requirements. In other cases, governments have demanded that an oil or gas company given a concession make certain minimal investments. But because the incentives of the private firm are not aligned with those of government (or society), they work to circumvent these requirements, giving rise to legal disputes. In the case of the investment requirements, for instance, the foreign firms may use "transfer" pricing schemes—the firm complies at the made-up prices the firm uses (which may even include charges for the time of the corporation's headquarter management). In other cases, the private firm may claim that the government did not comply with implicit or explicit provisions of the concession requirement; for instance, in Bolivia, some of the oil and gas companies claimed that they could not make the necessary investments because of the civil unrest in the country.

When there is actual or suspected bribery in the granting of a concession or in a privatization (suspected because the terms are so unfavorable to the country that it is hard to believe that they are simply a matter of incompetence), successor governments may be under political pressure to rectify the agreement. In some cases, they may have firm legal grounds; for instance, the agreement may not have satisfied certain constitutional provisions.[14]

No contract is ever complete.[15] Governments always have the power to impose regulations or undertake other actions that work to the disadvantage of the private firm. They may impose or enforce tougher environmental laws. If the government has a monopoly on electricity, it can fail to provide electricity on a regular basis, or it can demand higher prices. In short, there is always some leverage to force a renegotiation. More powerful governments, like Russia's, have used that power.

In recent years, many countries have signed bilateral investment agreements that provide for arbitration of these state-investor disputes. But these investment agreements have themselves provided a further argument against privatization. They are conducted by judicial processes that fall far short of the judicial standards expected in modern democracies (e.g., proceedings, and even the rulings, may be secret; there is no appellate process and no clear system of determining precedents).[16]

THE PRIVATIZATION PROCESS

Even if it could be shown that private ownership is more efficient than public ownership, it does not follow that privatization is desirable, for a simple reason: it is very difficult to do privatization well. Of obvious concern is the loss of revenue to the government in the process of privatization; also of concern are the resulting inequality and the undermining of confidence in the market system itself (as well as in democratic political processes). For markets to work well, there must be confidence in the legitimacy of property. If there is a widespread belief that those with wealth have obtained their wealth illegitimately, then there will be pressures for renationalization, or recapturing in some other way wealth that is viewed as having been stolen from society. But if investors believe that there is a significant risk of recapture (either through taxes or some other mechanism), incentives for investing will be attenuated, and incentives for asset stripping will be increased. But that, in turn, will mean that society will not reap many of the benefits that advocates of privatization promise; and as that happens, support for privatization and the market will wane.

NEGATIVE LUMP-SUM TAXES

There is a further problem when privatization occurs in ways that do not maximize government revenues, e.g., in voucher privatizations, in which state wealth is basically given back to citizens. It is equivalent to a negative lump-sum tax.

Governments need money to function, and most revenues are raised through distortionary taxation. Had the government continued to own the assets (assuming that it managed them reasonably well), they would have generated income that would have reduced the need for governments to raise distortionary taxes. Privatization results in the necessity of government to impose more distortionary taxation in the future, reducing the economy's efficiency.

SEQUENCING

Earlier I raised the concern that often privatization has occurred before the appropriate regulatory structure has been put into place. Privatization advocates have urged rapid privatization even before good legal frameworks are put into place, arguing that privatization would create a constituency in favor of the rule of law.[17] This has not turned out to be the case; in fact, there was neither theory nor historical experience in support of this view. On the contrary, once a monopoly has been privatized, it is in the interests of the monopolist to do what he can to maintain that monopoly—and that means using some of his profits to "invest" in the political process to ensure that his monopoly is maintained. By the same token, those who have excelled at stripping assets out of the firm, taking advantage of the lack of good corporate governance laws, have often not been part of the constituency for the establishment of the rule of law. On the contrary, they have benefited from the lack of good corporate governance laws, and they have especially benefited under the regime of capital market liberalization, which has meant that they could strip assets, take their money abroad, and enjoy strong property rights protection there, even as they abuse the property rights of others at home.[18]

Privatization is a more complex subject than simple ideologues—including the advocates of the Washington Consensus—thought a decade ago. The theoretical presumption is, at best, much weaker than they thought. At the same time, the theoretical and practical problems in privatization are greater than they thought.

There have been major government failures, and it is these that have contributed to the demand for privatization. But there have also been major market failures, especially in areas where market and social incentives may markedly differ. And in these areas, ensuring that the private sector acts in accordance with social needs and desires may not be easy.

NOTES

1. For a discussion of these experiences, see, for instance, Stiglitz (1991b, 2000a, 2000b) and Ellerman and Stiglitz (2001).

2. See Stiglitz (2002) and Humphreys, Sachs, and Stiglitz (2007).

3. In personal conversations in 1983, not long after he assumed office.

4. See Orszag and Stiglitz (2001) and references cited there.

5. Simon (1991).

6. Earlier, Berle and Means (1932) referred to the split between ownership and control. This has given rise to the general problem of corporate governance. See, e.g., Stiglitz (1985).

7. For a more extensive discussion of these theoretical issues, see Stiglitz (1991a, 1995).

8. See for instance, Stiglitz (1982a) and Grossman and Hart (1979).

9. See, e.g., Stiglitz (1972) and Grossman and Hart (1980).

10. See Edlin and Stiglitz (1995).

11. See, e.g., Stiglitz (1982b).

12. Indeed, the lack of coincidence of interests became clear, as USEC worked hard to keep out of the market the de-enriched warheads of deactivated Russian warheads; even though doing so had obvious risks for nuclear proliferation. See Stiglitz (2002).

13. See Stiglitz (2006).

14. For instance, many constitutions (such as Mexico's) do not allow the sale of a country's national resources; others (such as Bolivia's) allow the sale of certain resources only after ratification by the legislature. In the case of Bolivia, questions were raised about whether certain privatizations/concessions conformed to this constitutional provision.

15. The recognition of the impossibility of complete contracts—and the consequences of this—is one of the important advances of modern economic theory.

16. Elsewhere, I have written at length concerning the deficiencies of these agreements. See Stiglitz (forthcoming).

17. See, e.g., Shleifer and Vishny (1999).

18. See Hoff and Stiglitz (2004, forthcoming). The disappointments with the privatizations in Russia and elsewhere in the economies in transition has led to a large literature trying to explain the factors that contribute to a successful transition and a successful privatization. Godoy and Stiglitz (2007) argue that privatization played a far less important role than did the underlying institutional reforms. Stiglitz (2000a) argues, in particular, that the lack of good corporate governance meant that there were greater incentives for asset stripping and wealth creation; while Hoff and Stiglitz (2004, forthcoming) argue that the way privatization was conducted actually undermined the creation of a rule of law.

REFERENCES

Arrow, K. and G. Debreu. 1954. "Existence of an Equilibrium for a Competitive Economy." *Econometrica* 22(3): 265–290.

Berle, A. A. and G. C. Means. 1932. *The Modern Corporation and Private Property.* New York: Macmillan.

Edlin, A. and J. E. Stiglitz. 1995. "Discouraging Rivals: Managerial Rent-Seeking and Economic Inefficiencies." *American Economic Review* 85(5): 1301–1312.

Ellerman, D. and J. E. Stiglitz. 2001. "Not Poles Apart: 'Whither Reform?' and 'Whence Reform?'" *The Journal of Policy Reform* 4(4): 325–338.

Godoy, S. and J. E. Stiglitz. 2007. "Growth, Initial Conditions, Law and Speed of Privatization in Transition Countries: 11 Years Later." In *Transition and Beyond: Essays in Honour of Mario Nuti*, ed. S. Estrin, G. W. Kolodko, and M. Uvalić, 89–117. Hampshire, England: Palgrave Macmillan.

Greenwald, B. and J. E. Stiglitz. 1986. "Externalities in Economies with Imperfect Information and Incomplete Markets." *Quarterly Journal of Economics* 101(2): 229–264.

Grossman, S. and O. Hart. 1979. "A Theory of Competitive Equilibrium in Stock Market Economies." *Econometrica* 47(2): 293–329.

——. 1980. "Takeover Bids, the Free-Rider Problem and the Theory of the Corporation." *Bell Journal of Economics* 11(1): 42–64.

Grossman, S. and J. E. Stiglitz. 1977. "On Value Maximization and Alternative Objectives of the Firm." *Journal of Finance* 32(2): 389–402.

——. 1980. "Stockholder Unanimity in the Making of Production and Financial Decisions." *Quarterly Journal of Economics* 94(3): 543–566.

Hoff, K. and J. E. Stiglitz. 2004. "After the Big Bang? Obstacles to the Emergence of the Rule of Law in Post-Communist Societies." *American Economic Review* 94(3): 753–763.

———. Forthcoming. "Exiting a Lawless State." *Economic Journal.*

Humphreys, M., J. Sachs, and J. E. Stiglitz, eds. 2007. *Escaping the Resource Curse.* New York: Columbia University Press.

Orszag, P. and J. E. Stiglitz. 2001. "Rethinking Pension Reform: Ten Myths About Social Security Systems." In *New Ideas About Old Age Security*, ed. R. Holman and J. Stiglitz, 17–56. Washington, DC: World Bank.

Sappington, D. and J. E. Stiglitz. 1987. "Privatization, Information and Incentives." *Journal of Policy Analysis and Management* 6(4): 567–582.

Shleifer, A. and R. Vishny. 1999. *The Grabbing Hand: Government Pathologies and Their Cures.* Cambridge, MA: Harvard University Press.

Simon, H. 1991. "Organizations and Markets." *Journal of Economic Perspectives* 5(2): 25–44.

Stiglitz, J. E. 1972. "Some Aspects of the Pure Theory of Corporate Finance: Bankruptcies and Take-Overs." *Bell Journal of Economics* 3(2): 458–482.

———. 1982a. "The Inefficiency of the Stock Market Equilibrium." *Review of Economic Studies* 49(2): 241–261.

———. 1982b. "Ownership, Control and Efficient Markets: Some Paradoxes in the Theory of Capital Markets." In *Economic Regulation: Essays in Honor of James R. Nelson*, ed. Kenneth D. Boyer and William G. Shepherd, 311–341. East Lansing: Michigan State University Press.

———. 1985. "Credit Markets and the Control of Capital." *Journal of Money, Banking, and Credit* 17(2): 133–152.

———. 1991a. "The Invisible Hand and Modern Welfare Economics." In *Information Strategy and Public Policy*, ed. D. Vines and A. Stevenson, 12–50. Oxford: Basil Blackwell.

———. 1991b. "Some Theoretical Aspects of the Privatization: Applications to Eastern Europe." *Revista di Politica Economica* (December): 179–204.

———. 1995. *Whither Socialism?* Cambridge, MA: MIT Press.

———. 2000a. "Quis custodiet ipsos custodes? Corporate Governance Failures in the Transition." In *Governance, Equity and Global Markets: Proceedings from the Annual Bank Conference on Development Economics in Europe, June 1999*, ed. Pierre-Alain Muet and J. E. Stiglitz, 51–84. Paris: Conseil d'Analyse economique.

———. 2000b. "Whither Reform? Ten Years of Transition." In *Annual World Bank Conference on Economic Development*, ed. B. Pleskovic and J. E. Stiglitz, 27–56. Washington, DC: World Bank.

———. 2002. *Globalization and Its Discontents.* New York: W. W. Norton.

———. 2006. *Making Globalization Work.* New York: W. W. Norton.

———. Forthcoming. "Regulating Multinational Corporations: Towards Principles of Cross-Border Legal Frameworks in a Globalized World Balancing Rights with Responsibilities." *American University International Law Review.*

ACKNOWLEDGMENTS

This book is based on the work of the Privatization Task Force of the Initiative for Policy Dialogue (IPD). IPD is a global network of over 200 economists, researchers, and practitioners committed to furthering understanding of the development process. We would like to thank all task force members, whose participation in provocative and productive dialogues and debates on privatization informed the content of this book.

Special thanks goes to Shari Spiegel, who served as Executive Director of IPD during the course of this project.

We would also like to thank IPD staff members Sheila Chanani, Sarah Green, Siddhartha Gupta, Ariel Schwartz, Lauren Anderson, Shana Hoftsetter, and Sylvia Wu for their work organizing task force meetings and coordinating production of this book. Thanks also to IPD interns Vital Bord and James Giganti for their help in preparing the book.

We thank our editor, Myles Thompson, and the staff of Columbia University Press for bringing this book into publication.

Finally, we are most grateful to the Ford Foundation and the John D. and Catherine T. MacArthur Foundation for funding the work of the Privatization Task Force and supporting IPD activities.

PRIVATIZATION

———

Introduction

Gérard Roland

Privatization of large state-owned enterprises (SOEs) has been one of the most radical new policies of the last quarter century. While many countries engaged in large nationalization programs during the decades following World War II, Margaret Thatcher initiated a policy swing in the other direction in the 1980s by pushing for aggressive privatization of many of the large state-owned British firms. In the following two decades, privatization policies were implemented throughout the planet by left- and right-leaning governments alike. Right-wing governments engaged in privatization in an effort to keep down the size of government, while left-wing governments implemented privatization policies in order to generate revenues and also because they were persuaded of the virtues of markets and competition after being disappointed with the inefficiencies of large state-owned firms. In this way, privatization spread from Europe to Latin America, Asia, and Africa, reaching a high point with the transition from socialism to capitalism following the fall of the Berlin wall. Transition economies were then faced with the task of privatizing their whole economies. In these cases, quite diverse policies were put in place, ranging from a gradual sale of state property to foreign and domestic investors (as was the case in Hungary and Poland) to more radical "mass privatization programs" that resulted in the rapid giveaway of state-owned assets.

Privatization policies generated huge controversies. In many countries, they were criticized for their regressive redistribution effects. State ownership in many countries was used as a tool of redistribution that made it possible to provide cheap water, energy, or transportation for poorer segments of the population. Privatization has thus been associated with cutbacks in redistribution and has stirred popular discontent in many countries. Privatization programs were also systematically criticized for the rents they generated among the acquirers of state assets. Mass privatization in Russia, for example, fell under attack for fabulously enriching a small group of very powerful oligarchs in a very short period. Accusations of corruption and cronyism have stained the reputation of privatization programs in many countries. More blandly, the efficiency improvements expected from privatization have often been hard to detect or altogether absent.

In the spirit of the mission of the Initiative for Policy Dialogue (IPD), this volume, developed by the IPD Privatization Task Force, brings together some of the world's foremost experts on the subject. In the following essays, the contributors present their knowledge about privatization not just for an academic world, but also for a far wider audience. It would be presumptuous to assert that every single topic is covered, but the reader of this volume will find a comprehensive overview of the issues associated with privatization as well as coverage of specific privatization projects undertaken in different continents.

One of the main reasons that privatization programs were first pushed forward is the disappointment with the economic performance of SOEs. The proposition that private ownership is economically more efficient than state ownership might appear uncontroversial to the outside observer, yet this has not been the case in economic theory. In chapter 1, Gérard Roland reviews the economic literature on private and public ownership. Citing in particular general equilibrium theory—one of the central components of economic theory—Roland explains how ownership of firms plays no role at all, provided the firms act in a manner that maximizes their profits. What matters most is that firms face a perfectly competitive environment. In traditional industrial organization theory, there is a priori not much difference between a natural monopoly under government ownership and one under private ownership with government regulation. It has really only been in the last decades—with the advent of contract theory—that one has been able to pin down differences between private and public ownership in the context of imperfect competition. One branch of contract theory, complete contract theory, emphasizes the differences in information under public and private ownership and how they affect the incentives of the firms. Incomplete contract theory attaches great importance to ownership as residual rights of control in situations not provided for by the contract. The picture that emerges is that private ownership gives better incentives to invest, to innovate, to reduce costs, and to reduce inefficient government intervention in firms. On the other hand, this higher efficiency may come at the cost of quality and other socially valuable objectives and may even increase corruption within government. The analysis of the trade-offs between public and private ownership have become more sophisticated. Interestingly, many of the trade-offs pointed to by these theories can now be observed in the actual experience of privatization.

Western Europe is the world leader in privatization revenues, with roughly a third of privatization proceeds over the period from 1977 to 2002. In chapter 2, Bernardo Bortolotti and Valentina Milella remind us that Western Europe also implemented extensive nationalization programs after World War II. Later, when the United Kingdom initiated a large privatization program under Margaret Thatcher, continental Europe also experienced large programs of divestiture of state assets. High privatization revenues are associated, not surprisingly, with high per capita GDP and large and liquid stock markets, but they are also associated with a higher public debt and lower growth. The latter findings suggest that concerns for fiscal imbalances and deterioration of economic performance might have played an important role in triggering privatization programs. Privatization efforts were greater in countries with a majoritarian electoral rule. Interestingly, all else being equal, left-wing governments do not appear to have privatized less than right-wing governments. Surprisingly, there is scant evidence as to the macroeconomic effects of privatization in Western Europe. The only solid evidence is the negative impact of privatization on public debt, not an unexpected result. Privatization is associated with vigorous financial market development. It is also associated with better performance at the level of individual firms. However, the empirical evidence is often not convincing because it compares the performance of firms that were privatized with others that were not. The performance effect might reflect the fact that those enterprises that were privatized were either the most profitable or had the highest potential for profitability. There are as yet too few studies measuring correctly the causal effect of privatization on enterprise performance. An especially interesting finding reported by Bortolotti and Milella is that a large part of privatization deals (at least 30%) led to the divestiture of only a minority of shares of state-owned firms. Governments have kept sizable residual stakes in privatized firms and appear reluctant to lose their control over state assets. These interesting findings are quite recent and will undoubtedly be investigated in future research.

The most spectacular privatization experience is undoubtedly the one that took place in the transition process from socialism to capitalism in Central and Eastern Europe. In chapter 3, Jan Hanousek, Evžen Kočenda, and Jan Svejnar review this historical phenomenon. They insist that privatization policies must be seen within the general context of the transition strategy adopted in each country, including the relative role given to privatization of large state-owned firms and to the development of a new private sector. Economists were deeply divided between those who, on one hand, advocated very rapid privatization relying on giveaway schemes—the so-called mass privatization programs—and those who, on the other hand, advocated a more cautious approach based on the gradual sale of state assets. The literature abounds with various schemes on how to implement one of these two approaches. Countries like Poland, Slovenia, Estonia, and Hungary adopted the gradualist approach. Russia, Ukraine, the Czech Republic, Lithuania, and, to a certain extent, Slovakia adopted forms of mass privatization programs. Within that general classification, the details of the programs varied from country to country. The few studies on the determinants of privatization suggest that the more profitable firms were privatized first, which is consistent with political economic theories of privatization where the sequencing of privatization is used to gather support for further privatization. But there is astonishing diversity in the results of the studies on the effects of privatization on firm performance. Many studies were made very shortly after privatization first occurred. Other studies relied on rather rough measures of ownership, noting only a public-private distinction, and could not measure differences in ownership structure and corporate governance. Many studies suffer from a selection bias alluded to previously. If the more profitable firms were privatized first, superior performance in those firms cannot be causally attributed to privatization. The studies that correct for this bias generally find more modest effects of privatization. The strongest effects seem to be reached in cases where state assets were sold to foreign owners. Employee and manager ownership rarely has a significant positive effect on firm performance—be it total-factor productivity, labor productivity, or profitability. The survey by Hanousek, Kočenda, and Svejnar is quite thorough in terms of the performance variables analyzed.

In chapter 4, John Nellis gives a careful overview of privatization policies and their effects in Africa. African governments have as a rule not wholeheartedly embraced privatization of SOEs. Only a minority of SOEs have been subject to privatization in most African countries. Very little privatization has taken place outside of five countries: South Africa, Ghana, Nigeria, Zambia, and Côte d'Ivoire. Infrastructure is the sector where one finds the largest SOEs in Africa, but privatization in that sector has lagged behind. When privatization does take place, the government usually keeps a significant ownership share. In Africa there is much less evidence regarding the effects of privatization than in Europe, and the evidence, scarce as it is, is at best mixed. Privatization in Côte d'Ivoire seems to have had positive effects on firm performance. A similar picture emerges from Ghana. However there are many caveats. Positive effects seem to be observed only when privatization is associated with enhanced competition and a better quality of regulation. There is also evidence of rent seeking, regulatory capture, reduction in affordability of public services, and a loss of jobs—all of which further feed resentment within the country and increase the reluctance of African governments to go farther along the route of privatization. Nellis argues that even when negative effects are observed, it is not obvious that the counterfactual—namely, the absence of privatization—would have delivered better results. This is due in part to the general deterioration of public services and of the economy in general in many countries. The poor performance of privatization has in the Eastern European context often been attributed to weakness in institutions. This is likely to be even truer in Africa. However, it is not realistic to expect large institutional changes in Africa in the medium run. Nellis explores possible solutions to this problem, such as the outsourcing of institutional provision and the use of offshore commercial arbitration mechanisms or of NGOs to vet transactions. However, few of these solutions are likely to find much political support. It appears that the return of Africa to a path of growth and development cannot, in the near future at least, rely too much on privatization.

Chile was one of the first countries to start a large-scale privatization program. Chile began privatizing in 1974 after the Pinochet coup—many years before Thatcher started privatizing in the United Kingdom. In the late 1980s and early 1990s, many other Latin American countries also engaged in extensive privatization. Bolivia, Peru, Brazil, Argentina, and El Salvador, for example, all launched quite ambitious privatization programs. In chapter 5, Antonio Estache and Lourdes Trujillo detail Latin America's diverse experience with privatization and give a country-by-country account of its privatization policies. Privatization of infrastructure plays a special role in Latin America, pointing to politically delicate distributive issues such as access to water, electricity, and public transportation.

Indeed, it was only under extreme fiscal strain that large infrastructure privatization programs were launched. Because of fears of political backlash, assets were generally leased instead of sold, and concession contracts were widely used. Nonetheless, this has not prevented some forms of political backlash when, on several occasions, electricity or water shortages emerged. What has privatization achieved in Latin America? It seems to have been an effective tool to generate revenues. Moreover, overall we have seen a strong flow of investment in the privatized firms. Privatized firms have in general improved their profitability and productivity. Gains are mostly present in regulated sectors rather than in firms in competitive sectors. Estache and Trujillo also remind us that privatization often had quite a positive impact on the quality of goods and services in the privatized firms. In these cases, improvements were initially welcomed by the population and generated support for privatization. So, why has political support for privatization disappeared in recent years? One reason is that privatization has rarely put an end to subsidies or to government investment in the sectors concerned. While privatization has generated a stock of revenues, it has often not reduced the flow of government expenditures in the privatized sectors. Another reason why support for privatization has subsided relates to the redistribution of gains. Privatization has generated large rents for new owners, but these have not been shared with the general public. There are cases such as the Cochabamba water concession in Bolivia where the poorer segments of the population faced price increases for water. This is due to regulatory failure resulting, most often, from regulatory capture. Despite the organization of competitive bids, in practice there has been very little competition between bidders. The reason for this is not clear but might be due in part to collusion between private firms. It might also be a result of extreme international concentration in some markets. Related to the weakness of competition is the fact that many privatization deals were renegotiated only a few years after the initial privatization took place. This often led to higher prices and more rents for the private owners. Restructuring in privatized firms has led to job losses that have been quite salient. For example, in the international sanitation business (water, sanitation, and solid waste), the same five large companies have been involved in all privatization deals the world over.

Despite its strong economic dynamism, the Asian continent has not been at the forefront of the world's privatization efforts. This is especially the case for South Asia (Bangladesh, India, Pakistan, and Sri Lanka). In chapter 6, Nandini Gupta analyzes the experience of privatization in these countries. India, after its independence, developed a sizable public sector and adopted some form of central planning. But after the collapse of central planning in the former socialist economies, India's reforms efforts also gained strength. However, privatization achievements remained modest. Until very recently, most privatization was partial and consisted of the divestiture of minority shares in public enterprises. Nevertheless, Gupta gives extensive evidence that partial privatization has had positive effects. The floating of shares on the stock market has allowed for improvement in the monitoring of management. Privatization has also had a positive effect on the development of stock markets. Yet, limited capacities of financial markets as well as limited administrative capabilities and political obstacles have constrained the speed of privatization. An important reason for the reluctance of politicians to privatize is that SOEs are used for political patronage. Privatization therefore tends to be slower in provinces where there is sharp political competition.

Finally, the subject of privatization has been very controversial. Chapter 7 summarizes the perspective of one of privatization's most vocal critics, Jomo K. S. He puts the current debate in historical context and cites the literature providing evidence of how the effects of privatization on efficiency may not have been as positive as its advocates claim, even aside from the adverse equity implications. He also shows that, due to these revealed deficiencies, the debate over privatization has evolved over time.

Overall, some common themes emerge from the various contributions to this volume. First of all, partial privatization tends to be more widespread than one might think. Governments in Western Europe, India, and elsewhere are reluctant to relinquish control (partly or fully) over SOEs. This is not surprising but is still an important fact that has emerged from the privatization experience of the last decades. Whether partial privatization has beneficial effects or not depends on many factors, and one should be wary of making sweeping generalizations. Partial privatization may enhance the monitoring of enterprises, but it may also keep alive inefficient forms of government intervention. The efficiency effects of privatization are generally mixed but rarely negative. This is true even though many empirical studies tend to overestimate the efficiency effects due to sample selection bias that has plagued many econometric estimations of privatization. While privatization appears uncontroversial in competitive sectors (even though its effects may be small in relation to the incentive effects of competition), it becomes increasingly complex in more monopolistic sectors where good regulation is a necessary and crucial complement to privatization. However, creating good regulation is easier said than done. There is a real danger (documented in particular in the chapters on Africa and Latin America) that privatization will lead to a form of regulatory capture that generates large rents for the new private owners while creating welfare losses for consumers. This can especially harm the poorest segments of the population that may be hurt strongly by the regressive redistributive effects often generated by privatization. Calling for better regulation might be illusory because it would require a major institutional overhaul that is not in the cards in the immediate future. Thus, policy makers involved with privatization often face a large dilemma: be cautious with privatization and face the continued inefficiencies of SOEs with the prospect of further deteriorations, or be bold and risk major political backlash because of the redistributive effects of privatization, especially if rent seeking and regulatory capture are involved. This is a steep trade-off. However, in the larger context of development, focusing on the restructuring of large SOEs, by privatization and complementary policies, might prove to be misguided. Statist policies of development have focused on the creation of large SOEs in the hope that this would lead developing economies to close the gap between themselves and the developed economies. Liberalization policies based on the Washington Consensus have also focused on these large enterprises, hoping that the transfer of ownership to the private sector would foster accelerated growth in the economy. The privatization policies of particular countries might, however, at best have had second-order effects on growth. Countries that have experienced impressive growth in recent years, such as China, India, and Vietnam, have not had an impressive privatization policy. Rather, they have been able to unleash the productive energies of millions of small entrepreneurs, creating a vibrant and thriving sector of small and medium enterprises that serve both the domestic and the export market. One would hope that international financial organizations pay as much attention to the development of the small private sector as they have to privatization policies in the past.

CHAPTER 1

Private and Public Ownership
in Economic Theory

Gérard Roland

One of the major economic events of the end of the twentieth century was the wave of privatization that, starting in the United Kingdom under Margaret Thatcher, was followed by mass privatization experiences in Russia and other transition countries. To the outsider, it would seem that this change had been prepared by intensive economic research, that it must have been the natural outcome of years of debates in academic circles. Nothing could be further from the truth. Mainstream economic theory, as it stood in the early 1980s, did not have much to say about privatization or even about ownership of firms for that matter. This remains largely true today, however surprising it may seem to noneconomists. There has been much research in the wake of the privatization experiences, but today's economic theory still has big gaps when it comes to theories of ownership.

The main fields of economic theory relevant to the issue of privatization are reviewed below. The core of economic theory, and specifically general equilibrium theory, has surprisingly little to say about ownership. Nevertheless, in a competitive environment of profit-maximizing firms without market failures, there is no efficiency case against private ownership. Traditional industrial organization theory makes the argument for government intervention in the case of natural monopolies (i.e., in sectors where economies of scale are very large). However, it cannot distinguish between the effects of government ownership and the regulation of privately owned firms. It is only with the recent advent of contract theory that more in-depth theoretical research on the effects of private versus publicly regulated firms has been developed. Two strands of literature must be distinguished here. Complete contract theory emphasizes the informational differences stemming from different forms of ownership, while incomplete contract theory emphasizes the residual rights of control associated with different forms of ownership. In both cases, there are many trade-offs to be considered when determining which form of ownership is better for society.

GENERAL EQUILIBRIUM THEORY AND PRIVATIZATION

The core building block of economic theory developed from Léon Walras over 100 years ago to Arrow and Debreu (1954) is the theory of general equilibrium. The theory of general equilibrium answers a basic question of economics first asked over 200 years ago by Adam Smith: How is it possible that the market economy—where millions of economic agents as producers and consumers follow their narrow self-interest (maximize their profits or their satisfaction "utility" as consumers) and act in a totally uncoordinated way—does not lead to utter anarchy and chaos? Why does it, on the contrary, so often lead to very efficient outcomes? According to general equilibrium theory, competitive markets are the answer. Under certain assumptions, the theory states that in a purely competitive setting, where producers have no market power, when producers set their supply decisions in order to maximize their profits, and when consumer demand is driven by utility maximization, the outcome, called a *competitive equilibrium*, is efficient; resources are not wasted and are used in the most efficient manner. The implicit efficient coordination happens via the price system, which conveys information about changes in preferences or technology across different markets. In other words, it is impossible to make one agent better off without making another one worse off. This is what is called a *Pareto optimum*.

There is no mention at all in general equilibrium theory of the role of ownership of firms. The general presumption is that the profit-maximizing firms are under private ownership, but there is no intrinsic reason for them to be private as long as they maximize profits. For example, self-managed firms—on which a whole literature has developed in the light of Yugoslav self-management (Ward, 1967; Vanek, 1977)—are assumed to maximize not profits but income per worker. This leads to decision-making procedures different than those of profit-maximizing firms in terms of the amount of labor and capital used as well as in terms of the volume of production. However, if one assumes that firms under public ownership are instructed to maximize profits, then general equilibrium theory states that the outcome should be the same as if they were privately owned. It is this absence of the role of ownership in general equilibrium theory that has made it possible to develop models of market socialism within the theory (Bardhan and Roemer, 1993). Market socialism, an idea that was popular in the 1970s and 1980s, is an economy where the market is the main allocative device but where ownership of firms is public. It was never entirely implemented in any country, though the Hungarian reform experience has often been significantly associated with the ideas of market socialism, and debates on market socialism were probably the most developed among Hungarian economists.

The absence of the role of ownership in general equilibrium theory can be used in different ways. It clearly does not provide any argument against private ownership. Yet by the same token, it does not offer an argument in favor of public ownership. Advocates of market socialism argue that public ownership brings advantages other than economic efficiency, such as a more equal income distribution (see Bardhan and Roemer, 1993). But general equilibrium theory, in and of itself, does not provide any argument in favor of either private or public ownership.

TRADITIONAL INDUSTRIAL ORGANIZATION

The theory of general equilibrium has not been successfully extended to encompass imperfect competition. Models of imperfect competition are partial equilibrium models in the sense that they analyze only one market or a subset of markets and do not take interactions with other markets into account, as is the case with general equilibrium theory. The best illustration is the most extreme case of imperfect competition: the monopoly. Monopolies tend to produce less and charge higher prices than do firms in a competitive environment, everything else being equal. The situation is inefficient because, in a monopolistic equilibrium, the marginal cost of increasing production is lower than the marginal benefit for consumers. This is the reason why economists have always been obsessed with competition policy and antitrust laws. Markets should be kept competitive to prevent the emergence of monopolies. The problem is that some markets may be characterized by what is called, in economic theory, a "natural monopoly." In such a market, economies of scale are so large that there is no place for more than one firm. Take the case of water or electricity distribution, for example, which involves huge fixed costs in infrastructure to bring electricity or water to factories and private residences. Competition among different producers would involve huge duplication and would considerably increase unit costs of production. Competition would tend to drive out of business all producers except one, who is then in a position to act as a monopoly. In mainstream economic theory, the case of the natural monopoly has provided one of the strongest arguments for public ownership. The idea is that nationalization of sectors operating under conditions of natural monopoly would allow the government to impose pricing and production policies on firms in order to deviate from monopolistic profit maximization and to increase social welfare. This kind of argument was pervasive in the post–World War II economic literature (see, e.g., Lewis, 1949; Meade, 1948; Allais, 1947).[1] Note that this argument is distinct from the traditional and more general "Pigovian" argument for government intervention to correct market failures due to externalities. But that is a different discussion best left for another time.

An important question is, how far do natural monopolies reach? In recent years, economists have reevaluated earlier thinking. For example, while electricity *distribution* may be subject to natural monopoly, it is not the case for electricity *production*, where competition may in fact help reduce prices and costs. This is the kind of thinking that has provided the motivation for European programs to introduce competition in traditional utilities sectors.

While in the case of competitive markets, ownership does not matter for general equilibrium theory, the case of natural monopoly in traditional industrial organization theory provides a compelling argument that government ownership will lead to different—and presumably better, from the point of view of social welfare—allocative outcomes than the laissez-faire market solution. However, by no means does it follow from that argument that government ownership is the only way to improve on laissez-faire. Indeed, why can the government not regulate private monopolies and issue appropriate incentive contracts in order to achieve socially desirable outcomes (Laffont and Tirole, 1993)? Why should it be necessary to nationalize firms? Why not simply issue contracts that will give private monopolies the right incentives?

With appropriate incentive contracts, in-house provision of supply can be replaced by private supply. Thus, concerns that private firms fail to address social goals can be resolved through government contracting and regulation without resorting to government ownership. A key insight of the contracting approach is that under certain conditions, it does not matter whether the government delivers the good or service on its own or whether it contracts the provision to a private supplier. If the government knows exactly what it wants the producer to make, then it can specify this in a contract or a regulation and enforce it. In this case, there is no difference between in-house provision and contracting out. Shleifer (1998) argues that, from the contractual perspective, the argument that government ownership of postal service is necessary to force the delivery of mail to sparsely populated areas, where it would be unprofitable to deliver it privately (Tierney, 1988), is weak. The government can always bind private companies competing for mail delivery concessions to go wherever the government wants, or it can alternatively regulate these companies if market entry is free. Similarly, if the government can describe the products that the monopoly delivers, it can always regulate a private monopoly. Williamson (1985) and Grossman and Hart (1986) also emphasize that the ownership structure does not matter when complete contracts can be written. Thus, once regulation is allowed, the 1940s case for superiority of government ownership disappears. With perfect contracting and regulation, there is no difference between state and private provision of goods and services. We are in a sense back to the case of competitive markets where ownership also did not matter.

Thus, in traditional industrial organization theory, there is no good a priori case for either nationalization or privatization, depending on whether the initial situation is one of private or public ownership. It is important to note, however, that in a monopolistic environment, government intervention of one form or the other is warranted. This point is significant because much of the economic literature on privatization, in particular the contract-theoretic literature, has focused on situations of imperfect competition and monopoly.

CONTRACT AND INCENTIVE THEORY: THE INFORMATIONAL APPROACH

While the introduction of the contracting perspective has cast doubt on the traditional natural monopoly argument for public ownership, it has led to new perspectives in the comparison between public and private ownership. Contract theory has developed in the wake of the introduction of informational asymmetries in economic theory (e.g., Akerlof, Spence, and Stiglitz). Not surprisingly, contract-theoretic analysis of the difference between private and public ownership of monopolies has emphasized the informational differences stemming from different forms of ownership. This has led to a vast literature on the subject.

There are two major ideas in relation to informational asymmetries under public and private ownership. The first one is that government ownership reduces access to firm information for outsiders, namely, stock market participants. This in turn reduces opportunities for monitoring the managers of firms. Thus, monitoring in government firms is poorer, and incentives for efficiency are potentially lower. The second idea emphasizes the difference in information that government has about private and public firms. The main idea here is that the government is less informed about private firms than about public firms, because ownership of the latter gives government privileged access to the accounts of the firm. Because of this difference in information, privatization lowers government's ability to extract rents from firms. A final and related idea is that government is often unable to pre-commit to contractual arrangements. This commitment problem can be more or less severe, depending on how well informed the government is about firms. More information on government-owned firms makes the commitment problem worse. We develop these arguments in greater detail below.

OWNERSHIP AFFECTS THE MONITORING
OF FIRM MANAGERS

A popular criticism of public ownership is that it provides poor incentives to monitor managerial behavior, allowing managers the discretion to pursue personal agendas. This argument is not an obvious one. Managers of government firms are typically accountable to political decision makers. However, it is not obvious that this will lead to managerial discretion. In general, political fortunes might not be very sensitive to overall state enterprise performance. Politicians may thus lack strong incentives to monitor enterprise management. However, some decisions are politically very sensitive. When state budgets are being tightened, when enterprises are losing money, or when the closure of state firms is being considered, state enterprise performance can become a priority on the political agenda. In such situations, managerial discretion in public enterprises may be limited.

Vickers and Yarrow (1991) and Laffont and Tirole (1993) point to a different reason why privatization alters the means of monitoring managerial behavior, namely, capital market pressures. One of the crucial roles of a stock market is to give managers incentives that go beyond those provided by reward schemes based on accounting data.

There are two important arguments in favor of private ownership that are worth examining, the first being the fact that stock prices convey information about the level and quality of managerial investments. This information can be used in contracts between shareholders and managers (remuneration packages may be made sensitive to stock market prices), and it might have further incentive effects via the managerial labor market. Simply put, managers with good reputations for value maximization increase their own market value (Fama, 1980; Holmström, 1982a). The information about the value of the firm conveyed by the stock price disappears when the stock is not valued by the market, as in the case of a pure public firm. In this respect, pure public firms lack the tools for disciplining their managers that are present in private firms.

There are two criticisms of this argument. One is that it is based on an underlying assumption of the "efficient market" view of financial markets. The efficient market hypothesis states that all relevant information about firms is incorporated in the stock market price as soon as it becomes available. This includes information that affects, in one way or another, expectations of future performance. If the efficient market hypothesis is not true, then the information conveyed by stock prices has less value for monitoring purposes (Vickers and Yarrow, 1991). The second criticism is that the government could take control only of a majority of shares and have an active stock market for all remaining shares (Laffont and Tirole, 1993). This might suggest that managerial incentives are not affected when the government takes control as long as shares of the firm are traded on the stock market.

Holmström and Tirole (1991) nevertheless argue that ownership still matters because it affects market liquidity. High government stakes in firms will tend to reduce market liquidity, which will, in turn, lower the incentives of stock market participants to acquire information. The stock price will then be a very garbled measure of managerial performance, which will negatively affect monitoring. But Laffont and Tirole (1993) point out a limitation to the Holmström-Tirole analysis: "it takes for granted that a stock market is an (approximately) optimal institution to induce outsiders to acquire information about the firm's prospects. No such proposition has ever been proved" (p. 642). Even if this were true, liquidity is not necessarily reduced if government-owned firms can issue shares with nonvoting rights. The speculators will still buy and sell such shares and supply useful information about the firm, but they will leave ownership to the government. However, incentives of speculators will be dampened if the government intervenes on stock markets, for example, by selling assets or products to favored groups at artificially low prices. Such intervention may reduce the value of the shares and thus the incentives for speculators to search for information. In this respect, it has consequences similar to those of a reduction in market liquidity.

The second argument in favor of private ownership is that stock market participants may intervene in management through a proxy fight or a takeover. Such interventions will disappear under public ownership. Of course, political takeovers do exist (ministry personnel changes or administration changes), but they tend to be rarer and of a different nature. However, this argument has little relevance in countries where corporate takeovers have played a minor role, which is the case in most countries. Furthermore, takeovers of public utilities are quite rare even during periods of high takeover activity in other industries.

Vickers and Yarrow (1991) point out that the threats of takeover and bankruptcy become especially important in cases of privatization that concern large corporations with numerous shareholders. Dispersed shareholding was actively promoted in privatizations that aimed to widen share ownership, but it created an obvious free-rider problem for shareholder monitoring. The threat of takeover could raise managerial discipline. Vickers and Yarrow (1991) also emphasize the role of competition in improving monitoring possibilities. In particular, competition facilitates performance comparisons, which can generally improve trade-offs between incentives and risk when several managers facing correlated risks are being monitored (Hart, 1983; Holmström, 1982b; Nalebuff and Stiglitz, 1983). Improved information provided by stock markets can then be used to impose stronger incentive contracts on managers.

To summarize, contract theory states that private ownership can deliver better incentives than public ownership. This is possible when stock markets deliver better information on firm performance, which in turn helps design stronger incentive contracts for managers. Thus, the advantage of privatized firms hinges strongly on the efficiency properties of stock markets.

OWNERSHIP AFFECTS GOVERNMENT'S INFORMATION ABOUT FIRMS

Let us now review issues related to the difference in information that government has about private and public firms. Shapiro and Willig (1990) and Schmidt (1990, 1995) analyze the choice between public ownership on one hand and the regulation of a private firm on the other hand. One of the benefits of public ownership is that it allows the government to have more precise information about the firm's cost than it would have under regulation. This means that the firm's management will have lower informational rents under public ownership: a firm with lower than average or expected costs is not as able to pretend that it has higher costs in order to receive higher than necessary compensation to cover its costs and thus receive the informational rent.

The cost of public ownership differs depending on how one views the government's objective function. Shapiro and Willig allow that the government may sometimes be malevolent. The benefit of privatization is that reduced information acts as a constraint on a government that pursues objectives different from efficiency. One would prefer a malevolent government to be hampered by informational limitations and would thus prefer regulation and private ownership over public ownership. Schmidt presumes a benevolent regulator who cannot commit intertemporally to incentive schemes. This lack of commitment dulls the incentives of the manager to reduce costs, because reduction of costs would be less rewarded in the future once it is shown to be feasible. In a government-owned firm, the government has information about the cost structure and will always subsidize costs to implement ex post efficient production levels. This will lead to lower incentives for management to reduce costs. If the firm is privatized, the optimal regulation scheme will lead to better incentives for management to invest in cost-cutting technology. This, however, comes at a price. Where costs turn out to be unexpectedly high, the private firm will strongly reduce its production level, which can hurt society at large. The lack of information associated with private ownership in a sense commits the regulator not to expropriate too much of the firm's investment. Thus, following Schmidt, public ownership decreases managerial incentives to reduce costs but also reduces allocative inefficiency.

The same trade-off is seen in Laffont and Tirole (1993): nationalization decreases managerial investment but reduces allocative inefficiency. Laffont and Tirole also compare a government-owned firm with a regulated private firm. However, the cost and benefit of public ownership are different from Shapiro-Willig and Schmidt. In their setup, privately regulated firms suffer from a conflict of interest between shareholders and regulators. Thus, the cost of private ownership is that the firm's managers must respond to two masters with conflicting objectives. This conflict between regulators and shareholders tends to dilute incentives and yield low-powered managerial incentive schemes.

Taken together, the literature on government's informational advantage in state-owned firms has ambiguous implications for the relative cost efficiency of the public and private sectors.

THE PROBLEM OF GOVERNMENT COMMITMENT

A strong criticism of government ownership is related to government's inability to commit to incentive schemes and long-term contracts. This lack of government commitment is seen as the source of inefficiencies. In particular, when there is lack of commitment, the government may not be able to resist the temptation to renew incentive schemes on the basis of new information it receives about government-owned firms. In that sense, the informational advantage of government ownership mentioned above can be a definite disadvantage.

Two problems arise due to a lack of government commitment, the first being the ratchet effect and the second being the problem of soft budget constraints. In the ratchet effect problem, the lack of government commitment is a source of inefficiency even though the government pursues efficiency objectives, contrary to the Shapiro-Willig theory. In the case of the soft budget constraint problem, rational self-interested private agents can exploit the lack of government commitment to obtain economic rents.

To better understand the ratchet effect, we must look at the work of Berliner (1952), who coined the term while analyzing management behavior in Soviet-type firms. Under central planning, managers were given strong incentives to fulfill their production plans. They were also given bonuses for plan overfulfillment. Nevertheless, managers generally did not overfulfill their plans. The reason was that they were afraid that next year's plan targets would be increased—that is, the plan would be ratcheted up if they used all their capacity. The ratchet effect is a more general incentive problem reaching beyond just central planning. Examples include organizations that spend all of their budget at the end of the year, even on useless items, in order to avoid future budget cuts; workers who shirk responsibility to avoid higher workloads; and so on. Weitzman (1980), Keren, Miller, and Thornton (1983), Bain et al. (1987), and Roland and Szafarz (1990) model the ratchet effect in the context of Soviet planning. Freixas, Guesnerie, and Tirole (1985), Laffont and Tirole (1988,

1993), Hart and Tirole (1988), and Litwack (1993) model the ratchet effect in the framework of contract theory. Roland and Sekkat (2000) show that the ratchet effect will be prevalent when public sector managers do not have outside options and when the government is the main employer in the economy. This would be the case even in a market socialist economy, where managerial incentives are based on profit incentives. The ratchet effect has ceased to be a problem early in the transition process from socialism to capitalism. The very existence of a private sector affects managerial incentives by giving managers the option of leaving the public sector and going to work in the private sector. Also, managers could leave the state sector without leaving their enterprise if the latter is privatized. The introduction of the private sector gives managers incentives to put in high effort, but also gives incentives to the government to commit to its own incentive schemes. As soon as a private sector begins to develop at a sufficient rate, the government's monopsony power over managers disappears, thereby solving the commitment problem at the heart of the ratchet effect. Thus, the ratchet effect will be absent once there is a managerial labor market, and public sector efficiency will be enhanced if managers have the possibility, during their careers, of switching to the private sector. The ratchet effect is thus not a particular problem of government ownership in an economy with widespread government ownership as long as public sector managers can join the private sector.

A more persistent source of inefficiency in public firms stems from less-prosperous firms being allowed to rely on the government for funding. This leads us to the second issue concerning the lack of government commitment: that of soft budget constraints (see Roland, 2000, or Kornai, Maskin, and Roland, 2003, on the literature on soft budget constraints). The soft budget constraint view holds that bankruptcy is not a credible threat to public managers because it is in the interest of the central government to bail them out in the case of financial distress. Because the government is unlikely to allow a large state enterprise to face bankruptcy, the discipline enforced on private firms by the capital markets and the threat of financial distress is less important for state firms. Kornai (1993), Berglof and Roland (1998), and Frydman et al. (2000) suggest that soft budget constraints were a major source of inefficiency in socialist firms. Kornai (1980, 1992) explores the role of soft budget constraints in explaining the emergence and reproduction of shortages, the weakening of price responsiveness of firms, and various other inefficiencies in the socialist economy. Dewatripont and Maskin (1995) see the soft budget constraint as a very general dynamic incentive problem where the funding source—the government or a bank—cannot commit to hold an enterprise to a fixed initial budget and is led to bail it out ex post. Because any prior funds invested in the firm are sunk costs, it is ex post optimal for the funding source to bail the firm out instead of liquidating its activity. The funding source would like to commit ex ante not to bail out a firm, but if it cannot make such a commitment, it is tempted to ex post refinance the firm because the initial injection of funds is sunk. Hardening of budget constraints thus means creating conditions for a credible commitment to not refinance the firm. Precisely because the soft budget constraint is a very general incentive problem, it is not clear why it should apply more to government-owned firms than to private firms. Dewatripont and Maskin (1995) point to decentralization of credit as a major source of hardening of budget constraints. This would explain the difference but would also point to the existence of soft budget constraints in the private sector.

Vickers and Yarrow (1991) and Laffont and Tirole (1993) also point to some difficulties with using the soft budget constraint problem as an argument in the state versus private ownership debate. First, hard budget constraints have, at times, been successfully applied to state enterprises. Public firms can be shut down, although one would expect this to happen less frequently than with private firms. Second, the government has many ways to loosen the budget constraints for private firms, including subsidies, loan guarantees, trade protection, and ultimately nationalization. Regulators do bail out privately regulated firms, for example, by raising allowed prices. Regulators of privatized utility companies in Great Britain are effectively required to ensure that they do not go bankrupt (Vickers and Yarrow, 1991). For these reasons, the soft budget constraint argument does not clearly distinguish between a public enterprise and a privately regulated firm.

INCOMPLETE CONTRACTS AND OWNERSHIP

A simpler but perhaps more natural and powerful way to look at the difference between public and private ownership is to look less at informational differences and more at differences in who has control rights—the emphasis of what is called incomplete contract theory. For example, the difference between in-house government provision and contracting out becomes clear once we recognize that, in many instances, contracts are limited and that the government cannot fully anticipate, specify, regulate, and enforce exactly what it wants. Grossman and Hart (1986), Hart and Moore (1990), and Hart (1995) point out that ownership of assets gives the owner control and bargaining power in situations where contracts do not specify what has to be done. Different control rights are affected by differences in objectives. They are affected not only by differences in costs of government intervention and differences in incentives to innovate and invest but also by differences in the incentives for corruption.

DIFFERENCE IN OBJECTIVES

One of the criticisms of government ownership is based on the fact that the government's objectives are multiple and fuzzy and can change over time; this in turn exacerbates the problem of managerial control in public enterprises. A government naturally has objectives other than profit maximization. A government must prevent monopoly pricing, control quality, reduce negative externalities, encourage sectoral policies and national independence, and concentrate on investment and employment in recessions. Thus, government ownership of firms is problematic when defining the goals of the firms. Moreover, governments are subject to pressures from interest groups, which want to manipulate public enterprise behavior to enhance their own welfare. Further, government objectives may change from one administration to the next.

The problem with many government objectives is that, unlike profit maximization, they are hard to contract upon. Also, because emphasis on different objectives may change between successive administrations, legal limitations on the power to commit must be introduced. This could explain why it is often felt that regulators have fuzzy and time-varying objectives. Further complications arise if the government's goals are inconsistent with efficiency, inconsistent with maximizing social welfare, or even malevolent. Yet even in private firms, things are not so simple: managers also pursue their private agendas, and corporate governance arrangements are imperfect. Nevertheless, the objectives of the owners are relatively simpler than governmental objectives.

However, it would be an oversimplification to assume that privatization entails the transfer of all decision-making authority to private hands. In reality, government intervenes in the decisions made by firms through regulation. Government goals that are complex and vary over time will also affect the behavior of regulated firms. Similarly, interest groups successfully lobby governments to control regulated firms to their benefit.

Laffont and Tirole (1993) look at the case of contingencies that are not covered by the contract between the government and the firm. Residual rights of control determine who can dispose of the assets in such contingencies. They list four ways in which ownership will matter.

First, a benefit of public ownership is that the government can impose socially desirable adjustments to the firm in unforeseen contingencies, while it must bargain with a private firm under the same circumstances. Milgrom and Roberts (1990) and Holmström and Tirole (1989) point out that if bargaining takes place under asymmetric information, inefficiencies will typically result. This argument is similar to the argument of Williamson (1985) that, under identical conditions, when it is impossible to write complete contracts with the private owners, state enterprises will function at least as well as private firms, and "selective intervention" by the government in the case of unforeseen contingencies will actually make public ownership preferable.

Laffont and Tirole's second point regarding ownership explains how public ownership can lead to expropriation of managerial investments. Suppose the manager can initially make a nonverifiable investment that permits cost reduction and profit enhancement later. A nonverifiable action is an action that can be observed but cannot be verified in front of the courts. However, in a government-owned firm, the government could reallocate such an investment for an alternative use for which the manager is not rewarded. Such reallocation reduces the manager's incentive to invest and leads to a situation in which private ownership is superior (even though ex post the assets are not used in a socially optimal way).

Third, Laffont and Tirole discuss how the divergence of objectives between government and shareholders may explain why the shareholders of public utilities in the United States have the right of control over their managers' incentive schemes. The explanation they give is that it is difficult for the government and the shareholders to agree contractually on the details of managerial incentive schemes. Thus, if the government has residual rights of control over managerial incentive schemes, it might not induce managers to properly maintain the shareholders' assets and to make profit-maximizing investment decisions. This is an argument similar to Laffont and Tirole's second point—expropriation might occur if private shareholders leave residual rights of control to the government.

Fourth, the case against public ownership might be even stronger when the government does not maximize social welfare. Government decision making can be captured by interest groups; this, along with an increase in the power of a nonbenevolent government through nationalization, could in fact end up reducing welfare. Laffont and Tirole (1993) give the example of the pressure governments put on public enterprises in the military sector to not compete with private firms in civilian markets, even if the public firms have idle capacity and the machinery and expertise to produce the civilian goods.

GOVERNMENT INTERVENTION IN FIRM OPERATION

When governments or politicians pursue goals different from economic efficiency, they have incentives to intervene in firms in order to achieve these objectives. On their own, firm managers would tend to pursue efficiency objectives, but when governments intervene, they may be prevented from doing so. Thus, government power to intervene is a direct source of inefficiency. Governments can intervene in the operations of both public and private firms. However, the government's transaction costs of intervening in production arrangements and other decisions of the firm are greater when firms are privately owned. Thus, to the extent that government intervention has greater costs than benefits, private ownership is preferable to public ownership.

Sappington and Stiglitz (1987) argue that privatization affects the transaction costs of government intervention in enterprise decision making. For example, subsidization of loss-making enterprises is easier under public ownership, and cross-subsidies that serve political and distributional goals are often a feature of public enterprise pricing. Where monopoly power or other externalities are accruing, intervention by government is likely to be desirable on welfare grounds, and regulation is necessary. When a firm is both privatized and regulated, much depends upon the nature of the relationship between the firm and the government. For example, if the firm chooses to reduce costs by way of sunk investment expenditures, it runs the risk that the government might opportunistically decide to enforce low prices without allowing the firm to recover its costs, and this can lead to underinvestment. Therefore, the welfare effects of privatizing monopolies depend significantly upon how well regulatory problems are overcome. Regulation might, for example, reinstate the problem of public officials acting in their own interest—the very problem that privatization was intended to sidestep.

Shleifer and Vishny (1994) use the incomplete contract approach to emphasize the difference in control rights of government in public and privatized firms. Differences in ownership imply not only differences in cash flow rights, but also differences in control rights. When the government has control rights over the firm, it has power over the manager. Politicians derive political benefits from providing jobs to the unemployed; therefore they must persuade managers to hire excess labor by paying them a transfer. In a private firm, it is more costly to pay managers to convince them to hire excess labor and make inefficient decisions. The result is reduced levels of excess employment and increased net transfers to the firm. Thus, while government intervention is possible in private firms, it is more costly and thus less likely to accrue than in government-controlled firms. The government can more easily use its power to force public firms to hire excess labor. Allocation of cash flow rights does not influence the solution when control rights over the firm belong to the managers. This result suggests that the transfer of control rights is what counts most.

OWNERSHIP AND THE INCENTIVES FOR INNOVATION

Hart, Shleifer, and Vishny (1997) use the incomplete contracts approach to emphasize the effects of the difference in control rights of government in public and privatized firms. They analyze the difference between the provision of public goods by a private or by a public firm, examining prisons, police, schools, health care, and foreign policy. The manager of a firm can implement cost reductions and quality innovations. Under private ownership, the manager is fully the residual claimant of reductions in costs. However, it is in the manager's interest to renegotiate with the government over the quality innovation because it is not part of the initial contract. Under public ownership, the manager needs the approval of the government to implement both innovations. Moreover, the government can replace the manager and appropriate a fraction of the returns on his ideas. Thus, private provision will tend to excessively reduce costs, at the expense of quality, and to underinvest in quality innovation. Public provision will lead to underinvestment in both cost reduction and quality innovation because of blunted incentives. Yet in some cases, Hart, Shleifer, and Vishny argue that the quality spillover is strong enough so that public provision is preferable. This seems to be the case for prisons. In other instances, this spillover is not strong, and private provision is better—a finding that conforms to our intuition concerning public procurements. In still other cases, such as schools and health care, conclusions are less obvious.

Shleifer (1998) argues that the case for government production, even in situations where cost reduction does have an adverse effect on noncontractible quality, becomes even weaker when consumers buy the good and service themselves, when there is enough competition between suppliers so that consumers have some choice, and when reputation building is important.

Moreover, even when these conditions are not fulfilled, there is a private alternative to profit-maximizing suppliers that attenuates the incentives for cost reduction via reducing quality. This is the not-for-profit provision. Glaeser and Shleifer (1998) show that entrepreneurial not-for-profit firms can be more efficient than the government and the for-profit private suppliers precisely in the situations described above. Schools, universities, hospitals, day care centers, and other firms that might in principle raise concerns about private provision often have a not-for-profit status. Not-for-profit firms care about their perquisites, improving the lives of their employees, and increasing quality (Weisbrod, 1988). Presumably, the not-for-profit firms value the perquisites less than the for-profit firms value profits. Thus, a not-for-profit firm may care about quality for its own sake, which decreases its incentives to make quality-reducing cost cuts.

There are some situations, however, where innovation and cost efficiency are not crucial and contractual incompleteness comes from the government's not knowing exactly what it wants and its need for freedom to change its mind quickly. In these situations, there is a case for government ownership based on cost savings (Shleifer, 1998). The best examples are nationalization or heavy regulation in wartime.

OWNERSHIP AND CORRUPTION

An important issue that has often been neglected in debates on public versus private ownership is corruption. Privatization in transition countries and emerging market economies designed to improve efficiency has also often, though not necessarily, led to corruption scandals. This was the case in Russia, the Czech Republic, and Argentina.

A paper by Glaeser (2001) sheds interesting light on these issues. Glaeser argues that the history of American cities provides an example of how the transition from private to public ownership helped reduce bribery and corruption. In nineteenth-century America, private firms that sold to or bought from the government would frequently bribe government officials to get favorable prices. Glaeser focuses on three types of corruption:

underpricing of inputs bought from the government, overpricing of out-
puts sold to the government, and the perversion of attempts to use subsidies to internalize externalities.

Public ownership eliminates the first two problems because the public
manager has only weak incentives and will not risk prison for profits that
he does not himself enjoy. Public ownership does not, however, eradicate
corruption. When firms are government owned, the corruption only
moves upstream. Public firms may still overpay for inputs if those inputs
are privately provided because private providers can bribe the officials in
charge. Even if the public firms only use labor, there can be corrupt bargains between workers and firms, as public firms may overpay workers in
exchange for kickbacks or services in kind.

A key criterion to finding out whether private or public ownership is
preferable is whether the firm sells or buys significantly from the government. If the firm is particularly labor intensive, it may be hard to create
corrupt bargains with large numbers of workers. In that case, public ownership becomes optimal.

The third problem explains why government ownership may be a better response to externalities than are subsidies to private firms. If there is
massive corruption, subsidies will be roundly abused. For example, in
nineteenth-century America, the subsidies to railroads seem to have been
related more to the size of the bribes of railroad officials than to the externalities coming from railroads. If government subsidies are going to
be perverted through corruption, then public ownership provides a
solution.

When examining the history of New York City public ownership of
the major local government services—water supply, sanitation, street maintenance, public transportation, and power and light utilities—Glaeser
found that in almost all areas, the desire to eliminate corruption seems to
have played a role in shifting from private to public provision (although
eliminating corruption seems to have been least important in the provision of water and most important in public transportation).

This short survey of economic theory on the costs and benefits of private versus public ownership shows that it is mostly with the development of contract theory in recent years that economists have gained a
better understanding of the costs and benefits of public versus private
ownership. While the complete contract approach emphasizes the differences in information under different conditions of ownership, the

incomplete contract approach emphasizes differences in residual rights of control. While contract theory has clearly shown that previous presumptions in favor of public ownership of natural monopolies are not warranted, no clear picture emerges of a definite advantage of private ownership. It may have better incentives to invest, to innovate, and to reduce costs, and it reduces inefficient government intervention in firms—all aspects that undoubtedly increase economic efficiency—but it may entail distortions in the form of too low levels of production and excessive emphasis on cost reduction at the expense of quality and other socially valuable objectives, and under certain circumstances it may lead to corruption within government. The nature of the analysis has become more sophisticated.

What is strikingly missing is a comparative analysis of government ownership under different types of government. While there is often a tension in the literature between theories that assume a benevolent government maximizing social welfare versus a malevolent government seeking to prey on economic agents, there is no finer analysis of government ownership under specific kinds of government. What are the advantages, disadvantages, and trade-offs in governments characterized by widespread corruption and incompetence versus governments with Weberian-type bureaucracies? How are they affected by the degree of separation of powers, the degree of insulation of government from political pressure, and other factors? No one has yet begun to analyze these questions seriously.

NOTES

Acknowledgment: I thank Elena Duggar for extensive research assistance.

1. This should not be confused with the then-popular Marxist idea of nationalizing key industries in order to replace market allocation of resources by central planning.

REFERENCES

Aghion, P. and O. Blanchard. 1998. "On Privatization Methods in Eastern Europe and Their Implications." *Economics of Transition* 6(1): 87–99.

Allais, M. 1947. "Le Problème de la planification economique dans une economie collectiviste." *Kyklos* 2: 48–71.

Arrow, K. and G. Debreu. 1954. "Existence of an Equilibrium for a Competitive Economy." *Econometrica* 22(3): 265–290.

Auriol, E. and P. Picard. 2002. "Privatizations in Developing Countries and the Government's Budget Constraint." Working Paper 2002.75, Fondazione Eni Enrico Mattei.

Bain, J., M. Keren, J. Miller, and J. Thornton. 1987. "The Ratchet, Tautness and Managerial Behavior in Soviet-Type Economies." *European Economic Review* 31(6): 1173–1202.

Bardhan, P. and J. Roemer, eds. 1993. *Market Socialism.* Oxford: Oxford University Press.

Berglof, E. and G. Roland. 1998. "Soft Budget Constraints and Banking in Transition Economies." *Journal of Comparative Economics* 26(1): 18–40.

Berliner, J. 1952. "The Informal Organization of the Soviet Firm." *Quarterly Journal of Economics* 66: 342–365.

Bolton, P., F. Pivetta, and G. Roland. 1997. "Optimal Sale of Assets: The Role of Non Cash Bids." Brussels: European Center for Advanced Research in Economics and Statistics, Université Libre de Bruxelles, mimeo.

Davis, J., R. Ossowski, T. Richardson, and S. Barnett. 2000. "Fiscal and Macroeconomic Aspects of Privatization." IMF Occasional Paper 194. Washington, DC: International Monetary Fund.

Debande, O. and G. Friebel. 1995. "Privatization, Employment and Managerial Decision-Taking." Brussels: European Center for Advanced Research in Economics and Statistics, Université Libre de Bruxelles, mimeo.

Dewatripont, M. and E. Maskin. 1995. "Credit and Efficiency in Centralized and Decentralized Economies." *Review of Economic Studies* 62: 541–555.

Dewatripont, M. and G. Roland. 1997. "Transition as a Process of Large Scale Institutional Change." In *Advances in Economic Theory*, vol. 2, ed. D. Kreps and K. Wallis, 240–278. Cambridge: Cambridge University Press.

Fama, E. 1980. "Agency Problems and the Theory of the Firm." *Journal of Political Economy* 88: 288–307.

Freixas, X., R. Guesnerie, and J. Tirole. 1985. "Planning Under Incomplete Information and the Ratchet Effect." *Review of Economic Studies* 52: 173–191.

Frydman, R., C. Gray, M. Hessel, and A. Rapaczynski. 2000. "The Limits of Discipline: Ownership and Hard Budget Constraints in the Transition Economies." SCAE Working Paper 2. New York: Starr Center for Applied Economics, New York University.

Glaeser, E. 2001. "Public Ownership in the American City." NBER Working Paper 8613. Cambridge, MA: National Bureau of Economic Research.

Glaeser, E. and A. Shleifer. 1998. "Not-for-Profit Entrepreneurs." Mimeo.

Goldfelt, S. and R. Quandt. 1988. "Budget Constraints, Bailouts and the Firm Under Central Planning." *Journal of Economic Behavior and Organization* 14(2): 205–222.

——. 1990. "Output Targets, the Soft Budget Constraint and the Firm Under Central Planning." *Journal of Comparative Economics* 12(4): 502–520.

Grossman, S. and O. Hart. 1986. "The Costs and Benefits of Ownership: A Theory of Vertical and Lateral Integration." *Journal of Political Economy* 94(4): 691–719.

Hart, O. 1983. "The Market Mechanism as an Incentive Scheme." *Bell Journal of Economics* 14 (Autumn): 366–382.

———. 1995. *Firms, Contracts, and Financial Structure.* Oxford: Oxford University Press.

Hart, O. and J. Moore. 1990. "Property Rights and the Nature of the Firm." *Journal of Political Economy* 98(6): 1119–1158.

Hart, O., A. Shleifer, and R. W. Vishny. 1997. "The Proper Scope of Government: Theory and an Application to Prisons." *Quarterly Journal of Economics* 112(4): 1127–1161.

Hart, O. and J. Tirole. 1988. "Contract Renegotiation and Coasian Dynamics." *Review of Economic Studies* 55: 509–540.

Hillman, A., E. Katz, and J. Rosenberg. 1987. "Workers as Insurance: Anticipated Government Assistance and Factor Demand." *Oxford Economic Papers* 39(4): 813–820.

Holmström, B. 1982a. "Managerial Incentive Problems—A Dynamic Perspective." In *Essays in Honor of Lars Wahlbeck,* 169–182. Helsinki: Swedish School of Economics.

———. 1982b. "Moral Hazard in Teams." *Bell Journal of Economics* 13 (Autumn): 324–340.

Holmström, B. and J. Tirole. 1989. "The Theory of the Firm." In *Handbook of Industrial Organization,* ed. R. Schmalensee and R. Willig, 61–134. Amsterdam: North-Holland.

———. 1991. "Market Liquidity and Performance Monitoring." *Journal of Political Economy* 101(4): 678–709.

Kaufmann, D. and P. Siegelbaum. 1997. "Privatization and Corruption in Transition Economies." *Journal of International Affairs* 50(2): 419–464.

Keren, M., J. Miller, and J. Thornton. 1983. "The Ratchet: A Dynamic Managerial Incentive Model of the Soviet Enterprise." *Journal of Comparative Economics* 7(4): 347–367.

Kornai, J. 1980. *Economics of Shortage.* Amsterdam: North-Holland.

———. 1992. *The Socialist System: The Political Economy of Communism.* Oxford: Oxford University Press.

———. 1993. "Transformational Recession: A General Phenomenon Examined Through the Example of Hungary's Development." *Economie Appliquee* 46(2): 181–227.

Kornai, J., E. Maskin, and G. Roland. 2003. "Understanding the Soft Budget Constraint." *Journal of Economic Literature* 41(4): 1095–1136.

Laffont, J. and J. Tirole. 1988. "The Dynamics of Incentive Contracts." *Econometrica* 51: 1153–1175.

———. 1993. *A Theory of Incentives in Regulation and Procurement.* Cambridge, MA: MIT Press.

Lewis, A. 1949. *The Principles of Economic Planning.* London: George Allen & Unwin.

Litwack, J. 1993. "Coordination, Incentives and the Ratchet Effect." *RAND Journal of Economics* 24(2): 271–285.

López-de-Silanes, F. 1997. "Determinants of Privatization Prices." *Quarterly Journal of Economics* 112(4): 965–1026.

López-de-Silanes, F., A. Shleifer, and R. W. Vishny. 1997. "Privatization in the United States." *RAND Journal of Economics* 28(3): 447–471.

Lulfesman, C. 2001. "Benevolent Government, Managerial Incentives, and the Virtues of Privatization." University of Bonn, mimeo.

Meade, J. 1948. *Planning and the Price Mechanism: The Liberal Socialist Solution.* London: George Allen & Unwin.

Megginson, W. and J. Netter. 2001. "From State to Market: A Survey of Empirical Studies on Privatization." *Journal of Economic Literature* 39(2): 321–389.

Milgrom, P. and J. Roberts. 1990. "Bargaining and Influence Costs and the Organization of Economic Activity." In *Perspectives on Positive Political Economy*, ed. J. Alt and K. Shepsle, 57–89. Cambridge: Cambridge University Press.

Nalebuff, B. and J. Stiglitz. 1983. "Prizes and Incentives: Towards a General Theory of Compensation and Competition." *Bell Journal of Economics* 14 (Spring): 21–43.

Peltzman, S. 1989. "The Control and Performance of State-Owned Enterprises." In *Privatization and State-Owned Enterprises*, ed. P. MacAvoy et al., 69–75. Boston: Kluwer Academic Publishers.

Perotti, E. 1995. "Credible Privatization." *American Economic Review* 85(4): 847–859.

Qian, Y. 1994. "A Theory of Shortage in Socialist Economies Based on the Soft Budget Constraint." *American Economic Review* 84: 145–156.

Qian, Y. and G. Roland. 1998. "Federalism and the Soft Budget Constraint." *American Economic Review* 88(5): 1143–1162.

Qian, Y. and C. Xu. 1998. "Innovation and Bureaucracy Under Soft and Hard Budget Constraints." *Review of Economic Studies* 65(1): 151–164.

Roland, G. 2000. *Transition and Economics: Politics, Markets and Firms.* Cambridge, MA: MIT Press.

Roland, G. and K. Sekkat. 2000. "Managerial Career Concerns, Privatization and Restructuring in Transition Economies." *European Economic Review* 44(10): 1857–1872.

Roland, G. and A. Szafarz. 1990. "The Ratchet Effect and the Planner's Expectations." *European Economic Review* 34: 1079–1088.

Sappington, D. and J. Stiglitz. 1987. "Privatization, Information and Incentives." *Journal of Policy Analysis and Management* 6: 567–582.

Schmidt, K. 1990. *The Costs and Benefits of Privatization.* University of Bonn, Discussion Paper No. 330.

——. 1995. "The Costs and Benefits of Privatization: An Incomplete Contracts Approach." University of Bonn, mimeo.

——. 1996. "The Political Economy of Mass Privatization and the Risk of Expropriation." William Davidson Institute Working Paper 136, University of Michigan.

Segal, I. 1998. "Monopoly and Soft Budget Constraints." *RAND Journal of Economics* 29(3): 596–609.

Shapiro, C. and R. Willig. 1990. "Economic Rationales for the Scope of Privatization." In *The Political Economy of Private Sector Reform and Privatization*, ed. E. Suleiman and J. Waterbury, 55–87. Boulder, CO: Westview Press.

Sheshinski, E. and L. Lopez-Calva. 1998. "Privatization and Its Benefits: Theory and Evidence." Harvard Institute for International Development Discussion Paper 698. Cambridge, MA: Harvard University.

Shleifer, A. 1998. "State Versus Private Ownership." *Journal of Economic Perspectives* 12: 133–150.

Shleifer, A. and R. W. Vishny. 1993. "Corruption." *Quarterly Journal of Economics* 108(3): 599–618.

——. 1994. "Politicians and Firms." *Quarterly Journal of Economics* 109(4): 995–1025.

Stiglitz, J. 1998. "The Private Uses of Public Interests: Incentives and Institutions." *Journal of Economic Perspectives* 12: 3–22.

Tierney, J. 1988. *The U.S. Postal Service: Status and Prospects of a Public Enterprise.* New York: Auburn House.

Vanek, J. 1977. "The Yugoslav Economy Viewed Through the Theory of Labor Management." In *The Labor Managed Economy: Essays by Jaroslav Vanek*, 48–92. Ithaca, NY: Cornell University Press.

Vickers, J. and G. Yarrow. 1989. *Privatization: An Economic Analysis.* Boston: MIT Press.

——. 1991. "Economic Perspectives on Privatization." *Journal of Economic Perspectives* 5(2): 111–132.

Ward, B. 1967. *The Socialist Economy: A Study in Organization Alternatives.* New York: Random House.

Weisbrod, B. 1988. *The Nonprofit Economy.* Cambridge, MA: Harvard University Press.

Weitzman, M. 1980. "The Ratchet Principle and Performance Incentives." *Bell Journal of Economics* 11: 302–308.

Williamson, O. 1985. *The Economic Institutions of Capitalism.* New York: Free Press.

World Bank. 1995. *Bureaucrats in Business.* Oxford: Oxford University Press.

CHAPTER 2

Privatization in Western Europe

Stylized Facts, Outcomes, and Open Issues

Bernardo Bortolotti and Valentina Milella

Started in the United Kingdom at the end of the 1970s, privatization spread in continental Europe during the 1980s. Western European countries, hard-pressed to improve mounting fiscal deficits and to introduce major product market reforms as requisite to join the European Union, pushed ahead one of the most extensive and ambitious privatization programs around the world during the 1990s.

After more than a quarter of a century, it is possible to take stock of the main national experiences and to try to draw an overarching description of what has been achieved and not achieved through such a sustained divestiture policy.

This chapter presents quantitative information about the size and the extent of the state sell-offs and state ownership in major European countries and analyzes the most important stylized facts about the causes and consequences of the process.

The main findings can be summarized as follows. Privatization in Western Europe has been mainly driven by fiscal conditions and by the positive outlook in financial markets. The process has also been shaped by political preferences and institutional constraints because partisan politics and constitutional rules affected privatization choices.

As to the consequences, our knowledge about the real effects of privatization in terms of fiscal consolidation and the operating efficiency of firms is more limited, even if the impact of privatization on financial market development and on the spreading of equity culture has often been dramatic.

Surprisingly, the large-scale privatization process of the 1990s did not alter the prevailing corporate governance structures in privatized firms. At the turn of the century, we find European governments firmly controlling, by voting rights and golden shares (broadly defined as the complex of special powers granted to the state and the statutory constraints in privatized companies), a large part of privatized companies, especially in strategic sectors. Understanding whether the coexistence of private ownership and public control is a European transient anomaly or a functional pattern of governance is important for policy reasons and might be an exciting avenue for future research.

The chapter is organized as follows: The first section reports the main trends of privatization activity; the second section describes the emergence of the state-owned enterprise (SOE) sector; the third section analyzes the main privatization drivers; and the fourth section provides an account of the main findings on the effects of privatization at the macroeconomic and microeconomic levels.

PRIVATIZATION TRENDS

The first aggregation of data, which referred to the global number of transactions and revenues raised in the 1977–2004 period, provides a preliminary indication of the extent of privatization in Western Europe as compared to the rest of the world.

Western Europe appears to be the area mostly involved in the process, having implemented the greatest number of privatizations (29% of global deals) and raised 48% of global revenues (see table 2.1 and figure 2.1).

In terms of percentage of global proceeds, Western Europe is followed by Asia (24%) and Latin America (11%). As to the number of transactions, privatization sales were also numerous in Central and Eastern Europe and the former Soviet Union (28%) but limited in size (representing only 6% of global revenues). The opposite occurred in Asia (see table 2.1).

The data on the privatization methods adopted in Western Europe confirm a general trend, with private sales (PS), i.e., a private equity placement to strategic investors, accounting for the majority of cases. Privatization on public equity markets (public offerings [POs]) are less frequent (28%) and typically raise higher revenues (64%), being used for larger and often more profitable companies that can be easily floated in domestic and/or international exchanges.

The vast extent of European privatization (see figures 2.2 and 2.3) can be ascribed to the large size of the SOE sector of most European economies and to the exceptional weight of the British experience.

TABLE 2.1   Privatizations Around the World: Revenues and Transactions by Geographic Areas, 1977–2004

Area	Privatization Transactions			Privatization Revenues		
	Total Deals	%	PO/ Deals	Total Revenues	%	PO/ Revenues
Western Europe	1,183	29	0.36	647,647.75	48	0.73
Asia	569	14	0.53	322,349.60	24	0.85
Latin America	501	12	0.14	154,499.00	11	0.21
Oceania	200	5	0.08	88,237.78	7	0.36
CEE and the Former Soviet Union	1,145	28	0.12	84,471.25	6	0.25
North America and the Caribbean	115	3	0.21	24,187.56	2	0.57
MENA	185	5	0.61	20,767.39	2	0.64
Sub-Saharan Africa	156	4	0.30	7,930.07	1	0.33
Total	4,054	100	0.28	1,350,090.40	100	0.64

Note: In our classification, *Western Europe* includes Austria, Belgium, Denmark, Finland, France, Germany, Greece, Iceland, Ireland, Italy, Luxembourg, Malta, Monaco, the Netherlands, Norway, Portugal, Spain, Sweden, Switzerland, Turkey, and the United Kingdom; *Asia* includes Armenia, Bangladesh, Cambodia, China, India, Indonesia, Japan, South Korea, Malaysia, Pakistan, the Philippines, Singapore, Sri Lanka, Taiwan, and Thailand; *Latin America* includes Argentina, Bolivia, Brazil, Chile, Columbia, Ecuador, El Salvador, Guatemala, Guyana, Mexico, Panama, Paraguay, Peru, Uruguay, and Venezuela; *Oceania* includes Australia, Fiji, French Polynesia, New Zealand, and Papua New Guinea; *Central-Eastern Europe (CEE) and the Former Soviet Union* include: Albania, Bosnia, Bulgaria, Croatia, the Czech Republic, Czechoslovakia, East Germany, Estonia, Georgia, Hungary, Kazakhstan, Latvia, Lithuania, Macedonia, Moldova, Poland, Romania, Russian Federation, Slovak Republic, Slovenia, Soviet Union, Ukraine, Uzbekistan, and Yugoslavia; *North America and the Caribbean* include Barbados, Belize, British Virgin Islands, Canada, Dominican Republic, Haiti, Honduras, Jamaica, Netherlands Antilles, Nicaragua, St. Lucia, Trinidad, Tobago, and the United States; *the Middle East and North Africa (MENA)* include Algeria, Bahrain, Egypt, Israel, Jordan, Kuwait, Lebanon, Mauritania, Morocco, Oman, Qatar, and Tunisia; *sub-Saharan Africa* includes Benin, Cameroon, Chad, Congo, Ethiopia, Gabon, Ghana, Guinea, Côte d'Ivoire, Kenya, Lesotho, Malawi, Mali, Mauritius, Mozambique, Nigeria, Rwanda, Sao Tome, Senegal, Sierra Leone, South Africa, Sudan, Tanzania, Uganda, Zambia, and Zimbabwe.

Sources: Privatization Barometer (http://www.privatizationbarometer.net) and Securities Data Corporation.

Indeed, privatization was one of the building blocks of the Thatcherite reforms, which shrank the size of the SOE sector in the United Kingdom from 10% of GDP to virtually nil. The 1977 PO of British Petroleum is usually considered, after the failed German attempts of the 1950s under the Adenauer government, the first large-scale privatization in modern times.

Shortly after, in the mid 1980s, privatization started to spread out in continental Europe. In 1985 Italy undertook the long-lasting process of

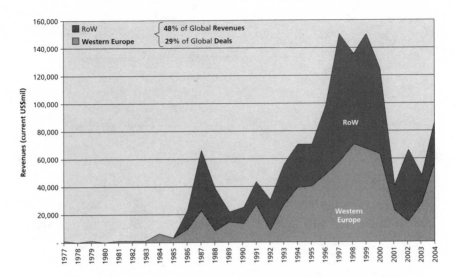

FIGURE 2.1 Revenues in Western Europe versus Rest of the World, 1977–2004

Sources: Privatization Barometer (http://www.privatizationbarometer.net) and Securities Data Corporation.

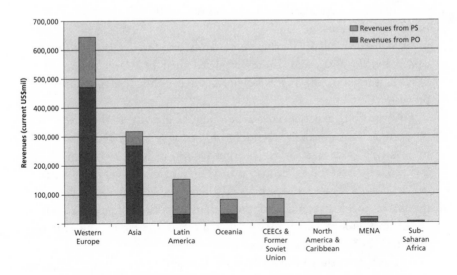

FIGURE 2.2 Privatizations Around the World: Ranking by Revenues, 1977–2004

Sources: Privatization Barometer (http://www.privatizationbarometer.net) and Securities Data Corporation.

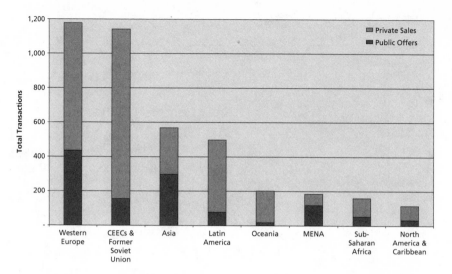

FIGURE 2.3   Privatizations Around the World: Ranking by Transactions, 1977–2004

Sources: Privatization Barometer (http://www.privatizationbarometer.net) and Securities Data Corporation.

denationalization of the state holding company IRI, with the partial sale of SIRTI and Alitalia, and in 1986 the newly elected French conservative government pushed ahead a highly politicized (re)privatization of its financial institutions.

In 1989 Portugal, Spain, the Netherlands, and Sweden entered the process. Italy, Portugal, and Turkey reported their first large-scale sales in 1993. Throughout the 1990s Belgium, Greece, and Ireland joined the process.

Privatizations experienced an exponential growth at the end of the 1990s, reporting a peak in revenues in 1998 due to a number of large POs in "strategic" sectors, such as ENI (petroleum) in Italy, Swisscom (tlc) in Switzerland, ENDESA (electric utility) in Spain, and France Telecom (tlc) in France. The year 1999 boasted a remarkable level of revenues, also thanks to the first tranche of the Italian electric generation company ENEL in October, which today still represents the largest initial public offering (IPO) in history.

At the turn of the century, the process abruptly slowed down. Between 2000 and 2002 sales and revenues decreased at an average rate of 34% and 50%, respectively. Privatization activity in 2002 fell to the levels reported at the initial stage of the cycle. After this striking dip, mainly due to the global economic downturn and negative stock market conditions, the

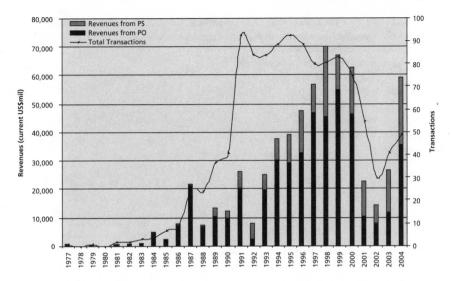

FIGURE 2.4   Privatization in Western Europe: Total Revenues and Transactions, 1977–2004

Sources: Privatization Barometer (http://www.privatizationbarometer.net) and Securities Data Corporation.

process resumed in 2003 and regained momentum in 2004 (see figure 2.4). Several large POs in the telecommunications sector (France Telecom, Deutsche Telekom, Telekom Austria, and Telia Sonera), in the financial sector (Eulia in France and Deutsche Postbank in Germany), and in the oil and gas industry (French Total and Norwegian Statoil) boosted privatization revenues to US$59 billion, a figure close to the historical peak levels of the European process.

Importantly, 2004 marked the resurgence of global offers and retail investors' appetite for privatized stocks, allowing, for example, the implementation of a large offering of shares of ENEL, the Italian electricity giant, which brought over US$9.5 billion into the government coffers.

A preliminary analysis of privatization trends at the national level shows that, within European countries, the United Kingdom leads the ranking by total revenues (see figure 2.5), and Italy boasts the second position, followed by Germany, France, and Spain.

However, revenues scaled by GDP provide a more appropriate measure for a cross-country comparison. Indeed, because the size of a country matters in explaining the extent of privatization (as it also affects the size of the SOE sector), the final ranking changes considerably when total revenues are scaled by GDP (see figures 2.5 and 2.6), even if

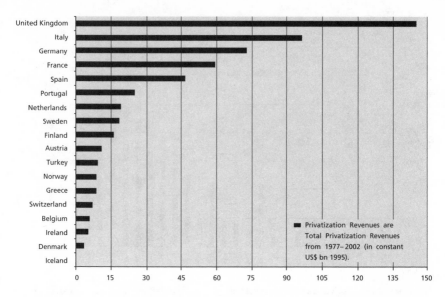

FIGURE 2.5   Privatization in Western Europe: Country Ranking by Revenues, 1977–2002

Sources: Privatization Barometer (http://www.privatizationbarometer.net), Securities Data Corporation, and World Bank.

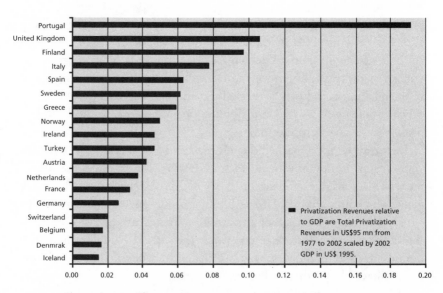

FIGURE 2.6   Privatization in Western Europe: Country Ranking by Revenues Relative to GDP

Sources: Privatization Barometer (http://www.privatizationbarometer.net), Securities Data Corporation, and World Bank.

countries such as the United Kingdom and Italy remain in prominent positions.

The comparison between the mean and median values of privatization revenues suggests that the distribution of total revenues is strongly affected by the presence of a few "deep" privatizing countries such as the United Kingdom, Italy, and Germany, which report values well above the sample mean. Italy boasts the highest value in average revenues, meaning that larger companies have been sold.

The ratio of public offers to total deals provides some information about the privatization methods. Austria and Portugal have opted more systematically for flotation in public equity markets, while in Germany, Belgium, and Sweden the resort to share issues has been much more limited.

The breakdown by industry (see figure 2.7) shows that almost no sector is left out of the privatization process. However, the greater part of revenues comes from telecommunications, utilities, the manufacturing industry, finance, petroleum, and transportation.[1]

As a general rule, the initial stage of the process involves the manufacturing and industrial sectors and financial institutions (the latter in a prominent position in terms of proceeds), while the privatization of telecommunications, energy, transportation, and utilities (i.e., "strategic sectors") typically step into the second stage.

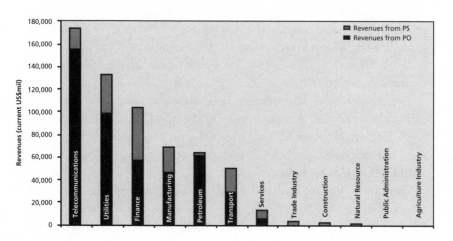

FIGURE 2.7   Privatization in Western Europe: Distribution of Revenues by Sector, 1977–2004

Sources: Privatization Barometer (http://www.privatizationbarometer.net) and Securities Data Corporation.

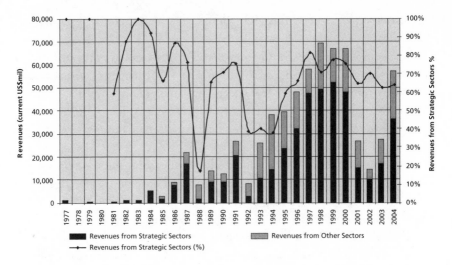

FIGURE 2.8   Strategic versus Other Sectors, 1977–2004

Note: Strategic Sectors include telecommunications, utilities, transportation industry, and petroleum. Other Sectors are all the other sectors.

Sources: Privatization Barometer (http://www.privatizationbarometer.net) and Securities Data Corporation.

However, the timing of the entry of sectors has been different in continental Europe with respect to the United Kingdom, which went farthest in the shortest time, privatizing its national oil company, British Petroleum, in 1977, telecommunications in 1981 (with the first tranche of Cable & Wireless), several water and electric utilities during the 1980s, and the railways shortly thereafter.

In the other European countries, apart from some scattered cases at the end of the 1980s (i.e., Alitalia in 1985; OMV, Cie Général Téléphoniques, and VEBA in 1987; and ENDESA in 1988), the telecommunications, utilities, transportation, and energy sectors were still firmly in public hands until the first half of the 1990s.

Only from 1994 onward, indeed, did strategic sectors actually become involved in the process. Among the oil companies outside the United Kingdom, Elf Aquitaine, ENI, OMV, Total, and Repsol were the first to be privatized during the early 1990s. Shortly after, coupled with the global context of technological innovation and trade liberalization pushed by WTO, several privatizations involved the telecommunications companies of Spain, Switzerland, Denmark, Finland, and the Netherlands.

During the second half of the 1990s, water, electric utilities, and transportation companies started to be privatized, and the percentage of revenues raised through the sales of public assets in strategic sectors appeared to be highly increasing over time, especially between 1994 and 1997, and remaining stable at quite high levels (well above 60% of yearly total revenues) from 1998 to today (see figure 2.8).

Overall, the privatization of strategic sectors raised 68% of European privatization revenues through 38% of the total area transactions. However, despite these significant results, it seems that European countries fell short of accomplishing ambitious privatization programs in strategic sectors, and only a few countries, such as the United Kingdom and Spain, have fully privatized strategic sectors such as energy, telecommunications, or transportation, while in some other countries, despite some recent announcements, the majority of assets in strategic sectors (particularly in energy) are still publicly owned.

THE STATE-OWNED ENTERPRISE SECTOR
IN WESTERN EUROPE

The aggregate data presented provide a preliminary description of European divestitures. However privatization processes would be more fully understood by relating the extent of state sell-offs to the size of the SOE sector pre-privatization.

To our knowledge, the only centralized source of comprehensive data on SOE activity is the World Bank (1995), reporting several indicators for industrialized and developing economies for the 1978–1991 period.[2] SOEs are defined as "government owned or controlled entities that generate the bulk of their revenues from selling goods and services" (ibid.).

We therefore used the World Bank database in order to build a proxy for initial conditions given by the value added of SOEs as a percentage of GDP in the year before the first operation reported by Securities Data Corporation databases (where possible), certainly the most comprehensive source for privatization information at the transaction level.

As shown in table 2.2, on average, SOEs accounted for a significant fraction of the economic activity in Western Europe pre-privatization. The European average, indeed, is about 10%, while for non-European Organisation for Economic Co-operation and Development (OECD) economies this figure narrows to approximately 7%. Several countries, such as the United Kingdom, Germany, France, Austria, Portugal, and

TABLE 2.2   Privatizations in Western Europe, 1977–2002

This table reports the aggregate figures on privatization in Western European countries for the 1977–2002 period. Countries are ranked by *Rev/GDP*. *Deals* is the total number of privatizations; *Revenues* is total revenues from privatizations for the period 1977–2002 (in US$ mn 1995); *PO/Deals* is the ratio of the number of privatizations by public offer to the total number of privatizations; *PO/Rev* is the ratio of revenues raised through public offers of shares to total revenues from privatizations; *Rev/GDP* is the ratio of total revenues cumulated in the period to 2002 GDP (in US$ mn 1995); *SOE/GDP* is the ratio of the SOE value added to GDP (in US$ mn 1995) reported the year before the first privatization; *Rev/SOE* is the ratio of revenues (in US$ mn 1995) reported the year before the first privatization, when possible.

Country	Deals	Revenues	PO/ Deals	PO/ Rev	Revenues/ Deals	Rev/ GDP	SOE/ GDP	Rev/ SOE
Portugal	78	25,453.65	0.51	0.80	326.33	0.19	0.15	1.87
United Kingdom	183	145,531.73	0.32	0.88	795.26	0.11	0.11	1.40
Finland	56	16,328.63	0.43	0.66	291.58	0.10	—	—
Italy	103	96,442.39	0.44	0.84	936.33	0.08	0.09	0.86
Spain	74	46,577.60	0.35	0.79	629.43	0.06	0.09	1.01
Sweden	56	18,625.54	0.20	0.70	332.60	0.06	0.10	0.73
Austria	51	11,503.06	0.57	0.51	225.55	0.04	0.14	0.52
Netherlands	29	19,182.48	0.38	0.66	661.46	0.04	0.06	1.15
France	97	59,875.26	0.53	0.92	617.27	0.03	0.11	0.48
Germany	150	73,302.53	0.14	0.66	488.68	0.03	0.10	0.79
Belgium	10	5,707.97	0.20	0.18	570.80	0.02	0.04	0.69
Mean	81	47,139.17	0.37	0.69	534.12	0.07	0.09	0.95
Median	74	25,453.65	0.38	0.70	570.80	0.05	0.10	0.82

Sources: Privatization Barometer (http://www.privatizationbarometer.net), Securities Data Corporation, and World Bank (1995, 2002).

Sweden, range between 10% and 15% of GDP. Only Belgium and the Netherlands appear remarkably below the European average.

However, these data suffer from several drawbacks. First, the definition used by the World Bank is limited to "commercial activities controlled by virtue of government's (direct and indirect) ownership stake alone." However, in several cases, SOEs are owned by regional and local bodies, which do not enter in the definition. In other cases, the database does not report the stakes owned by the government in financial entities and does not take into account the government's indirect ownership.

For example, the Swedish SOE share of value added would have certainly been higher—and probably larger than the EU average—if the ownership of local and regional bodies was included. Local municipal governments and the regions/county councils control about 1,777 local enterprises altogether, operating especially in the housing and energy sectors. The case of Portugal illustrates how the exclusion of the financial sector may distort the real size of the SOE sector. In the mid 1970s, the state nationalized the nine largest banks and eight insurance companies. As a consequence, the state indirectly owned hundreds of small and medium enterprises in which formerly private banks held controlling stakes (Baklanoff, 1986). Finally, the value-added figures for Belgium only refer to the transportation and telecommunications sectors, largely underestimating the size of the SOE sector in a historically highly interventionist state.

Due to these limitations, World Bank data partially fail to appreciate the real size of state ownership in Europe, suggesting the need for a more systematic data collection to fill the gap. Albeit biased, the data show quite clearly that at the beginning of the 1980s state ownership of productive assets was very large. What factors explain the emergence of such a large SOE sector in Europe?

At the risk of oversimplification, the rise of state ownership in Western Europe can be traced back to the twentieth century, and particularly to three waves of nationalizations that occurred (1) after the Great Depression of 1929–1933, (2) during the post–World War II period, and (3) after the oil shocks in the mid 1970s.

The economic downturn caused by the Great Depression led to a strong interventionist approach almost everywhere. In the 1920s, the French and the Belgian governments established financial institutions that took control of the banking sector. In Germany from the Weimar Republic to the National Socialist period, large-scale nationalizations were implemented to foster the industrialization process. Similarly, important nationalizations took place in Austria involving the telecommunications, transportation, and banking sectors.

Similarly, in 1933—in the fascist era—the state-owned industrial holding Istituto per la Ricostruzione Industriale (IRI) was created in Italy in order to recover the national economy. In Spain, the root of state-owned industry dates back to the establishment of Franco's dictatorship. After the Civil War, Spain imported the IRI model, creating the Instituto Nacional de Industria (INI) with the aim of strengthening domestic development, fostering import substitution, and injecting growth in underdeveloped areas. In Portugal, since 1933, the "corporative" ideology became the manifesto of Salazar's authoritarian regime, which aimed at keeping political and economic activity under tight public control.

As to northern European countries, SOEs in Sweden were established at the beginning of the twentieth century to better exploit national resources, in particular in the coal, timber, and steel industries. In Finland, the state's economic activities of the 1920s and 1930s were spurred by the lack of private venture capital and were mainly aimed at the exploitation of raw materials, development of infrastructure, achievement of self-sufficiency, financing of business activities, and implementation of regional policies.

The second wave of nationalizations were implemented after World War II and were carried on within the economic reconstruction. In the United Kingdom between 1945 and 1951, the SOE sector became one of the largest in Western Europe. In France in the 1945–1946 period, the state took control of economic sectors requiring heavy capital injection— such as coal, electricity, gas, and railways—along with the credit and insurance sectors. At that time, France established a centralized planning body, the Commissariat Général au Plan, with the mission of planning and coordinating the entire activity of the public sector. Belgium implemented important postwar nationalizations through the state holding company Societé Nationale d'Investissement (SNI), although the government already controlled indirectly a large number of enterprises through banks and credit institutions (Societé Générale de Belgique, Caisse Générale d'Epargne et de Retraite (CGER), Crédit Communal de Belgique). In Austria, nationalization basically involved all the formerly nationalized companies successively taken over by the German Reich. The former "German property"—including industrial enterprises founded by the Nazis—accounted for one-fifth of Austrian value added. It included the country's three largest banks, the entire coal and metal mining industry, all mineral oil extraction and processing facilities, and all the important companies in the heavy industry sector. Nationalized industry made the Austrian public sector one of the largest in continental Europe. The state holding company Österreichische Industrieholding (ÖIAG) played an important role in economic reconstruction in the occupation zones, also thanks to American reconstruction aid.

The third wave of nationalizations occurred in Europe in the aftermath of the oil shocks, in the period from the mid 1970s to mid 1980s. State-owned firms were increasingly used for stabilization and direct employment policies, to rescue ailing private firms, sustain investment, and support underdeveloped regions. In general, and in particular in Spain, Italy, and Sweden, noneconomic goals were put above corporate policy objectives.

In France, the promotion of "national champions," which competed with domestic and foreign rivals from a favored position, was an important

feature of the industrial policy of the period. Along with the direct ownership of the main economic sectors, including key industries, the state
control over the economy took the form of industrial protection and subsidies and control over foreign investments. This whole range of policy instruments typified the French Model of state intervention in the economy.
Finally, during the revolutionary period (1974–1976), Portugal launched a
massive nationalization program involving a large number of companies
that came under direct state control via the holding company IPE (Investi-
mentos e Participaçoes do Estado).

The abnormal growth of the SOE sector ensuing from these three
waves of nationalization clashed with the rising requirements of global
competitiveness. The pursued type of stabilization policy made it possible
to smooth the adjustment process but caused negative effects on the productivity and profitability of SOEs and on public finances.

In the early 1980s, the problem of the inefficiency of the SOE sector—
absorbing an increasing amount of public subsidies—became a priority in
the political agenda of most European countries, prompting the surge of
privatizations that began in the 1980s and gathered momentum from 1991
onward, after the ratification of the Maastricht Treaty. The restructuring
and privatization of the SOE sector became necessary not only to mod-
ernize the economy, but also to meet convergence criteria without politically costly tax increases.

DETERMINANTS OF PRIVATIZATION

The previous section has pointed out that common factors can explain the
rise of the SOE sector in Europe and that at the beginning of the 1980s,
with a few exceptions, European governments owned on average large
chunks of the national economy. Within this common pattern, historical
specifics matter and can be reflected in the cross-country variability in the
percentages of SOE value added that we observe in the European context.

Although some caution is needed in the interpretation of World Bank
data, it is certainly interesting to construct an indicator about the extent
of privatization in a given country that could take into account initial
conditions. In this direction, we have scaled the total revenues raised in a
given country in the 1977–2000 period by the total valued added of SOE
in the year preceding the first privatization sale (Rev/SOE in table 2.2).
The number obtained therefore provides a measure of the size of one
country's privatization process relative to what governments have to sell.

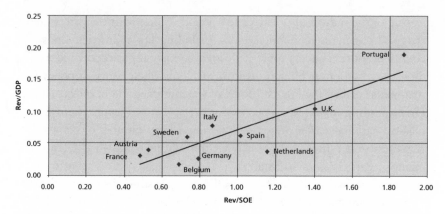

FIGURE 2.9   Privatizations in Western Europe: Revenues/GDP and Revenues/SOE, 1977–2002

Rev/GDP is the ratio of total revenues cumulated in the period 1977–2002 to 2002 GDP (in US$ mn 1995).

Rev/SOE is the ratio of revenues to the SOE value added reported in the year before the first privatization (in US$ mn 1995), when possible.

Sources: Privatization Barometer (http://www.privatizationbarometer.net), Securities Data Corporation, and World Bank.

The data show that Portugal has carried out the largest contraction in state property, followed by the United Kingdom and the Netherlands. Spain and Italy rank in middle high position, while France and Austria report the lowest scores.

Interestingly, as shown in figure 2.9, privatization revenues scaled by our proxy for the size of the SOE sector appear to be strongly correlated with the revenues to GDP ratio (corr.=0.87), a widely used measure in cross-country analyses of the size of privatization. Rev/GDP series can be easily constructed for a large number of countries and therefore allow for panel data empirical analyses. The positive correlation with a more proper measure of one country's privatization effort is reassuring and suggests the feasibility of comprehensive empirical analyses on the political and economic determinants of privatization in Europe.

Bortolotti and Pinotti (2003) perform an econometric analysis on a sample of 21 developed countries (16 European) for the 1977–1999 period, estimating in Tobit panel regressions the yearly ratio of revenues to GDP. Macroeconomic conditions appear particularly relevant. The extent of privatization appears higher in countries with higher per capita GDP and lower growth rates, which in turns means that privatization characterizes a relatively advanced stage of economic development. The inverse relation found between (lagged) growth rates and privatization could also indicate that governments tend to resort to privatization when the economic outlook deteriorates in order to foster economic activity via an increase in private investment. Fiscal conditions are also particularly relevant, as we find the debt ratio always highly statistically significant. Indeed, privatizing countries are often financially distressed, and they allocate revenues to amortization funds that allow them directly to reduce the debt, and indirectly to improve the fiscal budget due to lower interest payments.

Finally, and not surprisingly, privatization is more likely where large and liquid stock markets are in place. The coefficients of the (lagged) market capitalization and the turnover ratio are positive and statistically significant. Well-developed financial markets are key as they allow the absorption of big share issues. Liquidity is also particularly important as after market liquidity is discounted in privatization prices, allowing governments to raise more proceeds. The turnover ratio is also a measure of market activity, which typically increases with a bull market. The positive sign of the coefficient can also be interpreted as governments taking advantage of hot markets to float companies in order to fetch better prices.

Apart from macroeconomic factors, the paper takes into account political and institutional factors as possible determinants of privatization. Particularly, the authors develop an index that includes three components: (1) a measure of the disproportionality of the electoral rule (the Gallagher index); (2) the effective number of parties; and (3) an indicator of the type of executive. Higher values of the political institutional index are associated with a better fit with the majoritarian model, while lower values with the consensus model, which is characterized by strong veto players and a more dispersed decision-making power (Lijphart, 1999).

As predicted by the theoretical literature on the political economy of stabilization policies (Alesina and Drazen, 1991; Spolaore, 2004), majoritarian countries privatize more: where less power is granted by the electoral rule to minorities, minority will is underrepresented, and a lower number of veto players is found in the political arena. Therefore, large-scale reform packages (which typically include privatizations) are more likely to be implemented. The feasibility of a large-scale privatization program therefore is affected by institutional constraints.

THE OUTCOMES OF PRIVATIZATION PROCESSES

In this section we will try to investigate some of the main consequences of privatization in Europe at both the macroeconomic and microeconomic levels. At the macroeconomic level, we will try to shed some light on the effects of privatization (1) on fiscal conditions of European countries and (2) on financial market development. At the microeconomic level, we will try (1) to survey the evidence on the performance improvements of privatized SOEs, (2) to document the role of share issue privatizations in fostering popular capitalism and ownership diffusion, and (3) to understand whether privatization involved substantial changes in corporate governance structures of European privatized companies.

THE IMPACT ON MACROECONOMIC VARIABLES

To our knowledge, the effects of privatization on macroeconomic variables have never been the object of a formal analysis. The empirical literature addressing these issues is also quite limited, and no solid evidence has yet been produced in the context of Western European countries. This is rather surprising because macroeconomic conditions, especially high deficits and public debt, have been key drivers in the decision to privatize the European SOE sector.

In principle, the purpose of privatization is to achieve a redeployment of assets from the public to the private sector. Under the assumption that assets are used inefficiently by the public sector, privatization should spur productivity and the growth of aggregate output. Given that it may take some time for these effect to materialize, one could claim that a sustained privatization policy should foster long-term growth and increase output levels of the economy.

Apart from long-term considerations, as noted by Mackenzie (1998), privatization programs may have important macroeconomic consequences also in the short run, and especially on public finance aggregates.

To evaluate these effects, it is important first to establish the valuation differential of the assets in public versus private hands, namely, the difference between the present value of the income streams generated under public and private ownership. Second, an assumption should be made about the allocation of privatization proceeds.

Suppose that the valuation differential is negative and that revenues are used to retire outstanding debt. Then, the operation improves the public sector net worth and, thanks to lower interest payments, loosens the government inter-temporal budget constraint. Private sector wealth and consumption should not fall, because due to the operation the private sector reduces its holdings of money and increases its holdings of less liquid financial assets. Privatization may instead affect private investment in the sense that it could crowd out investment that would be otherwise undertaken. Aggregate demand could therefore fall unless the government sterilizes this effect by using the proceeds to finance new investments.

Suppose instead that the valuation differential is positive. This may stem from a different degree of risk aversion: public assets are discounted at higher rates by the private sector than by the government, and privatized assets are transferred at underpriced values. In this case, the operation worsens the public sector net worth and tightens the inter-temporal budget constraint because future income flows are not reflected in privatization prices. Under this circumstance, there may be a limited effect on investment, but a sizable wealth effect if the private sector perceives the windfall gain. Privatization policy may therefore have an expansionary impact in the short run.

Suppose instead that proceeds are treated as fiscal revenues (and so put "above the line") and are used to finance budget deficits. In this case, the public sector net worth would decrease (independently from the valuation) as the government sells fixed assets to finance public expenditure or tax cuts.

The final effects of privatization on public finances depend also on the possible reduction of state subsidies to SOEs, the increase on tax revenues due to the increased profitability of privatized firms, and importantly on the consequences of privatization in the labor market.

Indeed, privatization may involve layoffs and labor shedding in SOEs, with a possible increase in unemployment benefits in the short run. In the long run, it is likely that the positive effects of privatization in terms of increased productivity may spur economic growth and bring the economy to a lower equilibrium level of unemployment.

The overall macroeconomic effects of privatization have never been properly addressed in a general theoretical model that could provide testable predictions. However, a consensus view is that ceteris paribus privatization improves fiscal conditions when privatization proceeds are treated as financing and not as a source of budgetary revenue (Sheshinski and Lopez-Calva, 2002).

Some empirical work has been carried out to test the effect of privatization on fiscal deficit in Spain, Greece, Italy, and Portugal using data for the 1990–1997 period. Jeronimo, Pagán, and Gökçe (2000) find a negative and statistically significant relationship between privatization revenues and deficits for the 1990–1997 period. Katsoulakos and Likoyanni (2002) examine the impact of privatization on public deficit, on public debt, and on other macroeconomic variables (employment and growth) using country-level panel data of 23 OECD countries for the period from 1990 to 2000.

Katsoulakos and Likoyanni do not find any correlation of privatization variables with budget deficit, either for the whole OECD sample or for the four southern European countries. Thus, the results by Jeronimo, Pagán, and Gökçe (2000) do not seem to be robust to an extension of the sample period (1997–2000). However, Katsoulakos and Likoyanni document a statistically significant and negative relation between privatization revenues and public debt. Current privatization receipts have a statistically significant and negative effect on the current unemployment rate and a positive effect on previous period's unemployment rate. When privatization is announced, the announcement is typically followed by restructuring and layoffs, causing an increase in the unemployment rate. When privatization is instead implemented, output may grow, increasing the demand for labor and, thus, decreasing the unemployment rate. Finally, Katsoulakos and Likoyanni find, rather surprisingly, that the relations between GDP growth and current or past period's privatization receipts are statistically insignificant for the whole OECD sample.

These results suggest that privatization may be strongly correlated to macroeconomic variables, but certainly more theoretical and empirical work is needed to understand more fully the channels through which privatization affects aggregates.

FINANCIAL MARKET DEVELOPMENT

The development of equity markets has been one of the main objectives of divestiture throughout Europe. The British privatization program certainly represents one of the most successful experiences. However, the first experiment to strengthen equity culture through privatization in recent financial history was carried out during the 1960s in Germany by the Adenauer government. Subsequent and more ambitious programs to jump-start or revitalize national exchanges were reported in France in the

1980s under the Chirac government and especially in Italy throughout the 1990s.

But beyond national programs and announcements, it is important to examine first whether privatization is consistent with the objective of stock market development, and second how European governments designed sales to achieve it.

Obviously, as the U.S. experience clearly shows, stock markets could flourish without privatization. Furthermore, other policies, such as the reduction of tax rates on dividends, the establishment of efficient trading infrastructure, and the enactment of sound financial regulation are likely to promote financial market development. Yet a sustained privatization process based on the floatation of shares of SOEs in the stock market should have a strong effect in jump-starting a market caught in a low liquidity trap.

The theoretical models backing this prediction are Pagano (1993) and Subramanian and Titman (1999). The basic assumption is that the listing decision involves important positive externalities on other market participants. But when a company goes public, the entrepreneur fails to recognize the beneficial effect in terms of improved diversification opportunities stemming from his decision. Hence, financial markets can be trapped in a bad equilibrium with few listed firms and high risk premiums. The government, as the single owner of several companies, can shift away the market from this bad state through a sequence of IPOs and secondary offerings of privatized companies, and hence reduce the risk premium and improve overall market liquidity.

A second important aspect is related to the sheer size of SOEs. These companies are usually the largest firms in the country, and even a partial floatation may have a large effect on market capitalization and free float. Importantly, the limited absorption capacity of national stock markets have often induced government to tap major foreign exchanges by cross-listing shares at home and abroad. This privatization strategy stimulates the participation of foreign investors and may reduce the risk premium. Even though it concerns primarily the cross-listed firms, foreign participation will also benefit the liquidity of shares traded only in the local market. If the returns of privatized and local companies are positively correlated, foreigners will share some of the risk borne only by domestic investors prior to privatization. This reduces the required risk premium and thereby increases the value of domestic shares (Chiesa and Nicodano, 2003).

There are sound theoretical reasons to claim that share issue privatization, i.e., the privatization on public equity markets as opposed to private placements to strategic investors, promotes financial market development. It is now important to document whether the choice of the privatization method is consistent with this stated objective. One would expect privatization on public equity markets to be implemented more frequently in countries where governments are more eager to boost domestic financial development. Obviously this choice involves a trade-off. Share issue privatizations are likely to fail in fledgling stock markets for the simple reasons that it is more difficult to find buyers and that offerings have to be more strongly underpriced (Dewenter and Malatesta, 1997). Due to the costs of using the public capital markets, governments may opt for private sales in less developed capital markets.

To our knowledge, this trade-off has never been the object of empirical analysis in the European context. However, Megginson et al. (2000) study the choice of the privatization method for a large sample of (mainly developed) countries, finding that the objective of financial market development dominates—on average—revenue maximization. Indeed, share issue privatizations are more likely in countries with a lower turnover ratio, even controlling for public finance conditions via budget deficits.

Overall, these results suggest that financial market development matters in the choice of the privatization method. But have European governments been able to achieve it?

A bulk of evidence can be set forth to document the dramatic change in the European financial landscape in the last two decades, when large-scale privatization processes were in progress.

As table 2.3 shows, the average total market capitalization relative to GDP in Europe has increased five times from 1985 to 2000, from 18% to 91%. Finland boasts the largest leap throughout the period, from less than 10% to more than 200% of GDP. Financial market development has also been remarkable in France, Italy, and Spain, where the market capitalization has increased even more than the European average. It is not obvious to quantify the impact of privatization on market capitalization, given the presence of indirect effects via spillovers and cross-asset externalities. However, a first indication can be provided by looking at the change in the weight of privatized companies on total market capitalization. On average, the relative contribution of privatized companies has increased from 14% to 34%, which can partly be ascribed to privatization IPOs, but also to the enhancement of market value of newly privatized

TABLE 2.3 Financial Markets Development Indicators, 1985, 2000

| | Market Capitalization | | | | | Volume of Trades | | | | |
| | 1985 | 2000 | 1985 | 2000 | | 1985 | 2000 | 1985 | 2000 | |
	Mkt. Cap (as % of GDP)	Mkt. Cap (as % of GDP)	Mkt. Cap. of Privatized Companies as a % of Total Mkt. Cap (a)	Mkt. Cap. of Privatized Companies as a % of Total Mkt. Cap (b)	Difference (b)−(a)	Turnover Ratio	Turnover Ratio	Value of Trades of Privatized Companies as % of Total Volume of Trades (c)	Value of Trades of Privatized Companies as % of Total Volume of Trades (d)	Difference (d)−(c)
Austria	5.00	15.00	2.00	34.00	32.00	23.00	33.00	1.00	49.00	48.00
Belgium	0.00	1.00	1.00	8.00	7.00	11.00	23.00	1.00	11.00	10.00
Finland	9.00	236.00	1.00	14.00	13.00	10.00	72.00	2.00	20.00	18.00
France	11.00	99.00	26.00	83.00	57.00	25.00	84.00	3.00	35.00	32.00
Germany	18.00	64.00	4.00	22.00	18.00	55.00	89.00	4.00	15.00	11.00
Italy	10.00	62.00	17.00	41.00	24.00	33.00	117.00	2.00	34.00	32.00
Portugal	16.00	53.00	36.00	57.00	21.00	17.00	96.00	19.00	61.00	42.00
Spain	14.00	74.00	34.00	56.00	22.00	44.00	238.00	30.00	66.00	36.00
Sweden	30.00	136.00	1.00	6.00	5.00	31.00	125.00	3.00	18.00	15.00
United Kingdom	63.00	171.00	15.00	16.00	1.00	24.00	75.00	7.00	11.00	4.00
Average	17.60	91.10	13.70	33.70	20.00	27.30	95.20	7.20	32.00	24.80

Sources: Elaboration on World Bank (2002) and Datastream.

firms. Interestingly, countries such as France, Italy, and Spain report the highest increases in the relative weight of privatized companies together with above-average increases in market capitalization. Privatization activity may have therefore played an important role in deepening European stock markets.

Some interesting facts are also found by looking at the evolution of trading activity measured by the turnover ratio (the total value of trades relative to total market capitalization). On average, the turnover ratio increased about four times in the 1985–2000 period. The development of trading volume has been particularly marked in countries such as Finland, Spain, Portugal, and Sweden. The fraction of trading in shares of privatized companies has dramatically increased over this period, from a bare 7% in 1985 to 32% in 2000. Interestingly, countries such as Italy, Spain, and Portugal, where trading in privatized stocks increased the most, also report substantial variation in total trading activity, a preliminary finding which suggests that privatization may foster financial market development above the mechanic increase in market capitalization.

However, market capitalization and trading volumes fail to capture a fundamental aspect of financial market development, namely, *liquidity*. Liquidity is important because it allows companies to raise capital more cheaply (Ellul and Pagano, 2006) and to design stock-based managerial incentive schemes (Hölmstrom and Tirole, 1993), spurring company performance, efficiency, and ultimately economic growth. But liquidity is a quite elusive concept that is hard to define, let alone to quantify. The bid-ask spread has emerged as a conventional proxy for liquidity, but these spreads are difficult to compare across countries due to differences in market microstructure. Some of these difficulties can be circumvented by the use of price impact measures, given by the absolute value of return scaled by volume traded.

Bortolotti et al. (2007) estimate the effect of share issue privatization on stock market liquidity measured by the price impact in OECD countries, while accounting for other potential determinants set forth in the literature, such as the enforcement of insider trading regulation, political and country risk, and capital market liberalization. They find that privatization represents a source of variation of market liquidity. Particularly, as predicted by theory, the international profile of privatization matters the most. The price impact (hence liquidity) appears to be strongly and negatively (positively) correlated with the quantity of shares allocated to foreign investors in international exchanges. Importantly, the effect of cross-listings at the privatization stage survives when the liquidity of *private* companies is considered. A large-scale privatization program based on international share issue privatizations (SIPs) generates important positive externalities on the liquidity of private companies as well by improving diversification opportunities and by reducing risk premiums.

THE FINANCIAL AND OPERATING PERFORMANCE OF EUROPEAN PRIVATIZED FIRMS

There is no study available in the literature investigating the performance of European privatized firms in a single and comprehensive statistical analysis. However, some information could be grasped from Megginson, Nash, and van Randenborgh (1994) and D'Souza and Megginson (1999) (MNRD) papers dealing with the pre- and post-privatization performance changes in relatively large samples of privatized companies. The majority of these 133 companies are from industrialized economies, with a large predominance of European countries, so that the information coming from the papers—with a lot of caveats—could represent a useful starting point. We will then try to complement the analysis of performance reporting results of some country studies in the European context.

MNRD studies yield consistently positive results on the effectiveness of privatization in promoting improvements in the financial and operating performance of divested companies by documenting economically and statistically significant post-privatization increases in real sales (output), profitability, efficiency (sales per employee), and capital spending, coupled with significant declines in leverage. This point is made clear in table 2.4, which summarizes the results of the two studies.

Additionally, these two studies consistently document that output, efficiency, and capital spending increase dramatically and significantly after privatization. Meanwhile, leverage declines significantly. Megginson (2003) comments on these results, concluding that

> unlike profitability increases, these are all unambiguously socially beneficial outcomes, since they imply that privatized firms use resources more productively and also become financially healthier. That these benefits are achieved without systematically reducing employment also suggests that privatization yields important social benefits. In sum, the weight of evidence in these studies clearly indicates: (1) that privatization improves the operating and

TABLE 2.4 Results from Three Empirical Studies on the Financial and Operating Performance of Newly Privatized Firms

This table summarizes the empirical results of two directly comparable academic studies (Megginson, Nash, and van Randenborgh, 1994; D'Souza and Megginson, 1999) comparing the three-year average operating and financial performance of a combined sample of 133 newly privatized firms with the average performance of those same firms during their last three years as state-owned enterprises. The studies employ the Wilcoxon rank sum test (with its z-statistic) as the test of significance for the change in median value. All three studies employ multiple proxies for most of the economic variables being measured; this table summarizes only one proxy per topic and emphasizes the one highlighted in the studies (almost invariably, the variable that uses either physical measures—such as number of employees—or financial ratios using current-dollar measures in the numerator or denominator, or both). Profitability, investment, leverage, and dividend measures are in percent. Efficiency and output measures are index values, with the value during the year of privatization defined as 1.000; inflation-adjusted sales figures are used in the efficiency and output measures.

Variables and Studies Cited	Obs.	Mean Value Before Privatization	Mean Value After Privatization	Mean Change Due to Privatization	Z-Statistic for Difference in Performance	% of Firms with Improved Performance	Z-Statistic % Change
PROFITABILITY (Net Income ÷ Sales)							
Megginson, Nash, and van Randenborgh (1994); D'Souza and	55	0.0552 (0.0442)	0.0799 (0.0611)	0.0249 (0.0140)	3.15***	69.1	3.06***
Megginson (1999)	78	0.14 (0.05)	0.17 (0.08)	0.03 (0.03)	3.92***	71	4.17***
EFFICIENCY (Real Sales per Employee)							
Megginson, Nash, and van Randenborgh (1994); D'Souza and Megginson (1999)	51	0.956 (0.942)	1.062 (1.055)	0.1064 (0.1157)	3.66***	85.7	6.03***
	63	1.02 (0.87)	1.23 (1.16)	0.21 (0.29)	4.87***	79	5.76***
INVESTMENT (Capital Expenditures ÷ Sales)							
Megginson, Nash, and van Randenborgh (1994); D'Souza and	43	0.1169 (0.0668)	0.1689 (0.1221)	0.0521 (0.0159)	2.35**	67.4	2.44**
Megginson (1999)	66	0.18 (0.11)	0.17 (0.10)	-0.01 (-0.01)	0.80	55	0.81

	N						
OUTPUT (Real Sales [adjusted by CPI])							
Megginson, Nash, and van Randenborgh (1994); D'Souza and Megginson (1999)	57	0.899 (0.890)	1.140 (1.105)	0.241 (0.190)	4.77***	75.4	4.46***
Megginson (1999)	85	0.93	2.70	1.76	7.30***	88	10.94***
EMPLOYMENT (Total Employees)							
Megginson, Nash, and van Randenborgh (1994); D'Souza and Megginson (1999)	39	40,850 (19,360)	43,200 (23,720)	2,346 (276)	0.96	64.1	1.84*
Megginson (1999)	66	22,941 (9,876)	22,136 (9,106)	−805 (−770)	−1.62	36	−2.14**
LEVERAGE (Total Debt Total Assets)							
Megginson, Nash, and van Randenborgh (1994); D'Souza and Megginson (1999)	53	0.6622 (0.7039)	0.6379 (0.6618)	−0.0243 (−0.0234)	−2.41**	71.7	3.51***
Megginson (1999)	72	0.29	0.23	−0.06	−3.08***	67	3.05***
DIVIDENDS (Cash Dividends Sales)							
Megginson, Nash, and van Randenborgh (1994); D'Souza and Megginson (1999)	39	0.0128 (0.0054)	0.0300 (0.0223)	0.0172 (0.0121)	4.63***	89.7	8.18***
Megginson (1999)	51	0.015	0.04	0.025	4.98***	79	5.24***

*** Indicates significance at the 1% level.
** Indicates significance at the 5% level.
* Indicates significance at the 10% level.

Source: Megginson (2003).

financial performance of newly divested firms, (2) that these improvements are the result of socially beneficial improvements in
productive efficiency and entrepreneurial effort, and (3) that privatization "works" in a wide variety of countries, industries, and competitive environments.

The methodologies pioneered by MNRD have become standard in
the empirical analysis of the performance of privatized firms. However,
they suffer from several drawbacks. First, selection bias raises probably the
most serious concern, as the sample is made up of companies sold in public
equity markets via SIP programs. These companies tend to be the largest
and usually the most profitable SOEs, which due to intense restructuring
pre-privatization are certainly the easiest to privatize. Second, the two
snapshots taken on performance measures pre- and post-privatization do
not allow disentangling the possible sources of these improvements, which
may be ascribed to privatization per se, but also to other factors such as a
lack of competition or weak regulation.

Some steps in this direction have been made by Bortolotti et al. (2002)
in a study on the global telecommunications industry, including virtually all major European operators. Using panel data models, it is found
that some performance measures are more strongly affected by competitive conditions (with higher profitability associated with less-intense
competition in the product markets) rather than by the privatization
alone.

The existing evidence stemming from cross-country analyses does not
allow us to conclude that privatization per se has been the key in boosting
the financial and operating performance of firms, but rather the combination of liberalization and regulatory and ownership changes.

In what follows, we will try to complement this evidence by summarizing the main results of country studies on the economic and financial effects of privatization on the behavior of privatized SOEs in European
context, starting from the U.K. experience.

Several studies document significant performance improvements along
some key performance measures, but most of them conclude that the program could and should have been executed with more concern for distributional issues and/or with greater protection built for consumers.

Parker and Saal (2003) examine the productivity and price performance
of the privatized water and sewerage companies of England and Wales after the industry was privatized and a new regulatory regime imposed in

1989. They document that labor productivity improved significantly after privatization, but they find no evidence that total-factor productivity grew as a direct result of the ownership change. They also find that increases in output prices have outstripped increased input prices, leading to significantly higher economic profits after privatization.

Newbery and Pollitt (1997) perform a counterfactual analysis of the 1990 restructuring and privatization of the U.K. Central Electricity Generating Board and document significant post-privatization performance improvements. However, they find that the producers and their shareholders capture all of the financial rewards of this improvement and more, whereas the government and consumers lose out.

Price and Weyman-Jones (1996) measure the technical efficiency of the U.K. natural gas industry before and after its 1986 privatization and associated regulatory changes. They employ nonparametric frontier analysis to show that the industry's rate of productivity growth increased significantly after privatization—though not as much as it could have if the industry had been restructured and subjected to direct competition and more appropriate regulation.

In a comprehensive case study on the United Kingdom, Florio (2004) uses cost-benefit analyses to investigate the effect of privatization on firms, consumers, shareholders, workers, and taxpayers, concluding that the overall effect of "the Great Divestiture" on efficiency has been modest and that privatization had a substantial regressive effect on the distribution of incomes.

Studies conducted in other European countries provide very mixed evidence. Villalonga (2000) examines the effect of privatization on the operating efficiency of 24 Spanish firms that were fully divested between 1985 and 1993. Privatization seems to decrease efficiency over the intermediate term (five and six years after divestiture), but to increase efficiency over the longer term (seven and eight years) afterwards and in the period leading up to privatization (three and four years before).

Dumontier and Laurin (2002), investigate the value that was created or lost during the state ownership period for each of the 46 French companies (39 banks and 5 industrial firms) that were nationalized during 1982 and then reprivatized between 1986 and 1995. They analyze whether the subsequent privatization of these companies improved performance over that achieved during the post-1982 nationalized period. They find that the French government created value in the nationalized firms, but the state and taxpayers did not benefit because of the premium that was paid to shareholders upon nationalization (20%) and because of the underpricing of the IPOs at the time of privatization. The financial and operating performance of companies improved during the nationalization phase, then improved even more after privatization. Employment fell during the nationalization, but increased (due to higher sales) after privatization.

Goldstein and Nicoletti (2003) conduct a performance analysis based on a sample of 25 Italian privatized nonfinancial firms. Their analysis is important as it is one of the few based on a comparison with a control group of private companies, which allows it to take into account cyclical movements in the economy. Interestingly, none of the traditional indicators used in MNRD studies gains statistical significance, with the exception of investment indicators that show a marked improvement.

The evidence presented in this section does not allow us to provide an unambiguous answer about the role of privatization on the financial and operating performance of European SOEs. First, the bulk of the evidence coming from cross-country studies does not appear to be robust. Second, country studies provide mixed results. Importantly, the implications of privatizations in terms of allocative and productive efficiency have not yet been empirically documented in comprehensive statistical analyses.

POPULAR CAPITALISM AND OWNERSHIP DIFFUSION

The political economy approach to privatization points out that fostering popular capitalism and widening share ownership are possible objectives of divestiture that right-wing market-oriented governments may find particularly attractive. The reason for this preference is not purely ideological, but is grounded in self-interest and political opportunism. Indeed privatization, by making equity investment attractive for the middle classes, can create a constituency with an interest in increasing the value of its assets that is therefore averse to the redistribution policies of the left. In this way, privatization can be a rational strategy for raising the probability of electoral success of market-oriented coalitions. The key variable to achieve reelection via privatization is underpricing, which in turn depends on income distribution. Indeed, the poorer the median voter, the more underpricing is needed to entice him or her to become a shareholder in privatized firms (Biais and Perotti, 2002).

The English experience seems to fit quite well with the empirical implication of this model. The Thatcher government's privatization program, especially in the initial term, was implemented with the declared objective of expanding and spreading equity ownership. This was achieved through a massive program of SIPs characterized by substantial underpricing.[3] In this way, the distribution of equity at a discounted price made the renationalization (proposed in the Labour party's electoral program) costly while simultaneously increasing conservative support. Indeed, the five consecutive victories by the Conservatives indicate that strategic privatization (in combination with other market-oriented policies such as tax relief, reduction in public expenditures, and deregulation) may have paid off at the general elections.

Beyond the English experience, it is commonly recognized that privatization is politically motivated. A bulk of empirical papers has provided evidence that partisan politics matters in the choice of the privatization method. Particularly, privatization implemented by right-wing governments in developed (mainly European) countries tend to be structured as public offers instead of as private equity placements (Bortolotti and Siniscalco, 2004; Bortolotti and Pinotti, 2003), to be more strongly underpriced where the income inequality is higher (Jones et al., 1999), and to exhibit a preferential allocation of shares toward domestic retail investors (Bortolotti and Siniscalco, 2004).

The available evidence appears broadly consistent with the idea that political objectives shape privatization. However, the empirical literature has not established whether privatization contributed to widening share ownership and to promoting popular capitalism, nor that it has significantly shifted political preferences by creating support to market-oriented policies in Europe.

Boutchkova and Megginson (2000) analyze the evolution of share ownership in a sample of SIPs, concluding that the initial structure of shareholding does not appear to be stable over the long run. Indeed, the striking number of initial shareholders (often over 100,000) declines by 33% within five years of the offering. The privatization process in the United Kingdom seems to point this direction, as the inflation in the number of shareholders in privatized firms has been a temporary phenomenon. Clarke and Pitelis (1993) document substantial individual flipping such that the majority of initial investors immediately disposed of their holdings to cash in on the initial discount. The majority of shares ended up eventually with the financial institutions.

In a comprehensive analysis of retail incentives in share issue privatizations from 1981 to 2003, Kelohariju, Knupfer, and Torstila (2004) come to a sharply different conclusion with respect to the U.K. case study. First, they document a widespread use of retail incentives such as bonus shares, i.e., a free distribution of shares to investors holding shares for a given period (frequently 24–36 months). Second, they document that these measure are costly, but extremely effective in attracting retail investors. Particularly, they find that a dollar spent in retail incentives increases the number of investors participating in the offering 21 times more than a dollar spent on underpricing. Finally, in an interesting controlled experiment based on Finnish privatizations, they document that flipping is not simply postponed at the end of the lock-up period but is substantially reduced in bonus tranches as compared to regular tranches.

Retail incentives (which have been regularly used in share issue privatization) have worked well to meet the goal of widening the domestic shareholder base. The fact that these incentives are absent in private sector offerings confirms (again) that political objectives shape divestiture. It would be interesting to know more about the role of political preferences toward these incentives. Should bonus shares and incentives be systematically associated with share issue privatization by right-wing governments, then a final test could be provided about the link between partisan politics and the objective of spreading share ownership and equity culture.

OWNERSHIP AND CONTROL IN PRIVATIZED FIRMS

The wave of privatization that occurred in Europe during the 1990s definitively represents one of the greatest transfers of ownership in the history of the corporation. However, there is a lingering belief that privatization did not alter dramatically the corporate governance of SOE, which governments still hang on to control by direct and indirect means.

This section presents updated empirical evidence on the transfer of ownership and control in European privatized companies. The transfer of ownership is measured by the stake sold in the various operations in different countries. The transfer of control, instead, is analyzed through the government's voting rights in privatized companies and by the temporary or permanent restrictions to the control rights of the private investors, such as golden shares.

The divestiture of minority holdings, or partial privatization, appears to be quite common in Western Europe. From 1977 to 2003, 59% of the 1,133 deals involved the sale of the majority of stock. Interestingly, this percentage shrinks to 21% in the sample of privatizations

TABLE 2.5 Percentages of Capital Sold in European Privatizations, 1977–2003

This table reports aggregate figures on privatization in major Western European countries for the 1977–2003 period. Countries are ranked by average percentage of capital sold. *Deals* is the total number of privatizations.

Country	Deals	Average Percentage of Capital Sold	Average Percentage of Capital Sold Through PO	Average Percentage of Capital Sold Through PS
United Kingdom	186	89.92	73.84	96.95
Germany	156	78.08	29.31	84.99
Sweden	59	77.44	33.45	87.73
Ireland	17	65.20	38.35	73.46
Spain	80	63.65	30.01	79.22
Netherlands	32	60.64	24.92	82.08
Norway	34	59.95	34.16	76.07
France	114	59.26	37.81	75.99
Portugal	81	55.24	36.02	75.46
Italy	124	54.71	29.40	70.70
Finland	58	54.59	17.70	81.43
Denmark	9	46.14	32.71	68.53
Austria	58	45.70	32.73	61.77
Belgium	11	41.88	33.30	43.79
Mean	73	60.89	34.55	75.58

Sources: Privatization Barometer (http://www.privatizationbarometer.net) and Securities Data Corporation.

through public offer, where the average percentage of capital sold is 36%.

Table 2.5 shows the average percentage of capital sold in privatization deals in European countries. Obviously, a distinction has to be made between public offerings, which involve the largest companies and often more profitable SOEs floated in the stock market, and private placements, which instead are typically used to sell small-sized firms operating in nonstrategic sectors. The data show that privatization of the latter tends to be more complete, especially in countries such as the United Kingdom, Sweden, Germany, France, and Finland. On the contrary, partial privatization is typical of larger SOEs, which are usually sold by tranches. Indeed, lower averages of capital are sold through public offers of shares in almost all major European countries with the exception of the United Kingdom.

Partial privatization is certainly an interesting feature of a state's assets disposal. The effect of partial privatization should not be understated, given that the initial listing of the shares of the SOE can have first-order effects on managerial incentives and performance (Gupta, 2005). However, it is important to document whether partial sales are just a snapshot of a process that will end with a complete divestiture, or will tend to persist over the long run, as if governments were not really intended to give up ownership and control.

While privatizing the first tranche represents a win-win solution, allowing the government to raise revenues and to enhance the company value, the complete relinquishment of control is a politically costly decision given that governments lose a powerful instrument for targeted redistribution (as high wages and job security could be earmarked to special categories of workers), the right of having representatives on the boards in order to affect corporate decisions, and the power to safeguard public interests and national security.

Bortolotti and Faccio (2004) dig into the issue of government's control by analyzing the recent evolution of ultimate voting rights in 141 privatized companies, of which 81% are from Western Europe.

Ultimate (direct and indirect) control (voting) rights by private and public shareholders (including the central state, federal or regional bodies, central banks, etc.) are computed as the weakest link along the control chain, taking into account pyramiding and cross-holdings (as in La Porta et al., 1999). Then several categories of privatized firms are identified according to the identity of the largest ultimate controlling shareholder at the 10% cut-off level (see table 2.6).

In fact, the privatization process in developed economies (and particularly in Europe) does not seem to be accomplished. As of 2000, the state is *still* the largest shareholder in almost 30% of the privatized firms of our sample. The rest of the sample is split between family controlled (19%) and widely held firms (30%).

The high percentages of state-controlled firms observed in 2000 feed the suspicion that privatization was carried out reluctantly during the

TABLE 2.6 Type of Largest Shareholder in Privatized Firms

Data for 120 European privatized firms are used to construct this table. The table presents the percentage of firms controlled by the government, using 10% ownership as the threshold for a large shareholder. Large shareholders are classified into two types. *State*: a national government (domestic or foreign), a local authority (county, municipality, etc.), or a government agency. *Non-state*: any other shareholder.

Privatized Firms			
Time Period	Number of Firms	State	Non-state
End of 1996	120	36.67	63.33
End of 2000	120	30.83	69.17

Source: Privatization Barometer (http://www.privatizationbarometer.net).

1990s. In order to quantitatively assess this reluctance, we take a second snapshot in a previous year.

Data availability allows us to go back in time to 1996, when we find a higher number of state-controlled firms (34%) and a lower number of widely held (27%) and privately owned companies (16%). During the period, the government relinquished control only in 10 companies, which account for 7% of our sample.

The analysis of ultimate voting rights of the largest shareholders reported in table 2.7 yields some interesting results. In 2000, the largest shareholder on average controls 25% of voting rights. When the government is the largest shareholder, it controls more than 50% of voting rights. Government-controlled privatized firms show, therefore, a much higher concentration of power, which does not seem to decline over time.

We now raise a question: Is it possible to identify economic reasons to rationalize governments' reluctance to sell, or does it have to be traced back to their willingness to keep companies under political control? More precisely, are there idiosyncratic factors—perhaps related to a given country, sector, or business activity—that could explain why some SOEs are so tightly controlled?

One possible way of testing this hypothesis is to construct a control sample of private firms and then to compare the evolution of the ultimate ownership within the two samples.

Table 2.7 reports some statistics on the ultimate ownership of privatized companies as opposed to their respective matching private firms.[4] The pooled data suggest a quite strong convergence between the privatized firms and the control sample. The samples report a statistically significant difference in means of approximately 7% in 1996, which becomes insignificant and negligible in 2000.

In the subsample of government-controlled firms, control structures do not converge at all. On average, in 1996 the public shareholder owns a control stake that is 30% higher than the one owned by the largest ultimate shareholder in private firms. This difference shrinks only marginally at the end of the period, while remaining highly statistically significant.

This evidence about the dynamics of ownership in privatized companies allows a deeper understanding of government's reluctance to sell. On average, the European privatization process has contributed to the rollback of the state in the ownership of productive assets. Several companies have been sold off, and in these companies the governments do

TABLE 2.7 Ultimate Control Rights in Privatized Firms

Data relating to 120 European privatized corporations and 120 matching firms are used to construct this table. *Largest shareholder voting rights* is the percentage of voting rights ultimately controlled by the largest ultimate shareholder. *Government voting rights* is the percentage of voting rights controlled by a government, when a government is the largest shareholder. *Private voting rights* is the percentage of voting rights controlled by the largest shareholder in the matching firms of companies in which the government is the largest shareholder.

Panel A: Privatized Firms

	All Privatized Companies			Companies in Which the Government is the Largest Shareholder			
	Number of Firms	Largest Shareholder Voting Rights (Mean)	Median Voting Rights	Number of Firms	Government Voting Rights (Mean)	Median Voting Rights	Firms Using Control-Enhancing Devices (%)
End of 1996	120	28.91	23.01	44	52.49	51.00	8.65
End of 2000	120	25.92	16.61	37	45.08	47.28	16.73

Panel B: Matching Firms

	Number of Firms	Largest Shareholder Voting Rights (Mean)	Median Voting Rights	Number of Firms	Private Voting Rights (Mean)
End of 1996	120	19.54	10.12	44	14.62
End of 2000	120	26.44	12.81	37	31.26

Panel C: Difference Between Privatized and Matching Firms

	Voting Rights (Mean)	Voting Rights (Mean)
Diff. end 1996	9.37	37.87
Diff. end 2000	−0.52	13.82

Source: Privatization Barometer (http://www.privatizationbarometer.net).

not appear as the major shareholders post-privatization. However, there is also a hard core of companies that remain tightly controlled by the state over time.

The previous analysis has shown that several SOEs have been fully privatized during the 1990s. However, the sale of a majority holding is not itself a sufficient condition to avoid government interference in privatized companies. Governments can grant themselves wide discretionary powers over partially or even fully privatized companies by the use of golden shares. By exerting its rights, the "special" shareholder can often influence the choice of management and exert veto power over the acquisition of relevant stakes by private shareholders even without owning the majority of stock in the company or a single share of capital.

As stated earlier, golden shares can broadly be defined as the complex of special powers granted to the state and the statutory constraints in privatized companies. Typically, special powers include (1) the right to appoint members in corporate board; (2) the right to express consent or to veto the acquisition of relevant interests in the privatized companies; (3) other rights such as consent on the transfer of subsidiaries, dissolution of the company, and ordinary management. The above-mentioned rights may be temporary or not. Statutory constraints instead include (1) ownership limits, (2) voting caps, and (3) provisions of national control.

As table 2.8 shows, golden shares are widespread in Western European countries. In 1996, they are found in more than 42% of the companies in our sample and in each country. Furthermore, they are highly concentrated in some sectors, such as defense, where 100% of the privatized companies have golden shares, telecommunications (83%), oil and gas (62%), utilities (64%), and transportation (40%).

Indeed, governments resort to golden shares in order to protect a broadly defined concept of national security to shield privatized companies operating in the defense business from hostile (foreign) takeovers and also utilities providing public services such as gas, electricity, water, telecommunications, and transportation. The provision of such services but also the safeguard of essential facilities are certainly strategic, especially when privatization did not proceed in parallel with adequate liberalization and effective regulation.

Table 2.8 provides a comprehensive account of government power in privatized firms by taking into account in combination voting rights and golden shares mechanisms. As of 2000, 64.9% of the 118 privatized companies for which reliable information is available are either directly

TABLE 2.8 Country Distribution of Privatized Firms by Control Type

Government-controlled firms are those whose largest shareholder (at the 10% threshold) is a national government (domestic or foreign), local authority (county, municipality, etc.), or government agency. *Golden share* is a dummy that takes the value of 1 if the government enjoys special powers or there are statutory constraints in privatized companies.

Country	Obs.	Obs. in the Country as % of all Privatizations	Government-Controlled (as of end 1996)	Golden Share (as of end 1996)	Government-Controlled or Golden Share (as of end 1996)	Government-Controlled or Golden Share as % of Privatized Firms in the Country (as of end 1996)	Government-Controlled (as of end 2000)	Government-Controlled or Golden Share (as of end 2000)	Government-Controlled or Golden Share as % of Privatized Firms in the Country (as of end 2000)
Austria	11	7.80	9	2	9	81.80	9	9	81.80
Belgium	2	1.40	1	1	2	100.00	1	2	100.00
Denmark	2	1.40	2	1	2	100.00	1	1	50.00
Finland	4	2.80	4	1	4	100.00	4	4	100.00
France	20	14.20	6	5	9	45.00	5	8	40.00
Germany	10	7.10	5	2	5	50.00	5	5	50.00
Greece	2	1.40	2	1	2	100.00	2	2	100.00
Ireland	2	1.40	0	2	2	100.00	0	2	100.00
Italy	12	8.50	6	6	8	66.70	4	7	58.30
Netherlands	3	2.10	1	1	1	33.30	1	1	33.30
Norway	6	4.30	3	2	3	50.00	2	3	50.00
Portugal	9	6.40	1	4	4	44.40	1	4	44.40
Spain	5	3.50	2	2	3	60.00	1	3	60.00
Sweden	3	2.10	2	1	2	66.70	1	1	33.30
Turkey	3	2.10	0	2	2	66.70	0	2	66.70
United Kingdom	24	17.00	0	17	17	70.80	0	17	70.80
Whole Sample	118	100.00	44	50	75	70.90	37	71	64.90

Source: Privatization Barometer (http://www.privatizationbarometer.net).

controlled by the state or warrant special powers to the public share-holder through additional control devices.

This combined evidence shows that governments are reluctant to privatize, and this reluctance appears particularly strong in the so-called strategic sectors. This protectionist attitude can certainly be attributed to governments' willingness to firmly maintain political control over one country's largest and most valuable corporations. However, the failure to relinquish control has also to be traced back to the various economic and institutional constraints shaping economic policy. Indeed, genuine privatization is problematic if markets are not competitive and regulation is weak.

These new results on the corporate governance of privatized firms raise a final question: does reluctant privatization matter in the valuation of firms?

According to a largely held view, a principal-agent plagues government-controlled firms, as the owners (the taxpayers) have different objectives from the bureaucrat or the politician controlling the firm. In these firms, the manager may run the company to achieve political objectives such as keeping redundant workers, not to maximize profits. When control rights are transferred to the private sector, more emphasis will be placed on efficiency (Shleifer and Vishny, 1994). This theory has a straightforward empirical implication: in privatized firms, government voting rights are negatively related to the market valuation of a company.

Bortolotti and Faccio (2004) test this hypothesis by regressing ultimate voting rights on (adjusted) market-to-book ratios in a large sample of privatized firms, and find a quite surprising result: higher government control rights are *not* negatively discounted in market values. On the contrary, government-controlled privatized companies appear on average more valuable than fully privatized firms. Results do not appear to be driven by reverse causality or by the agency costs of private ownership, and they survive when several control variables (including sector dummies) are included.

Indeed, it is possible that governments grant special benefits to privatized companies in which they retain control, regardless of industries. The potential benefits include subsidizing loans, guaranteeing contracts, and shielding companies from competition.

A caveat is in order. This analysis on the effect of government power in firms is performed on a sample of privatized companies listed on the stock market. The reader should not jump to the conclusion that state ownership is superior because the empirical literature has documented major performance improvements in state-owned companies when they are initially privatized. Rather, the previous result points out the existence of a nonlinear relation between government rights and market valuation, which should be investigated in a richer theoretical setting where the "grabbing hand" hypothesis is complemented with other hypotheses on the behavior of politicians in firms.

Privatization was certainly one of the main events of the economic and financial history of the twentieth century. Western Europe had a great bearing in such a process, having raised half of worldwide proceeds. The relevance of Western Europe in the process can be ascribed to several factors, the main one being the abnormal growth of the SOE sector that occurred during the century to foster industrialization and stabilize the European economies severely hit by adverse shocks.

At the turn of the century, the process abruptly slowed down at the global scale, especially in Western Europe, the continent that launched the process.

This stylized fact raises an important question: is privatization in Western Europe a long-term trend proceeding in parallel with the advancing of market capitalism, or is it rather a cycle following the short- or medium-term fluctuations of economic fundamentals?

The empirical analysis shows that privatization processes are shaped by economic and political determinants. Particularly, they are affected by market conditions, so that large privatization waves are systematically associated with bull stock markets. But budget constraints and political institutions also matter. Weak fiscal conditions and the urge to meet Maastricht criteria have certainly been major drivers in the privatization decision, as financially distressed governments have been more eager to privatize. However, government preferences face institutional constraints so that large privatization programs have been more smoothly implemented in countries endowed with majoritarian political institutions, curbing the veto powers of averse constituencies and entrenched interests.

We can therefore tentatively conclude that the big privatization wave of the 1980s and especially the 1990s has mostly been a cyclical phenomenon, where the engine of sales have been booming stock markets and worsening fiscal conditions. However, within this common trend, the extent to which governments privatize depends upon exogenous political and institutional determinants, which tend to persist in the long run.

As to the effects of privatization, more research is needed to understand the profound consequences of divestiture in Western Europe. However, on the basis of the existing evidence, we can tentatively conclude that the effects at the macroeconomic level have been important, especially in terms of stock market development.

The microeconomic effects of privatization are less visible, both in terms of the performance of privatized firms and corporate governance structures. First, the financial and operating performance has apparently improved in the aftermath of privatization. However, only limited efforts have been displayed to quantify these improvements using private firms as benchmarks, and to isolate the possible sources of these improvements. Indeed, it is not clear whether they stem from the additional monitoring role played by the stock market, from intentional structural reforms, or from the dilution of government ownership.

As to ownership and control in privatized companies, the empirical literature has provided solid evidence that privatization in Western Europe has been partial and incomplete. In most cases, privatization did not entail a dramatic change in governance structures, as private ownership and public control actually seem to coexist.

The final question that we raise is the following: is the coexistence of private ownership with public control just a transient European anomaly or a functional pattern of governance?

Providing tentative answers to this question is certainly an important avenue for future research, both on the theoretical and empirical sides. For the time being, we conjecture that genuine privatization (i.e., the transfer of ownership and control to the private sector) appears difficult to achieve and sustain, as several conditions must be met. First, markets should be competitive or suitably regulated. Second, private investors should be adequately protected by the law in order to avoid expropriation. Third, political institutions should be designed to limit the veto power of constituencies ousting full divestiture. Fourth, governments should be credibly committed to not interfere in the operating activity of the companies postprivatization. Finally, and more cynically, the financial incentives for full divestiture may be limited if governments' stakes in privatized firms turn out to be valuable for shareholders because special benefits could be targeted to (partially) privatized firms.

The most recent trends document a strong resurgence of privatization activity in Europe, especially through public offering of shares to retail investors. European governments, severely hit by the global economic crisis and envisaging fiscal operations to improve budgetary figures, have once again resorted to privatization sales. The positive outlook in stock markets and investor's appetite for high-quality stocks have been key drivers in the resumption of the process. It is hard to predict whether this new trend represents the beginning of a new cycle or simply a readjustment after a negative shock. Certainly, the stage of increasing returns of privatization is probably over, and this makes privatizing the "second tranche" a difficult challenge for European governments.

NOTES

Acknowledgment: Research assistance from Luca Farinola is gratefully acknowledged.

1. Industrial sectors are defined as follows: Agriculture Industry (SICs 01XX–09XX) includes: Agricultural Production Crops; Agricultural Production Livestock; Agricultural Services; Forestry; Fishing, Hunting, and Trapping. Natural Resource (SICs 10XX; 12XX; 14XX) includes: Metal Mining; Coal Mining; Nonmetallic Minerals, except Fuels. Petroleum Industry (SICs 13XX; 29XX) includes: Oil and Gas Extraction; Petroleum and Coal Products. Construction (SICs 15XX–17XX) includes: General Building Contractors; Heavy Construction, Except Building; Special Trade Contractors. Finance (SICs 60XX–67XX) includes: Depository Institutions; Non Depository Institutions; Security and Commodity Brokers; Insurance Carriers; Insurance Agents, Brokers, & Service; Real Estate; Holding and Other Investment Offices. Manufacturing (SICs 20XX–28XX; 30XX–39XX) includes: Food and Kindred Products; Tobacco Products; Textile Mill Products; Apparel and Other Textile Products; Lumber and Wood Products; Furniture and Fixtures; Paper and Allied Products; Printing and Publishing; Chemical and Allied Products; Rubber and Miscellaneous Plastic Products; Leather and Leather Products; Stone, Clay, and Glass Products; Primary Metal Industries; Fabricated Metal Products; Industrial Machinery and Equipment; Electronic and Other Electric Equipment; Transportation Equipment; Instruments and Related Products; Miscellaneous Manufacturing Industries. Public Administration (SICs 91XX–97XX) includes: Executive, Legislative, & General; Justice, Public Order, & Safety; Finance, Taxation, & Monetary Policy; Administration of Human Resources; Environmental Quality & Housing; Administration of Economic Programs; National Security & International Affairs; Nonclassifiable Establishments. Services (SICs 70XX–89XX) includes: Hotels and Other Lodging Places; Personal Services; Business Services; Auto Repair, Services, and Parking; Miscellaneous Repair Services; Motion Pictures; Amusement & Recreation Services; Health Services; Legal Services; Educational Services; Social Services; Museums, Botanicals, Zoological Gardens; Membership Organizations; Engineering & Management Services; Private Households; Services, Misc. Telecommunications (SICs 48XX) includes: Communications. Trade Industry (SICs 50XX–59XX) includes: Wholesale Trade—Durable

Goods; Wholesale Trade—Nondurable Goods; Building Materials & Garden Supplies; General Merchandise Stores; Food Stores; Automotive Dealers & Services Stations; Apparel and Accessory Stores; Furniture and Home Furnishings Stores; Eating & Drinking Places; Miscellaneous Retail. Transportation Industry (SICs 40XX–42XX; 44XX; 45XX; 47XX) includes: Railroads Transportation; Local and Interurban Passenger Transit; Trucking and Warehousing; Water Transportation; Transportation by Air; Transportation Services. Utilities (SICs 46XX; 49XX) includes: Pipelines, Except Natural Gas; Electric, Gas, and Sanitary Services.

2. See also Nicoletti and Scarpetta (2003); Haggarty and Shirley (1995).

3. See Biais and Perotti (2002); Jenkinson and Ljungqvist (2000).

4. For a detailed description of the methodology used to identify the control group, see Bortolotti and Faccio (2004).

REFERENCES

Alesina, A. and A. Drazen. 1991. "Why Are Stabilizations Delayed?" *American Economic Review* 81: 1170–1188.

Baklanoff, E. N. 1986. "The State and Economy in Portugal: Perspectives on Corporatism, Revolution and Incipient Privatization." In *State Shrinking: A Comparative Inquiry into Privatization*, ed. W. P. Glade. Austin: Institute of Latin American Studies, University of Texas, Austin.

Biais, B. and E. C. Perotti. 2002. "Machiavellian Privatization." *American Economic Review* 92: 240–258.

Bortolotti, B., F. De Jong, G. Nicodano, and I. Schindele. 2007. "Privatization and Stock Market Liquidity." *Journal of Banking and Finance* 31(2): 297–316.

Bortolotti, B., J. D'Souza, M. Fantini, and W. L. Megginson. 2002. "Sources of Performance Improvements in Privatized Firms: A Clinical Study of the Global Telecommunications Industry." *Telecommunications Policy* 26: 243–268.

Bortolotti, B. and M. Faccio. 2004. "Reluctant Privatization." Working Paper 2004.130, Fondazione Eni Enrico Mattei.

Bortolotti, B., M. Fantini, and D. Siniscalco. 2003. "Privatisation Around the World: Evidence from Panel Data." *Journal of Public Economics* 88: 335–366.

Bortolotti, B. and P. Pinotti. 2003. "The Political Economy of Privatization." Working Paper 2003.45, Fondazione Eni Enrico Mattei.

Bortolotti, B. and D. Siniscalco. 2004. *The Challenges of Privatization: An International Analysis*. Oxford: Oxford University Press.

Boutchkova, M. K. and W. L. Megginson. 2000. "Privatization and the Role of Global Capital Markets." *Financial Management* (Winter): 32–76.

Chiesa, G. and G. Nicodano. 2003. "Privatization and Financial Market Development: Theoretical Issues." Working Paper 2003.1, Fondazione Eni Enrico Mattei.

Clarke, T. and C. Pitelis, eds. 1993. *The Political Economy of Privatization*. London: Routledge.

Dewenter, K. and P. H. Malatesta. 1997. "Public Offerings of State-Owned and Privately Owned Enterprises: An International Comparison." *Journal of Finance* 57: 1659–1679.

D'Souza, J. and W. L. Megginson. 1999. "The Financial and Operating Performance of Newly Privatized Firms in the 1990s." *Journal of Finance* 54: 1397–1438.

Dumontier, P. and C. Laurin. 2002. "The Financial Impacts of the French Government Nationalization—Privatization Strategy." Working Paper, University of Geneva.

Ellul, A. and M. Pagano. 2006. "IPO Underpricing and After-market Liquidity." *Review of Financial Studies* 19(2): 381–421.

Florio, M. 2004. *The Great Divestiture.* Cambridge, MA: MIT Press.

Goldstein, A. and G. Nicoletti. 2003. "Privatization in Italy 1993–2002: Goals, Institutions, Outcomes, and Outstanding Issues." Working Paper, OECD Development Centre, Paris.

Gupta, N. 2005. "Partial Privatization and Firm Performance." *Journal of Finance* 60(2): 987–1015.

Haggarty, L. and M. Shirley. 1995. *Bureaucrats in Business.* Washington, DC: World Bank.

Hölmstrom, B. and J. Tirole. 1993. "Market Liquidity and Performance Monitoring." *Journal of Political Economy* 101: 678–709.

Jenkinson, T. and A. P. Ljungqvist. 2000. *Going Public.* London: Oxford University Press.

Jeronimo, V., J. A. Pagán, and S. Gökçe. 2000. "Privatization and European Economic and Monetary Union." *Eastern Economic Journal* 26: 321–333.

Jones, S., W. L. Megginson, R. Nash, and J. Netter. 1999. "Share Issue Privatizations as Financial Means to Political and Economic Ends." *Journal of Financial Economics* 53: 217–253.

Katsoulakos, Y. and E. Likoyanni. 2002. "Fiscal and Macroeconomic Effects of Privatization." Working Paper, Athens University of Economics and Business.

Kelohariju, M., G. Knupfer, and S. Torstila. 2004. "Do Retail Incentives Work in Privatizations?" CEPR Discussion Paper 4612. London: Centre for Economic Policy Research.

La Porta, R., F. López-de-Silanes, A. Shleifer, and R. W. Vishny. 1999. "Corporate Ownership Around the World." *Journal of Finance* 54: 471–518.

Lijphart, A. 1999. *Patterns of Democracy.* New Haven, CT: Yale University Press.

Mackenzie, G. A. 1998. "The Macroeconomic Impact of Privatization." IMF Staff Paper 45(2). Washington, DC: International Monetary Fund.

Megginson, W. L. 2003. "Macroeconomic Effects of Privatization." Mimeo.

Megginson, W. L., R. Nash, J. M. Netter, and A. B. Poulsen. 2000. "The Choice Between Private and Public Markets: Evidence from Privatizations." Working Paper, University of Georgia.

Megginson, W. L., R. Nash, and M. van Randenborgh. 1994. "The Financial and Operating Performance of Newly Privatised Firms: An International Empirical Analysis." *Journal of Finance* 49: 403–452.

Megginson, W. L. and J. Netter. 2001. "From State to Market: A Survey of Empirical Studies on Privatization." *Journal of Economic Literature* 39: 321–389.

Newbery, D. and M. G. Pollitt. 1997. "The Restructuring and Privatization of Britain's CEGB—Was It Worth It?" *Journal of Industrial Economics* 45: 269–303.

Nicoletti, G. and S. Scarpetta. 2003. "Regulation, Productivity and Growth: OECD Evidence." Economics Department Working Paper 347. Paris: Organisation for Economic Co-operation and Development.

Pagano, M. 1993. "The Floatation of Companies and the Stock Market: A Co-ordination Failure Model." *European Economic Review* 37: 1101–1125.

Parker, D. and D. Saal. 2003. *International Handbook on Privatization.* Cheltenham, England: Edward Elgar.

Price, C. W. and T. Weyman-Jones. 1996. "Malmquist Indices of Productivity Change in the UK Gas Industry Before and After Privatization." *Applied Economics* 28: 29–39.

Sheshinski, E. and L. F. Lopez-Calva. 2002. "Privatization and Its Benefits: Theory, Evidence, and Challenges." In *Markets and Governments*, ed. K. Basu, P. Nayak, and R. Ray, 185–242. New Delhi: Oxford University Press.

Shleifer, A. and R. Vishny. 1994. "The Politics of Market Socialism." *Journal of Economic Perspectives* 8(2): 165–176.

Spolaore, E. 2004. "Adjustments in Different Government Systems." *Economics and Politics* 16(2): 117–146.

Subramaniam, S. and S. Titman. 1999. "The Going Public Decision and the Development of Financial Markets." *Journal of Finance* 54: 1045–1082.

Villalonga, B. 2000. "Privatization and Efficiency: Differentiating Ownership Effects from Political, Organizational and Dynamic Effects." *Journal of Economic Behavior and Organization* 42: 43–74.

World Bank. 1995. *Bureaucrats in Business: The Economics and Politics of Government Ownership.* New York: Oxford University Press.

——. 2002. *World Development Indicators.* Washington, DC: World Bank.

Wright V., ed. 1994. *Privatisation in Western Europe.* London: Pinter Publishers.

CHAPTER 3

Privatization in Central and Eastern Europe and the Commonwealth of Independent States

Jan Hanousek, Evžen Kočenda, and Jan Svejnar

The wisdom and economic effects of privatization in Central and Eastern Europe (CEE) and the Commonwealth of Independent States (CIS) are currently the subject of intense reexamination. While today privatization is under debate, in the early 1990s privatization was widely considered one of the keystones of the entire transition process. This view was advocated strongly by proponents of the so-called Washington Consensus, which emphasized fast transfer of ownership via privatization and the belief that private ownership, together with market forces, would ensure better and more efficient performance of the economy (see, e.g., Roland, 2001, for a discussion). The belief that privatization would be conducive to development of the former centrally planned economies was quite broad-based. In fact, efficiency was the most important argument for privatization. The transfer of ownership rights was viewed as crucial for the efficient allocation of resources. This way, the argument went, long-term economic growth would be initiated and sustained.

From the start it was clear, however, that privatization in and of itself would not be sufficient to ensure an effective functioning of the newly created market economies. In particular, most of the early writing on the subject of an optimal strategy for the transition stressed an entire series of interrelated systemic changes and policy reforms that were a prerequisite for a successful transition. Because the impact of privatization was often viewed as dependent on the presence of specific accompanying policies and systemic changes, we include in this chapter a brief evaluation of such policies and changes that presumably influenced the effects of privatization.

This chapter is structured as follows. In the first section we discuss the key systemic changes and policies that, along with privatization, were carried out, in full or in part, during the transition in CEE and the CIS. In the second section we examine the macro- and microeconomic evidence about the determinants, extent and effect of privatization. We conclude our study with a number of policy-oriented observations.

POLICIES, INSTITUTIONS, AND PRIVATIZATION

POLICIES

In the late 1980s and early 1990s, the new policy makers in the countries of the former Soviet bloc and Yugoslavia formulated initial strategies that focused on macroeconomic stabilization and microeconomic restructuring; they then enforced institutional and political reforms to support these strategies. The implementation of the strategies varied from country to country, both in speed and in the specifics of the actual changes that occurred. Almost all the transition governments in the former Soviet bloc and former Yugoslavia plunged ahead in rapid big-bang style with what Svejnar (2002) calls *Type I* reforms, namely macro stabilization, price liberalization, and the dismantling of the institutions of the communist system. The macroeconomic strategy emphasized restrictive fiscal and monetary policies, wage controls, and in most cases a fixed exchange rate as well. The micro strategy entailed a quick move toward price liberalization even though a number of key prices like those of energy, housing, and basic consumption goods often remained controlled along with wages and exchange rates. The institution that governed the Soviet bloc trading area, namely the Council for Mutual Economic Assistance, was abolished, and most countries rapidly opened up to international trade. This induced the immediate collapse of traditional trade and gradually allowed for a more efficient allocation of resources based on world market prices and new trade patterns. Most countries also quickly reduced direct subsidies to trusts and state-owned enterprises (SOEs) and allowed them to restructure or break up. Similarly, they removed or stopped altogether the enforcement of barriers to the creation of new firms and banks and carried out small-scale privatizations. Moreover, early on, most governments broke up the "monobank" system, whereby a single state bank (or a system of tightly knit and only nominally independent banks) functioned as a country's central bank as well as a nationwide commercial and investment bank. The breakup of the monobank system allowed for the creation of new and independent banks. The final feature of Type I reforms was the introduction of at least some elements of a social safety net in order to make citizens more willing to accept the disruptions associated with the introduction of a market economy. The Type I reforms proved relatively sustainable and were associated with improving economic performance in Central Europe and in the Baltic countries, although they were less successfully implemented in the Balkans and the CIS.

Svejnar's *Type II* reforms involved the development and enforcement of laws, regulations, and institutions that would ensure a successful functioning of a market-oriented economy. These reforms included not only the privatization of large and medium-sized enterprises, but also the establishment and enforcement of a market-oriented legal system and accompanying institutions, the further (in-depth) development of a viable commercial banking sector, and the appropriate regulatory infrastructure. This included labor market regulations, as well as the creation of parameters and institutions related to the unemployment, social security, and retirement systems. The important point is that these other features of transition, especially the development of institutions and a legal framework, were not absent from the recommendations and policy documents at the time, but they did prove to be particularly difficult to implement (see Svejnar, 2002).

LEGAL AND INSTITUTIONAL FRAMEWORK

Various approaches emerged with respect to the implementation of both types of reforms. In reviewing the first two years of transition, Fisher and Frenkel (1992) argued that policy makers cannot afford to move gradually and indeed must work fast because of the collapse of the previous nonmarket system. At the time, a similar view was advanced by Aslund (1991a). Yet, Aslund (1992a) argued that a sequencing of political and economic reforms might be desirable, with democratization being a crucial precondition to a change in the economic system. A recent counterpoint to these views was provided by Stiglitz (1999).

Contrary to a widely held view, most of the early advisers stressed the importance of developing and enforcing a market-oriented legal framework that would establish a level playing field, create well-defined property rights, permit the enforcement of contracts, and limit corruption.[1]

Unfortunately, virtually no country succeeded in rapidly developing a legal system and institutions that would be conducive to the preservation of private property and to the functioning of a market economy—although some countries did much better than others. In retrospect, this lack of a market-oriented legal structure appears to have been the Achilles heel of the first dozen years of the transition. Many policy makers underestimated the importance of a well-functioning legal system or believed too readily that free markets would take care of all major problems. In addition, many newly rich individuals and groups in the transition economies—especially those who contributed to the corruption of public officials—did not desire the establishment of a strong legal system. Finally, lawyers in the former Soviet bloc countries tended not to propose legal reforms or spontaneously draft bills and other reform measures, unlike economists who were a fertile source of reform proposals. Overall, the countries that have made the greatest progress in limiting corruption and establishing a functioning legal framework and institutions are the Central European and Baltic countries. In recent years, an important impetus for carrying out legal and institutional reforms in many of these countries has been the need to develop a system that conforms to that of the European Union (EU) as a prerequisite for accession. The required terminal (EU) conditions, as opposed to initial (communist) conditions, thus gradually became important determinants of progress in reforms.

In general, the ability of transition governments to carry out Type I and Type II reforms turned on two factors: their ability to collect taxes and finance public programs, and their ability to minimize corruption and rent-seeking behavior. Type I reforms aimed at reducing subsidies and centrally planned regulation. Most transition governments quickly abolished central planning. However, a number of them, especially in the CIS, had considerable difficulty setting up a reliable tax system. Many of these governments were practically forced to reduce subsidies and the scope of government. Type II reforms emphasized not only the withering away of an omnipresent dictatorial state, but also the creation of an efficient state apparatus able to provide a level playing field for and regulation of the market economy. Type II reforms hence required that government have some resources and enforce competition and market-friendly laws, and that they not be dominated or captured by special interests. In this area, most transition economies have faced a major challenge and may still have a long way to go.

PRIVATIZATION AND ENTERPRISE RESTRUCTURING

Virtually all advisers and many local policy makers stressed the need to privatize SOEs. The motivation for privatization ranged from perceived gains in economic efficiency, to gains in much needed government revenues, to political appeal (Lipton and Sachs, 1990; Gupta et al., 2001). It is important to note that even those who advocated a rapid approach to the transition (e.g., Svejnar, 1989; Kornai, 1990; Lipton and Sachs, 1990) differed on the desirable method and speed. Across the board, they all warned that it would take a while to privatize the large state sector and generate capable managers and entrepreneurs.

Along with the accent on privatization, the issue of restructuring of SOEs emerged. The advice on restructuring SOEs took a number of forms. Svejnar (1989) cautioned that in the short run most existing firms would have to be run as state enterprises. Svejnar stressed the need to restructure these enterprises by making all of them adopt a standard accounting system, by embedding them in a competitive environment, by gradually phasing out their subsidies according to a pre-announced plan, and by introducing a system of supervisory boards with external directors as well as strong incentives for managers. Lipton and Sachs (1990) argued that privatization would take a number of years to implement and that in the meantime "state enterprises will have to be kept on a tight leash—with wage controls and curbs on investment—to check their wasteful tendencies." In this context, Hanousek, Kočenda, and Svejnar (2004) found that spinoffs preceding privatization increased the firm's profitability but did not alter its scale of operations, while the effect of privatization depends on the resulting ownership structure—sometimes improving performance and sometimes bringing about decline that is consistent with tunneling (looting) by managers or partial owners.[2] As it turned out, most transition countries quickly reduced direct subsidies to trusts and SOEs and allowed SOEs to restructure and even break up. Most countries also removed or stopped enforcing barriers to the creation of new firms.

No matter how intricate the very early stages of the transition process was, the principal question relating to privatization centered on the speed of its conduct. The principal arguments for fast privatization were that (1) price liberalization and other reforms would not provide sufficient incentives for SOEs to restructure and become competitive, (2) the state would not be able to resist intervening in SOEs (Frydman and Rapaczynski, 1991; Boycko et al., 1993) and (3) managers would decapitalize firms in the absence of a rapid clarification of property rights (Frydman et al., 1993). In contrast, Dewatripont and Roland (1992a, b) and Roland (1994) argued that gradual privatization was needed to avoid a political backlash to rapid privatization of all firms—and hence the closing down of many of them—which could lead to the need to renationalize. In particular, Dewatripont and Roland's (1992a, b) first argument for gradualism was that it allowed the government to pursue a strategy that necessitated fewer workers/voters being immediately laid off and also permitted adequate compensation of the ones who were laid off. Their second argument was that rapid privatization brought about major uncertainty that might be unacceptable. Gradualism presumably generates less uncertainty and allows any potential difficulties to be at least in part resolved before the process is fully launched. As a result, Roland (1994) stressed the need to divide firms into "well" and "poorly" performing ones, privatize the good ones, and keep these privatized firms under hard budget constraints (i.e., extend no more subsidies to them). As to the bad firms, the state should keep control of the bad firms for a while and restructure them before privatizing. This line of reasoning of course presupposes that the state is politically strong enough to impose financial discipline on both sets of firms. In a number of countries, including pre-1997 Bulgaria and Russia, the state was unable to do so.

When approaching the practical aspects of privatization, a question that arose from the start was how to privatize thousands of state firms in a manner that would be equitable and politically viable and would result in higher efficiency due to effective corporate governance. There was a major concern that managers could seize state property and claim it as their own through the so called popular privatization—as occurred early on in Hungary and to some extent in a few other Central European economies (Svejnar, 1989; Lipton and Sachs, 1990). Some also feared that workers would claim ownership of their firms (Hinds, 1990; Lipton and Sachs, 1990), although others have argued that both economic theory and empirical evidence indicated that the possibility of this happening was exaggerated (Prasnikar and Svejnar, 1991; Ellerman, 1993).

Numerous proposals for privatization appeared. Svejnar (1989) proposed a method that relied on first establishing a market-oriented legal and institutional framework and then combining competitive bidding by foreign investors on majority stakes in state firms with free distribution of significant minority stakes in the form of diversified portfolios to citizens at large. The majority stakes could be offered to strategic partners as well as used in part for funding pensions, health benefits, and unemployment insurance. Svejnar's proposal was motivated by the goals of (1) improving economic performance through Western capital and management, (2) ensuring fairness and minimal risk for citizens by the allocation of shares, (3) achieving the maximum price by the government from sales to foreigners, while enabling citizens to participate in the process and obtaining collateral for bank credit that was needed for launching small enterprises, (4) preventing asset stripping by managers or other insiders, and (5) contributing to the development of a capital market.

Lipton and Sachs (1990) argued that to obtain political acceptability of privatization would require at least a partial transfer of ownership to stakeholders such as workers, state banks, and local government. They also pointed out that some shares might stay in the treasury and/or that the government could sell a leveraged firm and become a rentier rather than a capitalist. In his comment on Lipton and Sachs (1990), Stiglitz (1990) argued against the "give-away" of firms, stressing the importance of denoting the proper signals about each firm's profitability.

Blanchard et al. (1991) started from the premise that there was no unique path to privatization or "best" structure of ownership. In particular, they argued that the establishment of a clear system of ownership was urgent to avoid plundering of assets, but that restructuring of firms, by necessity, had to proceed slowly. The need for speed on establishing ownership led them to argue that privatization should proceed by distribution rather than sale of ownership claims. They also stressed that large shareholders were necessary for efficient management. These two propositions, together with a need for fairness, led them to conclude that the best program would emphasize the role of holding companies, with shares traded on the stock market and a mandate to restructure and divest themselves of firms in their portfolio over some period of time.

The closure of persistently loss-making enterprises was advocated by a number of advisers, including Gomulka (1989) and Svejnar (1989). In practice, relatively few firms were completely closed down, although many scaled down their operations and closed individual plants. The one country that moved aggressively to force bankruptcies on loss-making firms was Hungary in 1992.

Many advisers used the CEE experience in formulating their recommendations for privatization in Russia and the CIS in general. Hence, drawing on CEE evidence, Aslund (1992b) saw Russian privatization as proceeding excellently and advised Boris Yeltsin and Yegor Gaidar to stick to their policies. Sachs (1992) reviewed the early Polish privatization experience and warned against the method that gave a veto to every group of stakeholders as well as any method relying on sales of individual firms. He viewed the not-yet-implemented voucher privatization program in Czechoslovakia and the investment fund program in Poland as promising. Given that Russia was facing a much larger scale privatization (45,000 state enterprises as compared to around 8,000 in Poland), Sachs argued that Russia needed to adopt across-the-board mechanisms in which thousands of industrial enterprises would be moved through the privatization process simultaneously, in a manner that reflected the implicit ownership claims that existed without letting these claims derail the process. He also suggested that for large enterprises the key initial step should be a mass commercialization of these enterprises in which thousands of them would be transformed into joint-stock companies, with the initial claims over the shares reflecting the balance of interests in the enterprises. Once mass commercialization was accomplished and managers and workers received an initial distribution of the shares, new supervisory boards could be assigned the responsibility for privatizing another tranche of the shares, sufficient to bring the privatized equity to over 51%. Sachs (1992) also noted that the crucial aspect of mass commercialization would be the introduction of corporate governance where no clear governance existed. The Russian government could then divest itself of the remaining minority equity stakes.

In practice, remarkable differences existed in the strategies for privatization across the transition economies. Poland and Slovenia, while quick to undertake Type I reforms, moved decidedly slowly in terms of privatization of SOEs, relying instead on their commercialization and on the creation of new private firms. Estonia and Hungary were equally vigorous Type I reformers, but they also proceeded assiduously and surprisingly effectively when privatizing individual SOEs by selling them one by one to outside owners. As mentioned above, this method of privatization was originally viewed by many strategists and advisers as too slow. Yet it provided much needed managerial skills and external funds for investment in the privatized firms, and it generated government revenue and effective corporate governance. It also turned out to be relatively fast when carried out by determined governments. Russia and Ukraine are examples of countries that opted for rapid mass privatization and relied primarily on subsidized management-employee buyouts of firms. This method had the advantage of speed, but it led to poor corporate governance in that management usually was not able or willing to improve efficiency. The method also did not generate new investment funds and skills, and it provided little revenue for the government. The Czech Republic, Lithuania, and to a lesser extent Slovakia carried out rapid equal-access voucher privatization, whereby a majority of shares of most firms were distributed to citizens at large.[3] While this approach may have been the best in terms of fairness and speed,[4] it did not generate new investment funds, nor did it bring revenue to the government. Instead, it resulted in dispersed ownership of shares. Together with a weak legal framework, it imposed little control on management and resulted in poor corporate governance.[5] This poor corporate governance resulted in the appropriation of profits or even assets of the firms (by way of tunneling) by large shareholders at the expense of the minority shareholders.

In retrospect, it appears that despite clear advice and genuine efforts on the part of a number of policy makers, the creation and enforcement of an adequate legal and institutional framework that would underpin privatization was, in most transition economies, inadequate. Hence, Roland (2001) for instance stresses this lesson when he wrote that "the policies of liberalization, stabilization and privatization that are not grounded in adequate institutions may not deliver successful outcomes." Similarly, Zinnes, Eilat, and Sachs (2001) argued that "privatization involving change-of-title alone is not enough to generate economic performance improvements." What they call "deep" privatization, including institutional and "agency"-related reforms, was in many cases inadequately implemented.

The situation was further aggravated by two developments. First, in a number of countries, the governments tended to use instruments such as golden shares to maintain significant control over the privatized SOEs. The state thus created a contradiction in initiating privatization while trying to maintain its control over certain key companies.[6] Second, after the privatization process had begun, a number of governments, recognizing the inadequacy of the existing legal and institutional framework, quickly established institutions whose quality was often inferior to institutions that could have been established had they taken more time to develop them. If North (1994) was correct in arguing that the long-run economic performance of a country depends crucially on the way institutions evolve, then the institutional approach to privatization left much to be desired. This is especially poignant when we note that one of the frequently used methods was mass privatization, which usually covered a large part of the economy and depended crucially on a functioning legal and institutional system.

As may be seen from table 3.1, many transition economies moved fast to convert their virtually fully state-owned economies into economies based overwhelmingly on private ownership. As mentioned in the first section, numerous reasons were advanced for carrying out privatization—proposals about the extent and speed of the process, and expectations about the effects of privatization on performance. In this section, we provide a critical review of these three aspects of privatization.

DETERMINANTS AND SEQUENCING OF PRIVATIZATION

The number of studies examining the determinants and sequencing of privatization is relatively limited. Prior to the start of the transition process, privatization occurred in developing as well as developed countries. Plane (1997) explores the determinants of privatization in a sample of 35 developing market economies over the period from 1988 to 1992. He used probit and tobit models to identify the determinants of successful privatization programs and found that privatization (through divestiture) has a stronger positive effect on economic growth when it takes place in industry or infrastructure rather than in other sectors. This

TABLE 3.1 Private Sector Share of GDP

	1992	1994	1996	1998	2000	2001	2002
Czech Republic	30	65	75	75	80	80	80
Hungary	40	55	70	80	80	80	80
Poland	45	55	60	65	70	75	75
Slovak Republic	30	55	70	75	80	80	80
Slovenia	30	45	55	60	65	65	65
Estonia	25	55	70	70	75	75	80
Latvia	25	40	60	65	65	65	70
Lithuania	20	60	70	70	70	70	75
Bulgaria	25	40	55	65	70	70	75
Romania	25	40	55	60	60	65	65
Russia	25	50	60	70	70	70	70
Ukraine	10	40	50	55	60	60	65

Source: European Bank for Reconstruction and Development, *Transition Report*, various issues.

study hence suggests that if economic performance is the goal of the government, privatization should occur in industry and infrastructure first.

Glaeser and Scheinkman (1996) were the first authors to theoretically address sequencing. Their paper examines sequencing strategies that would increase efficiency. They argue that a primary advantage of private ownership is that it enhances efficiency by improving firms' acquisition of, and responsiveness to, information. In their model, private firms respond to demand and cost shocks, but this information is unobserved or ignored by public firms. In particular, the authors assume that SOEs produce a fixed level of output based on the expected values of demand and cost, while private owners observe the actual values and adjust their production when demand and cost conditions change. Thus, if the government is concerned about increasing efficiency in this sense, the Glaeser-Scheinkman (GS) model predicts that privatization should begin where demand or cost volatility is the greatest and where it maximizes the flow of information.

In the GS model, there are three sectors: upstream, downstream, and retail. In our analysis, we test two predictions of the model pertaining to sequencing privatization across industries. First, Glaeser and Scheinkman argue that when demand uncertainty is greater than cost uncertainty, downstream industries should be privatized before upstream industries, because downstream industries are better positioned to transmit information between the retail and upstream sectors. When the retail sector is private, the authors show that privatizing downstream firms should occur before upstream privatization so that the flow of information between the private upstream and the private retail sectors is not disrupted by the intermediate state-owned downstream sector. Second, Glaeser and Scheinkman argue that industries that experience the highest demand or cost volatility should be privatized first because firms in these industries need to respond to changing market conditions and hence are likely to benefit the most from privatization. The authors also note that the informational gains from privatization may be offset by a loss of consumer surplus if firms with significant market power are privatized and are allowed to engage in monopoly pricing.

The GS model provides a different set of predictions than have been obtained in the previous models. In the empirical section, we test whether downstream industries and industries that faced the greatest demand shocks were privatized first or not. We also test whether the market share of a firm affects the probability of its being privatized early. If the government maximizes public goodwill or privatization revenues, firms with high market share should be privatized first because this variable may also act as a proxy for profitability. Thus, the market share variable also allows us to compare the relative priority placed on revenue and public goodwill versus efficiency.

Gupta, Ham, and Svejnar (2008) note that while privatization of SOEs has been one of the most important aspects of the economic transition from a centrally planned to a market system, no transition economy has privatized all its firms simultaneously. This raises the question of whether governments privatize firms strategically. Gupta, Ham, and Svejnar examine theoretically and empirically the determinants of the sequencing of privatization. This is the first study to obtain theoretical predictions regarding a firm's characteristics by ascertaining whether these characteristics are likely to determine the sequence of privatization and finally to test these predictions. By identifying the nature of sequencing of privatization, our analysis contributes to a better understanding of the behavior of governments and firms.

To obtain testable predictions about the factors that may affect sequencing, Gupta, Ham, and Svejnar (2008) investigate theoretical models that consider the following competing government objectives: (1) maximizing efficiency through resource allocation; (2) maximizing public goodwill from the free transfers of shares to the public; (3) minimizing political costs stemming from unemployment; (4) maximizing efficiency through information gains (Glaeser-Scheinkman), and (5) maximizing privatization revenues. Next, they use firm-level data from the Czech Republic to test the competing theoretical predictions about the sequencing of privatization. The authors find strong evidence that the government first privatized firms that were more profitable, firms in downstream industries, and firms in industries subject to greater demand uncertainty. Privatizing more profitable firms first is inconsistent with maximizing Pareto efficiency, but it is consistent with the model of maximizing privatization revenues, maximizing public goodwill, and minimizing the political cost of unemployment. However, the implication of the political cost model—that employment growth in the firm's industry should affect sequencing—is not supported by the results. Gupta, Ham, and Svejnar's finding that firms in downstream industries and in industries with greater demand uncertainty were more likely to be privatized early suggests that the government placed emphasis on efficiency in the Glaeser and Scheinkman (1996) sense, namely, by first privatizing firms that required flexible management. However, in contrast to the GS model recommendation, but consistent with the general evidence regarding profitability, firms with higher market share were more likely to be privatized first.

In the noneconomic literature, Appel (2000) explores how ideology interacts with the distribution of power and the formation of material interests in society. She suggests that there are four mechanisms by which ideology determines the design and implementation of privatization programs: (1) The ideology determines how privatization programs are drafted. (2) The ideological context shapes the definition of interests and the distribution of power in society. (3) The ideological compliance reflects how leaders attempt to gain support for and agreement to a new property rights system. (4) The ideological compatibility addresses how privatization policies and ideas and beliefs in society differ. Appel provides several empirical examples of how these ideological factors interfere with privatization policies; in particular she discusses how these factors affect the ease of implementation and the distortion of privatization programs over time.

Another approach worth examining is taken by Feigenbaum and Henig (1994), who argue that privatization takes the form of a strategy that realigns institutions so as to privilege the goals of some groups over the competing aspirations of other groups. They develop a political typology that distinguishes between privatizations undertaken for different reasons—whether pragmatic, tactical, or systemic. In terms of determinants, it means that conventional assumptions about political rationality become problematic in the face of opportunities to achieve privatization. Further, structural shifts in governmental capacity and responsibility should be the central focus in distinguishing between types of privatization. Also, the most important political criterion for evaluating privatization alternatives is whether they represent substantial and not easily reversible reduction in state responsibility and capacity. Finally, some policy decisions are less readily reversible than others.

A philosophically similar approach is taken by De Castro and Uhlenbruck (1997), who examine how the characteristics of a county relate to the nature of the privatization deal of a formally state-owned enterprise and the strategy of the acquiring firm. They claim that there are differences with respect to the characteristics of privatization and government policies that translate into differences in firm strategy in former communist, less-developed, and developed countries. Country characteristics, government privatization policies, and firm strategies play a prominent role.

EXTENT OF PRIVATIZATION

Theoretical models have come up with a number of competing predictions about the extent of privatization that is most desirable. At the early stage of the transition, Fershtman (1990) analyzed the interdependence between the ownership status and market structure. Using the Dixit's (1980) framework, he examined a duopolistic market and considered the implications of privatization on the attractiveness of entry, the possibility of deterring entry, and the incumbent position as a natural monopoly. He demonstrated that a partly state-owned firm might realize higher profits than its private, profit-maximizing, competitor.[7] This implies that partial rather than full privatization may be desirable in the conditions of imperfect competition, which is a feature of the early transition stage.

McFaul (1995) reviews early transition events in Russia and demonstrates that future progress in developing private property rights will require not only sound economic policies but also more robust state institutions. Based on his research, McFaul claims that the set of political institutions comprising the first postcommunist Russian state were not capable of dismantling Soviet institutions, governing property rights, or creating and supporting new market-based economic institutions regarding private property. The conclusion one walks away with is that the extent of privatization ought to be limited.

Leamer and Taylor (1994) develop a Bayesian pooling technique to estimate aggregate production functions for the previously centrally planned economies (PCPEs) of Eastern Europe, for Western economies, and even for a group of developing countries. This technique adjusts for the low quality of the PCPE data and also possible differences between PCPE and Western and developing-country technologies. They find that if the transferability of assets to the new technology is low and Western capital is unavailable, it can be better not to privatize than to have full (big-bang) privatization. Large-scale privatization is also less desirable if Western capital is available for new projects. Thus, in some instances it may be desirable to use Western support to slow the rate of privatization rather than to hasten it. This study predicts that large-scale privatization may be more desirable in the CEE countries than in the CIS because Western capital is more available for the former than for the latter.

EFFECTS OF PRIVATIZATION ON PERFORMANCE

Theory

A number of theoretical models provided competing predictions about the effects of privatization on performance; these predictions range from positive, to negative, to ambiguous. In Gylfason's work (1998), privatization is shown to increase national economic output in a two-sector full-employment general-equilibrium model by enhancing efficiency as if a relative price distortion were being removed through price reform, trade liberalization, or stabilization. Gylfason shows that the static output gain from privatization may be large; he also shows that the potential dynamic output gain from privatization appears to be substantial. Hansen (1995) presents a general equilibrium imperfect competition model and shows that a broad distribution of ownership rights can have a favorable influence on microeconomic efficiency and may therefore lead to a "good" aggregate outcome. Yet the sales to single or core investors, if accompanied by workers' equity shares, may perform worse. Furthermore only a so-called big-bang rapid approach to privatization might lead to favorable outcomes.

Macro Evidence

A number of studies use aggregate data to assess the effect of privatization on economic performance. Using data from developing as well as developed countries, Plane (1997) finds that privatization (through divestiture) has a significant positive effect on economic growth. Berkowitz and de Jong (2001) analyze whether regional differences in reform policies in Russia can account for regional differences in growth rates and conclude that to a considerable degree they can. The authors find that regions with significant large-scale privatization create a greater number of new legal enterprises, which in turn exhibits a strong positive correspondence with growth. The inequality due to privatization is studied by Alexeev (1997), who examines the Russian privatization process through the end of voucher privatization and considers how its deviation from the competitive sale standard was likely to affect inequality. He argues that empirical evaluation is all but impossible due to the lack of reliable data. But he finds that it is feasible to analyze the institutional features of Russian privatization in terms of their effect on the redistribution of wealth. Alexeev claims that, given the rent-seeking character of the privatization process and differences in opportunities for various wealth groups, privatization systematically redistributes wealth and causes an increase in wealth inequality.

Privatization and economic growth are also often related through fiscal performance. Barnett (2000) carried out an empirical investigation of the relationship between privatization and measures of fiscal performance. Using macroeconomic and privatization data from 18 countries, he found that when privatization proceeds are transferred to the budget, they tend to be saved and used to reduce domestic financing. His other main finding was that total privatization, as opposed to just the proceeds transferred to the budget, correlates with an improvement in macroeconomic performance as manifested by higher real GDP growth and lower unemployment. However, this result needs to be interpreted cautiously, as the evidence it provides is not sufficient to establish causality. King (2003) provides more evidence on fiscal issues. He argues that the neoliberal policy package of "shock therapy"[8] creates severe supply-and-demand shock for enterprises and induces firm failure. This leads to a fiscal crisis for the state and an erosion of its bureaucratic character and capabilities. The author tests the neoliberal theory against a neoclassical sociological theory by examining the experience of 12 postcommunist countries and two reform Asian communist countries. He concludes that the application of the neoliberal transition program results in a less liberal outcome than neoliberal theory has envisaged.

In a cross-country aggregate study, Sachs, Zinnes, and Eilat (2000) find that privatization does not in and of itself increase GDP growth, but they suggest that a positive effect is present when privatization is accompanied by in-depth institutional reforms.

Finally, Bennett et al. (2004) classify 25 of the 27 transition economies according to the type, extent, and timing of the privatization that was carried out in each country. The authors then pool the data across countries and over time and regress the rate of growth of GDP on the privatization variables and controls. They find that mass-voucher privatization is the privatization form most conducive to economic growth. This is a provocative finding that deserves further study.

Because in a number of economies pre-privatization firms were to a large extent controlled by workers, Albrecht and Thum (1994) discuss how policy measures such as labor participation (with wage ceilings) can help avoid the destructive trend towards mass bankruptcy and the resulting negative macroeconomic impact. Gupta, Schiller, and Ma (1999) discuss the impact of privatization on labor markets as well as other fiscal issues. This work is further expanded by Gupta et al. (2001) when they examine policy makers' different options for mitigating the social impact of privatization. Gupta et al. discuss the adverse impacts of privatization in the form of economic efficiency and growth versus job losses and wage cuts, then survey the existing empirical evidence. They find that public sales and auctions can have strong negative effects on workers but maximize the government's revenue.

Micro Theory and Evidence

A theoretical analysis and overview of privatization and firm performance in transition is provided by Roland (2000). Surveys of firm-level studies examining the effects of privatization on a firm's performance provide a considerable range of results. Some find a large variation of outcomes but no systematically significant effect of privatization on performance (Bevan, Estrin, and Schaffer, 1999); others cautiously conclude that privatization improves firm performance (Megginson and Netter, 2001), and still others are fairly confident that privatization tends to improve performance (Shirley and Walsh, 2000; Djankov and Murrell, 2002).

This astonishing variation in the interpretation of results is brought about in part by the fact that those conducting early studies had access to different and often very limited data on firm ownership. For these reasons, many studies treat ownership as a relatively simple categorical concept (e.g., private versus state or state versus foreign, domestic private outsider versus domestic private insider). Such studies are often unable to distinguish the exact extent of ownership by individual owners or even relatively homogeneous groups of owners.

Equally important is the fact that three types of interrelated analytical problems generate the diversity of interpretations and findings. These problems may be expected in early studies, especially those in the context of the rapidly changing transition economies. First, the early studies examine only short time periods, with most observations concentrated immediately before and after the privatization. Second, the early studies (1) use small and often unrepresentative samples of firms, (2) are frequently unable to identify accurately who has ownership because privatization is still ongoing or because the frequent post-privatization changes of ownership are hard to detect, and (3) often combine panel data from different accounting systems. Third, many of the early studies were not able to control adequately for endogeneity of ownership (firms not being selected for privatization at random), and their estimates of the effects of privatization may hence be biased. Indeed, Djankov and Murrell (2002, 744) note that almost half (47%) of the surveyed studies do not take into account the fact that firms may not be assigned for privatization at random and that as a result many of the remaining studies treat the problem in an inadequate way. In view of this limitation of the existing literature and the vast effect this literature has on policy making around the world, Gupta, Ham, and Svejnar (2008) analyze the problem of ignoring the fact that better firms may be privatized first. They show that even one of the most popular methods for controlling for selection or endogeneity in the existing studies—namely, a difference-in-difference estimation (equivalent to fixed effects) approach—is unlikely to address this problem. Hence the entire literature on privatization suffers from a serious problem of potential selection (endogeneity) bias. Gupta, Ham, and Svejnar's study provides econometric evidence that better-performing firms tend to be privatized first, thus indicating that studies that treat the sequencing of privatization as random are likely to overstate the positive effect of privatization on performance.

Hanousek, Kočenda, and Svejnar (2007) alleviate the aforementioned methodological and data problems by using a virtually complete sample of privatized firms in the Czech Republic. They also implement an instrumental variable technique to account properly for ownership endogeneity bias. As a result they find present a positive effect of foreign owners—yet contrary to a number of previous studies, it is not that overwhelming. In a similar manner, the effect of the state is not only negative, as indicated earlier. The effect of domestic owners was largely favorable and far from being solely harmful. All these provocative results were made possible by the meticulous methodological account of ownership endogeneity. The authors also presented results from estimations by the ordinary least squares where ownership endogeneity was not fully accounted for. This approach is in line with the majority of previous studies that found a positive effect of foreign ownership and a negative effect of the state. Had the appropriate control for endogeneity been adopted, the earlier results might have shifted more toward the conclusions made by Hanousek, Kočenda, and Svejnar (2007).

In view of these problems, we have enlarged the survey of privatization studies reported by Djankov and Murrell (2002) to include additional studies and pertinent information about the data and econometric techniques used by the various authors. On the basis of this new information, collected as of December 2003, we came up with a relatively sobering assessment of the effects of privatization on the total-factor productivity (TFP), labor productivity, profitability, sales, revenues, employment, wages, and other indicators of performance in the transition economies of Central and Eastern Europe.

TOTAL-FACTOR PRODUCTIVITY

Seventeen studies have analyzed the impact of ownership on TFP, using value added, total product, or sales as the dependent variable; 14 studies control for endogeneity, and all but one use sample sizes with several hundred or more firms. The results are mixed. The overall effects of private or non-state ownership range from positive to insignificant to negative. The diversity persists across regions (CEE versus CIS), although relatively few studies analyze the CIS countries. Foreign ownership is mostly found to have a non-negative effect, but in a number of instances the effect is statistically insignificant. The effect of employee ownership is estimated in seven instances, with six being statistically insignificant and one being positive.

LABOR PRODUCTIVITY

Estimates related to the effect of ownership on labor productivity are based on 21 studies, with 13 controlling for endogeneity/selection of ownership. The results are again mixed, but private ownership in these cases registers primarily positive and insignificant effects. The diversity again persists across regions (CEE versus CIS), and there are now more studies analyzing the CIS countries. Foreign ownership is again found to have a non-negative effect, while the effects of employee and management ownership are estimated to be almost statistically insignificant. Finally, newly established firms are found to be less efficient than others.

PROFITABILITY

The effects on profitability were examined in 11 studies, and once again the results are mixed. But these studies consider specific ownership categories and the extent of ownership concentration. Concentrated foreign ownership (especially by industrial companies) appears to have a positive effect on profitability, and in some studies a positive effect of municipal ownership was found. The effect of domestic private ownership is for the most part insignificant or depends on the particular type of ownership (bank, fund, individual, etc.). In this finer categorization, however, the effects vary across studies.

SALES

Estimates of the effect of ownership on sales are based on 10 studies, with all but one controlling for endogeneity/selection of ownership. The results are again mixed, with private ownership (of all types) displaying a positive effect in the study of Poland by Angelucci et al. (2002), the paper on Russia by Bhaumik and Estrin (2003), the study of Lithuania by Grigorian (2000), and the study of Estonia by Jones and Mygind (2002). However, the effect of private ownership is insignificant or negative in the other studies. Among the recent studies that control for endogeneity of ownership, Kočenda and Svejnar's (2003) study finds ownership by foreign industrial firms to have a positive effect but ownership by foreign nonindustrial firms to be insignificant. Further, Hanousek, Kočenda, and Svejnar (2007) find a positive effect of foreign owners on firms' performance, yet contrary to a number of previous studies the conclusion is not overwhelming.

REVENUES

Six studies deal with the effect of ownership on revenues. In some cases revenues overlap with sales, and in some cases it covers non-sale revenues as well. Most of the estimated effects are small or nearly insignificant. This suggests that different types of ownership do not exert systematically different effects on revenues. The exception is when there is ownership by an outsider, which is found to have a significant positive effect, such as in Frydman et al.'s (1999, 2000) studies of Central Europe, but a negative effect in Jones's (1998) study of Russia.

EMPLOYMENT

Fourteen studies have examined the effect of ownership on employment. The results are again quite varied, but there is a discernible tendency for privatized firms, especially those with foreign owners, to increase employment relative to firms with state ownership. Worker ownership and control appear to have zero effect, or in one case a positive effect, on employment.

WAGES

Studies of the effects of ownership on wages find that state ownership is associated with lower wages in Russia and former Czechoslovakia, but not so in Poland. Moreover, SOEs are more likely to exhibit wage arrears than are firms with mixed ownership and de novo firms, but not domestic private and foreign-owned firms. The fact that domestic private and foreign-owned firms are about as likely to generate wage arrears as state-owned firms is interesting.

OTHER INDICATORS OF PERFORMANCE

Finally, a number of studies have analyzed the effect of ownership on other dependent variables. The results are again diverse, but the following patterns of private ownership effects do emerge when we examine the data: private ownership does not have a major effect on return on assets, investment, environmental emissions, and the price cost margin, but it has a zero or negative effect on costs and a positive effect on exports.

While the earlier surveys of CEE and the CIS differed in their conclusions about the effects of privatization on performance, most of them created a general presumption that the effect was positive. More recent studies have used larger data sets and controlled more thoroughly for potential endogeneity/selection of ownership. The results presented in these surveys suggest that the estimated effects of ownership on performance vary with data sets, econometric techniques, and the time period under consideration. Moreover, while foreign ownership is at times associated with superior economic performance, domestic private ownership has much less definite impact on performance than had been claimed in some of the earlier surveys. Our study hence suggests that privatization of state-owned firms to domestic owners in CEE and the CIS—one of the largest transfers of wealth in history—did not have the strongly positive effect on economic performance that was expected.

NOTES

Acknowledgment: We would like to thank Natalia Khorunzhina for valuable research assistance and Faith Vlcek for valuable secretarial assistance. While preparing this chapter, Svejnar benefited from NSF Grant No. SBR-951-2001, while Hanousek and Svejnar also benefited from NSF grant SES-0111783, and Hanousek and Kočenda benefited from GACR grant 402/06/1293.

1. Svejnar (1989) stressed that the "first step in the transformation process is the establishment of a clear set of laws on economic activity." He argued that defining the rules of the (new) game was essential for reducing uncertainty and providing an environment that would be conducive to economic decision-making. He also emphasized the importance of having incentives for achieving economic efficiency embedded in the legal system and he recommended that the drafting of laws be carried out as a joint process between lawyers and economists.

2. As we also show, the effects of privatization are hence much less clear-cut than was suggested in earlier studies. Methodologically, the Hanousek, Kočenda, and Svejnar (2004) study provides evidence that it is important to control for changes in ownership when analyzing spinoffs and generally to control for endogeneity, selection, and data attrition when analyzing the effects of spinoffs and privatization.

3. A general outline of a mass privatization using vouchers emerged in 1988. According to Lewandowski (1997, 35): "Mass privatization was a unique response to the post-communist challenge. The idea of distributing vouchers to promote equitable popular participation in privatization was elaborated by market-oriented advisers to the Solidarity movement in Gdansk, Poland, in mid-1988. Vouchers were intended to make up for insufficient supply of capital; as a special type of investment currency, they would be allocated to all citizens and tradable for shares of privatized companies. The concept was presented at a conference in November 1988—when communists were still in power—in response to a solicitation for proposals on how to transform Polish economy." Description of the method was published by Lewandowski and Szomburg (1990). Voucher schemes were then creatively adopted in several European transition countries.

4. Filer and Hanousek (2001) show that the voucher scheme is able to rapidly incorporate all available information, public and private. Hanousek and Kočenda (2005) present persuasive evidence that uninformed individuals learned quickly during the voucher scheme and were able to outperform many privatization funds.

5. For the assessment of the governance of privatization funds in the Czech Republic, see Kotrba, Kočenda, and Hanousek (1999).

6. This argument is supported by calculations and more details in Kočenda (1999) and Kočenda and Valachy (2002).

7. This result is to a certain extent supported by Kočenda and Svejnar (2003), who study the performance of privatized firms and provide results that portray the state as a more economically and socially beneficial agent than do other recent studies.

8. Shock therapy consists of the radical transition to a market economy through rapid and extensive price and trade liberalization, stringent monetary and fiscal stabilization, and the implementation of a mass privatization program.

REFERENCES

Aghion, P. and O. Blanchard. 1994. "On the Speed of Transition in Central Europe." *NBER Macroeconomics Annual*: 283–320.

Aghion, P. and W. Carlin. 1996. "Restructuring Outcomes and the Evolution of Ownership Patterns in Central and Eastern Europe." *Economics of Transition* 4(2): 371–388.

Aghion, P. and J. Tirole. 1997. "Formal and Real Authority in Organizations." *Journal of Political Economy* 55: 1–27.

Ahuja, G. and S. Majumdar. 1998. "On the Sequencing of Privatization in Transition Economies." *Industrial and Corporate Change* 7: 109–151.

Albrecht, B. and M. Thum. 1994. "Privatization, Labor Participation, and the Threat of Bankruptcy: The Case of Poland." *Journal of Institutional and Theoretical Economics* 150(4): 710–725.

Alesina, A., S. Danniger, and M. V. Rostagno. 2001. "Redistribution Through Public Employment." *IMF Staff Papers* 48(3): 447–473.

Alesina, A. and B. Wider. 2002. "Do Corrupt Governments Receive Less Foreign Aid?" *American Economic Review* 92: 1126–1137.

Alexeev, M. 1997. "The Effect of Privatization on the Wealth Distribution in Russia." William Davidson Institute Working Paper 86, University of Michigan.

Allen, F. and D. Gale. 1995. "A Welfare Comparison of Intermediaries in Germany and the US." *European Economic Review* 39(2): 179–209.

Amemiya, T. 1978. "Estimation of a Simultaneous Equation Generalized Probit Model." *Econometrica* 46: 1193–1205.

Angelucci, M., S. Estrin, J. Konings, and Z. Zólkiewski. 2002. "The Effect of Ownership and Competitive Pressure on Firm Performance in Transition Countries: Micro Evidence from Bulgaria, Romania and Poland." William Davidson Institute Working Paper 434, University of Michigan.

Appel, H. 2000. "The Ideological Determinants of Liberal Economic Reform: The Case of Privatization." *World Politics* 52(4): 520–549.

Ashenfelter, O. and D. Card. 1985. "Using the Longitudinal Structure of Earnings to Estimate the Effect of Training Programs." *Review of Economics and Statistics* 67(4): 648–660.

Aslund, A. 1991a. "The Case for Swift Currency Reform in the New Republics." *Transition* 2(8): 4–5.

——. 1991b. "Four Key Reforms: The Eastern European Experiment Phase II." *The American Enterprise* (July): 49–55.

——, ed. 1992a. "A Critique of Soviet Reform Plans." In *The Post-Soviet Economy: Soviet and Western Perspectives*, 167–180. London: Pinter Publishers.

——. 1992b. "Go Faster on Russian Reform." *New York Times*, December 7.

——. 1992c. "Debate: Anders Aslund." *Acta Oeconomica* 44: 231–235.

Aslund, A. and R. Layard. 1991. "Help Russia Now." *New York Times*, December 5.

Atkeson, A. and P. J. Kehoe. 1996. "Social Insurance and Transition." *International Economic Review* 37: 377–402.

Barberis, N., M. Boycko, A. Shleifer, and N. Tsukanova. 1996. "How Does Privatization Work? Evidence from the Russian Shops." *The Journal of Political Economy* 104(4): 764–790.

Barnett, S. 2000. "Evidence on the Fiscal and Macroeconomic Impact of Privatization." IMF Working Paper 130. Washington, DC: International Monetary Fund.

Barrell, R. and N. Pain. 1997. "Foreign Direct Investment, Technological Change, and Economic Growth Within Europe." *The Economic Journal* 107(445): 1770–1786.

Barro, R. and X. Sala-i-Martin. 1995. *Economic Growth.* Advanced Series in Economics. New York: McGraw-Hill.

Basu, S., S. Estrin, and J. Svejnar. 2000. "Employment Determination in Enterprises Under Communism and in Transition: Evidence from Central Europe." *Industrial and Labor Relations Review* 58(3): 353–369.

Bennett, J., S. Estrin, W. James, and G. Urga. 2004. "Privatization Methods and Economic Growth in Transition Economies." CEPR Discussion Paper 4291. London: Centre for Economic Policy Research.

Berkowitz, D. and D. de Jong. 2001. "Policy Reform and Growth in Post-Soviet Russia." William Davidson Institute Working Paper 405, University of Michigan.

Bevan, A., S. Estrin, and M. Schaffer. 1999. "Determinants of Enterprise Performance During Transition." CERT Working Paper 03. Birmingham, England: Centre for Environmental Research & Training, University of Birmingham.

Bhaumik, S. and S. Estrin. 2003. "Why Transition Paths Differ: Russian and Chinese Enterprise Performance Compared." William Davidson Institute Working Paper 525, University of Michigan.

Bilsen, V. and J. Konings. 1998. "Job Creation, Job Destruction, and Growth of Newly Established, Privatized, and State-Owned Enterprises in Transition Economies: Survey Evidence from Bulgaria, Hungary, and Romania." *Journal of Comparative Economics* 26: 429–445.

Black, B., R. Kraakman, and A. Tarassova. 1999. "Russian Privatization and Corporate Governance: What Went Wrong?" William Davidson Institute Working Paper 169, University of Michigan.

Blanchard, O. 1997. *The Economics of Post-Communist Transition.* Oxford: Clarendon Press.

Blanchard, O., R. Dornbusch, P. Krugman, R. Layard, and L. Summers. 1991. *Reform in Eastern Europe.* Cambridge, MA: MIT Press.

Blanchard, O. and M. Kremer. 1997. "Disorganization." *Quarterly Journal of Economics* 112(4): 1091–1126.

Boeri, T. 2000. *Structural Change, Welfare Systems and Labor Allocation.* Oxford: Oxford University Press.

Boeri, T. and K. Terrell. 2002. "Institutional Determinants of Labor Reallocation in Transition." *Journal of Economic Perspectives* 16(1): 51–76.

Bofinger, P. 1991. "Options for the Payments and Exchange Rate System in Eastern Europe." CEPR Discussion Paper 545. London: Centre for Economic Policy Research.

Bohata, M., P. Hanel, and M. Fischer. 1995. "Performance of Manufacturing." In *The Czech Republic and Economic Transition in Eastern Europe*, ed. J. Svejnar, 255–283. San Diego: Academic Press.

Bolton, P. and E-L. von-Thadden. 1998. "Blocks, Liquidity, and Corporate Control." *Journal of Finance* 53(1): 1–25.

Bonamo, M. 1997. "Poland's Privatization Process: A View from the Inside." *Journal of International Affairs* 50(2): 573.

Bornstein, M. 2001. "Post-Privatization Enterprise Restructuring." *Post-Communist Economies* 13(2): 189–203.

Boubakri, N. and J-C. Cosset. 1998. "The Financial and Operating Performance of Newly Privatized Firms: Evidence from Developing Countries." *Journal of Finance* 53(3): 1081–1110.

Boycko, M., A. Shleifer, R. W. Vishny, S. Fischer, and J. D. Sachs. 1993. "Privatizing Russia." *Brookings Papers on Economic Activity* 1993(2): 139–192.

Brada, J., A. King, and A. Kutan. 2000. "Inflation Bias and Productivity Shocks in Transition Economies: The Case of the Czech Republic." *Economic Systems* 24(2): 119–138.

Brainard, L. 1991. "Reform in Eastern Europe: Creating a Capital Market." *Economic Review* (January/February): 49–58.

Burkart, M., D. Gromb, and F. Panunzi. 2000. "Agency Conflict in Public and Negotiated Transfer of Corporate Control." *Journal of Finance* 55(2): 647–677.

Calvo, G. 1990. "Financial Aspects of Socialist Economies: From Inflation to Reform." Presented at the conference on Adjustment and Growth: Lessons for Eastern Europe for the IMF, October.

Calvo, G. and F. Coricelli. 1992. "Capital Market Imperfections and Output Response in Previously Centrally Planned Economies." In *Building Sound Finance in Emerging Market Economies*, ed. G. Caprio, D. Folkerts-Landau, and T. Lane. Washington DC: International Monetary Fund.

Calvo, G. and J. Frenkel. 1991. "Credit Markets, Credibility, and Economic Transformation." *Journal of Economic Perspectives* 5(4): 139–148.

Carlin, W., S. Fries, M. E. Schaffer, and P. Seabright. 2001. "Competition and Enterprise Performance in Transition Economies: Evidence from a Cross-Country Survey." CEPR Discussion Paper 2840. London: Centre for Economic Policy Research.

Caves, D. W. and L. Christensen. 1980. "The Relative Efficiency of Public and Private Firms in a Competitive Environment: The Case of Canadian Railroads." *Journal of Political Economy* 88(5): 958–976.

Chakraborty, A., N. Gupta, and R. Harbaugh. 2006. "Best Foot Forward or Best for Last in a Sequential Auction?" *RAND Journal of Economics* 37(1): 176–194.

Claessens, S. 1997. "Corporate Governance and Equity Prices: Evidence from the Czech and Slovak Republics." *Journal of Finance* 52(4): 1641–1658.

Claessens, S. and S. Djankov. 1999. "Ownership Concentration and Corporate Performance in the Czech Republic." *Journal of Comparative Economics* 27: 498–513.

Coffee, J. 1996. "Institutional Investors in Transitional Economies: Lessons from the Czech Experience." In *Corporate Governance in Central Europe and*

Russia, Volume 1: Banks, Funds, and Foreign Investors, ed. R. Frydman, C. Gray, and A. Rapaczynski, 111–186. Budapest: Central European University Press.

Coricelli, F. and R. Rocha. 1990. "Stabilization Programs in Eastern Europe: A Comparative Analysis of the Polish and the Yugoslav Programs of 1990." Presented at the conference on Adjustment and Growth: Lessons for Eastern Europe for the IMF, October.

Cornelli, F., R. Portes, and M. E. Schaffer. 1996. "The Capital Structure of Firms in Central and Eastern Europe." CEPR Discussion Paper 1392. London: Centre for Economic Policy Research.

de Castro, J. and K. Uhlenbruck. 1997. "Characteristics of Privatization: Evidence from Developed, Less-Developed, and Former Communist Countries." *Journal of International Business Studies* 28(1): 123–143.

Demsetz, H. and K. Lehn. 1985. "The Structure of Corporate Ownership: Causes and Consequences." *Journal of Political Economy* 93: 1155–1177.

Desai, P. 1992. "Reforming the Soviet Grain Economy: Performance, Problems and Solutions." *American Economic Review, Papers and Proceedings* 82(2): 49–54.

Desai, P. and T. Idson. 2000. *Work Without Wages: Russia's Nonpayment Crisis.* Cambridge, MA: MIT Press.

Dewatripont, M. and G. Roland. 1992a. "Economic Reform and Dynamic Political Constraints." *Review of Economic Studies* 59(4): 703–730.

——. 1992b. "The Virtues of Gradualism and the Legitimacy in the Transition to a Market Economy." *The Economic Journal* 102: 291–300.

——. 1995. "The Design of Reform Packages Under Uncertainty." *American Economic Review* 85: 1207–1223.

DeWenter, K. and P. Malatesta. 2001. "State-Owned and Privately Owned Firms: An Empirical Analysis of Profitability, Leverage, and Labor Intensity." *American Economic Review* 91(1): 320–334.

Diamond, P. 1992. "Pension Reform in a Transition Economy: Notes on Poland and Chile." Presented at the National Bureau of Economic Research Conference on Transition in Eastern Europe, February 26–29.

Dixit, A. 1980. "The Role of Investment in Entry-Deterrence." *The Economic Journal* 90(357): 95–106.

Djankov, S. and P. Murrell. 2002. "Enterprise Restructuring in Transition: A Quantitative Survey." *Journal of Economic Literature* 40(3): 739–792.

D'Souza, J. and W. Megginson. 1999. "The Financial and Operating Performance of Privatized Firms During the 1990s." *Journal of Finance* 54(4): 1397–1438.

Dyba, K. 1996. *The Czech Republic: 1990 to 1995.* Turin, Italy: Schuster Foundation Press.

Dyba, K. and J. Svejnar. 1991. "Czechoslovakia: Recent Economic Developments and Prospects." *American Economic Review* 81(2): 185–190.

——. 1995. "A Comparative View of Economic Developments in the Czech Republic." In *The Czech Republic and Economic Transition in Eastern Europe*, ed. J. Svejnar, 21–45. San Diego: Academic Press.

Dyck, I. and J. Alexander. 1997. "Privatization in Eastern Germany: Management Selection and Economic Transition." *American Economic Review, Papers and Proceedings* 87(4): 565–597.

Edwards, S. 1990. "Stabilization and Liberalization Policies in Eastern Europe: Lessons from Latin America." Paper presented at the American Economic Association Annual Meetings, Washington, DC, December 27–30.

Ellerman, D., ed. 1993. "Management and Employee Buy-Outs in Central and Eastern Europe: Introduction." In *Management and Employee Buy-Outs as a Technique of Privatization*. Ljubljana: Central & Eastern European Privatization Network.

Estrin, S., ed. 1994. *Privatization in Central and Eastern Europe.* London: Longman.

European Bank for Reconstruction and Development. *Transition Report*, various annual issues. London: European Bank for Reconstruction and Development.

Feigenbaum, H. and J. Henig. 1994. "The Political Underpinnings of Privatization: A Typology." *World Politics* 46(2): 185–208.

Fershtman, C. 1990. "The Interdependence Between Ownership Status and Market Structure: The Case of Privatization." *Economica* 57(227): 319–328.

Filer, R. and J. Hanousek. 2000. "Output Changes and Inflationary Bias in Transition." *Economic Systems* 24(3): 285–294.

——. 2001. "Efficiency of Price Setting Based on a Simple Excess Demand Rule: The Natural Experiment of Czech Voucher Privatization." *European Economic Review* 45(9): 1619–1646.

Fischer, S. 1990. "Comment on 'Creating a Market Economy in Eastern Europe: The Case of Poland.'" *Brookings Papers on Economic Activity* 1990(1): 75–147.

Fischer, S. and J. Frenkel. 1992. "Macroeconomic Issues of Soviet Reform." *American Economic Review, Papers and Proceedings* 82(2): 37–42.

Fisher-Vanden, K. 2003. "The Effects of Market Reforms on Structural Change: Implications for Energy Use and Carbon Emissions in China." *Energy Journal* 24(3): 27.

Frydman, R., C. W. Gray, M. Hessel, and A. Rapaczynski. 1999. "When Does Privatization Work? The Impact of Private Ownership on Corporate Performance in Transition Economies." *Quarterly Journal of Economics* 114: 1153–1191.

Frydman, R., M. Hessel, and A. Rapaczynski. 2000. "Why Ownership Matters? Entrepreneurship and the Restructuring of Enterprises in Central Europe." C. V. Starr Center for Applied Economics Working Paper, New York University.

Frydman, R., E. Phelps, A. Rapaczynski, and A. Shleifer. 1993. "Needed Mechanisms of Corporate Governance and Finance." *Economics of Transition* 1: 171–208.

Frydman, R. and A. Rapaczynski. 1991. "Markets and Institutions in Large Scale Privatization: An Approach to Economic and Social Transformation in Eastern Europe." In *Reforming Central and Eastern European Economics: Initial Results and Challenges*, ed. V. Corbo, S. Corbicelli, and J. Bossak. Washington, DC: World Bank.

Galal, A., L. Jones, P. Tandon, and I. Vogelsang. 1994. *Welfare Consequences of Selling Public Enterprises: An Empirical Analysis.* London: Oxford University Press.

Glaeser, E. L. and J. A. Scheinkman. 1996. "The Transition to Free Markets: Where to Begin Privatization." *Journal of Comparative Economics* 22: 23–42.

Gomulka, S. 1989. "Shock Needed for Polish Economy." *The Guardian*, August 19.

——. 1994. "Obstacles to Recovery in Transition Economies." In *Obstacles to Enterprise Restructuring in Transition*, ed. P. Aghion and N. Stern. London: European Bank for Reconstruction and Development

Gong, C. and S. Li. 1994. "Transition with Growth: The Chinese Experience in the World Economy." University of Minnesota Center for Economic Research Discussion Paper 271.

Gordon, R. and W. Li. 1995. "The Change in Productivity of Chinese State Enterprises." *Journal of Productivity Analysis* 6: 5–26.

Gray, C. and A. Holle. 1997. "Bank-Led Restructuring in Poland." *Economics of Transition* 5: 25–44.

Gregory, P. and R. Stuart. 1997. *Comparative Economic Systems*, 6th ed. Boston: Houghton Mifflin.

Grigorian, D. A. 2000. "Ownership and Performance of Lithuanian Enterprises." World Bank Policy Research Working Paper Series 2343. Washington, DC: World Bank.

Grosfeld, I. and J. F. Nivet. 1997. "Firm's Heterogeneity in Transition: Evidence from a Polish Panel Data Set." William Davidson Institute Working Paper 47, University of Michigan.

Grosfeld, I. and J. Roland. 1997. "Defensive and Strategic Restructuring in Central European Enterprises." *Journal of Transforming Economies and Societies* 3(4): 21–46.

Grosfeld, I. and T. Tressel. 2001. "Competition and Corporate Governance: Substitutes or Complements? Evidence from the Warsaw Stock Exchange." William Davidson Institute Working Paper 369, University of Michigan.

Gupta, N., J. Ham, and J. Svejnar. 2008. "Priorities and Sequencing in Privatization: Theory and Evidence from the Czech Republic." *European Economic Review*, Forthcoming.

Gupta, S., C. Schiller, and H. Ma. 1999. "Privatization, Social Impact, and Social Safety Nets." International Monetary Fund Working Paper 68. Washington, DC: International Monetary Fund.

Gupta, S., et al. 2001. "Privatization, Labor and Social Safety Nets." *Journal of Economic Surveys* 15(5): 647–669.

Gylfason, T. 1998. "Privatization, Efficiency and Economic Growth." CEPR Discussion Paper 1844. London: Centre for Economic Policy Research.

Ham, J., J. Svejnar, and K. Terrell. 1998. "Unemployment and the Social Safety Net During Transitions to a Market Economy: Evidence from the Czech and Slovak Republics." *American Economic Review* 88(5): 1117–1142.

——. 1999. "Women's Unemployment During the Transition: Evidence from Czech and Slovak Micro Data." *Economics of Transition* 7(1): 47–78.

Hanousek, J. and R. K. Filer. 2003. "Investment, Credit Rationing, and the Soft Budget Constraint: What Would a Well-Functioning Credit Market Look Like?" *Economic Letters* 82(3): 385–390.

Hanousek, J., D. Hajkova, and L. Nemecek. 2002. "The Czech Republic's Banking Sector: Emerging from Turbulent Times." *EIB Cahiers Papers* 7(1): 55–74.

Hanousek, J. and E. Kočenda. 2005. "Learning by Bidding: Evidence from a Large-Scale Natural Experiment." CERGE-EI Working Paper 247. Prague: Center for Economic Research and Graduate Education.

Hanousek, J., E. Kočenda, and J. Svejnar. 2004. "Spinoffs, Privatization and Corporate Performance in Emerging Markets." William Davidson Institute Working Paper 685, University of Michigan.

———. 2007. "Origin and Concentration: Corporate Ownership, Control and Performance in Firms After Privatization." *Economics of Transition* 15(1): 1–31.

Hansen, N. 1995. "Privatization, Technology Choice and Aggregate Outcomes." Discussion Paper 474 Series A, University of Bonn.

Hashi, I., J. Mladek, and A. Sinclair. 1997. "Bankruptcy and Owner-Led Liquidation in the Czech Republic." In *Enterprise Exit Processes in Transition Economies: Downsizing, Workouts and Liquidations,* ed. L. Balcerowicz, C. W. Gray, and I. Hashi. London: CEU Press.

Hausman, J. 1978. "Specification Tests in Econometrics." *Econometrica* 46(6): 1251–1271.

———. 1979. "Sample Selection Bias as a Specification Error." *Econometrica* 47(1): 153–161.

Heckman, J. and V. Hotz. 1989. "Choosing Among Alternative Nonexperimental Methods for Estimating the Impact of Social Programs: The Case of Manpower Training." *Journal of the American Statistical Association* 84(408): 862–874.

Heckman, J. and R. Robb. 1985. "Alternative Methods for Evaluating the Impact of Intervention." In *Longitudinal Analysis of Labor Market Data*, ed. J. Heckman and B. Singer. New York: Cambridge University Press.

Hinds, M. 1990. "Issues in the Introduction of Market Forces in Eastern European Socialist Economics." In *Managing Inflation in Socialist Economies in Transition.* Washington, DC: The Economic Institute of the World Bank.

Holmström, B. and J. Tirole. 1983. "Market Liquidity and Performance Monitoring." *Journal of Political Economy* 101: 678–709.

Huber, P. J. 1967. "The Behavior of Maximum Likelihood Estimates Under Nonstandard Conditions." In *Proceedings of the Fifth Berkeley Symposium on Mathematical Statistics and Probability,* 221–223. Berkeley: University of California Press.

Iskander, M. and N. Chamlou. 2000. *Corporate Governance: A Framework for Implementation.* Washington, DC: World Bank.

Jensen, M. 2000. *A Theory of the Firm: Governance, Residual Claims, and Organizational Forms.* Cambridge, MA: Harvard University Press.

Jones, D. 1998. "The Economic Effects of Privatization: Evidence from a Russian Panel." *Comparative Economic Studies* 40(2): 75–102.

Jones, D. and N. Mygind. 2000. "The Effects of Privatization on Productive Efficiency: Evidence from the Baltic Republics." *Annals of Public and Cooperative Economics* 71(3): 415–440.

Junz, H. 1991. "Integration of Eastern Europe into the World Trading System." *American Economic Review, Papers and Proceedings* 81(2): 176–180.

Jurajda, S. and K. Terrell. 2002. "What Drives the Speed of Job Reallocation During Episodes of Massive Adjustment?" William Davidson Institute Working Paper 432, University of Michigan.

Katz, B. and J. Owen. 1993. "Privatization: Choosing the Optimal Time Path." *Journal of Comparative Economics* 17: 715–736.

Kikeri, S., J. Nellis, and M. Shirley. 1992. *Privatization: The Lessons of Experience.* Washington, DC: World Bank.

King, L. P. 2003. "Explaining Postcommunist Economic Performance." William Davidson Institute Working Paper 559, University of Michigan.

Kočenda, E. 1999. "Residual State Property in the Czech Republic." *Eastern European Economics* 37(5): 6–35.

Kočenda, E. and J. Svejnar. 2003. "Ownership and Firm Performance After Large-Scale Privatization." CERGE-EI Working Paper 209. Prague: Center for Economic Research and Graduate Education.

Kočenda, E. and J. Valachy. 2002. "Firm Ownership Structures: Dynamic Development." *Prague Economic Papers* 11(3): 255–268.

Kornai, J. 1990. *The Road to a Free Economy. Shifting from a Socialist System: The Example of Hungary.* New York: W. W. Norton; Budapest: HVG Kiadó.

———. 1992. "The Postsocialist Transition and the State: Reflections in the Light of Hungarian Fiscal Problems." *American Economic Review, Papers and Proceedings* 82(2): 1–21.

Kotrba, J. 1995. "Privatization Process in the Czech Republic: Players and Winners." In *The Czech Republic and Economic Transition in Eastern Europe,* ed. J. Svejnar, 159–198. San Diego: Academic Press.

Kotrba, J., E. Kočenda, and J. Hanousek. 1999. "The Governance of Privatization Funds in the Czech Republic." In *The Governance of Privatization Funds: Experiences of the Czech Republic, Poland and Slovenia,* ed. M. Simoneti, S. Estrin, and A. Boehm, 7–43. London: Edward Elgar.

Kotrba, J. and J. Svejnar. 1994. "Rapid and Multifaceted Privatization: Experience of the Czech and Slovak Republics." *Nomisma/Most* 4: 147–185.

Kruskal, W. H. and W. A. Wallis. 1952. "Use of Ranks in One-Criterion Variance Analysis." *Journal of the American Statistical Association* 47: 583–621.

LaPorta, R. and F. Lopez-de-Silanes. 1999. "The Benefits of Privatization: Evidence from Mexico." *The Quarterly Journal of Economics* 114: 1193–1242.

Lau, L., Y. Qian, and G. Roland. 2000. "Reform Without Losers: An Interpretation of China's Dual-Track Approach to Transition." *Journal of Political Economy* 108: 120–143.

Leamer, E. and M. Taylor. 1994. The "Empirics of Economic Growth in Previously Centrally Planned Economies." CEPR Discussion Paper 976. London: Centre for Economic Policy Research.

Lewandowski, J. 1997. "The Political Context of Mass Privatization in Poland." In *Between State and Market: Mass Privatization in Transition Economies,* ed. I. W. Lieberman, S. Nestor, and R. Desai, 35–39. Washington, DC: World Bank.

Lewandowski, J. and J. Szomburg. 1990. "Dekalog prywatyzacji." *Tygodnik Solidarnosc* 45: Supplement.

Li, W. 1999. "A Tale of Two Reforms." *RAND Journal of Economics* 30(1): 120–136.

Lipton, D. and J. Sachs. 1990. "Creating a Market Economy in Eastern Europe: The Case of Poland." *Brookings Papers on Economic Activity* 1990(1): 75–147.

Lipton, D., J. Sachs, and L. H. Summers. 1990. "Privatization in Eastern Europe: The Case of Poland." *Brookings Papers on Economic Activity* 1990(2): 293–341.

Litwack, J. 1991. "Legality and Market Reform in Soviet-Type Economies." *Journal of Economic Perspectives* 5(4): 77–90.

Lízal, L. and E. Kočenda. 2001. "State of Corruption in Transition: The Case of the Czech Republic." *Emerging Markets Review* 2(2): 138–160.

Lízal, L. and J. Svejnar. 2001. "Investment, Credit Rationing and the Soft Budget Constraint: Evidence from Czech Panel Data." *The Review of Economics and Statistics* 84(2): 353–370.

Ma, S. 1998. "The Chinese Route to Privatization: The Evolution of the Shareholding System Option." *Asian Survey* 38(4): 379–397.

Mackenzie, G. 1997. "The Macroeconomic Impact of Privatization." IMF Paper on Policy Analysis and Assessment 9. Washington, DC: International Monetary Fund.

Mann, C. 1991. "Industry Restructuring in East-Central Europe: The Challenge and the Role for Foreign Investment." *American Economic Review, Papers and Proceedings* 81(2): 181–185.

McFaul, M. 1995. "State Power, Institutional Change, and the Politics of Privatization in Russia." *World Politics* 47(2): 210–243.

Megginson, W., R. Nash, and M. van Randenborgh. 1994. "The Financial and Operating Performance of Newly Privatized Firms: An International Empirical Analysis." *Journal of Finance* 49: 403–452.

Megginson, W. and J. Netter. 2001. "From State to Market: A Survey of Empirical Studies on Privatization." *Journal of Economic Literature* 39(2): 321–389.

Mejstrik, M., A. Marcincin, and R. Lastovicka. 1997. "Voucher Privatization, Ownership Structures, and Emerging Capital Market in the Czech Republic." In *The Privatization Process in East-Central Europe: Evolutionary Process of Czech Privatizations*, ed. M. Mejstrik. Norwell, MA: Kluwer Academic Publishers.

Murrell, P. 1991. "Can Neoclassical Economics Underpin the Reform of Centrally Planned Economies?" *Journal of Economic Perspectives* 5(4): 59–76.

North, D. 1994. "Privatization, Incentives and Economic Performance." Economics Working Paper Archive, Economic History Series 9411002, Washington University, St. Louis, MO.

Oi, J. 1992. "Fiscal Reform and the Economic Foundations of Local State Corporatism in China." *World Politics* 45(1): 99–126.

Perotti, E. 1995. "Credible Privatization." *American Economic Review* 85: 847–859.

Pissarides, F., M. Singer, and J. Svejnar. 2003. "Objectives and Constraints of Entrepreneurs: Evidence from Small and Medium Size Enterprises in Russia and Bulgaria." *Journal of Comparative Economics* 31: 503–531.

Plane, P. 1997. "Privatization and Economic Growth: An Empirical Investigation from a Sample of Developing Market Economies." *Applied Economics* 29(2): 161–178.

Pohl, G., R. Anderson, S. Claessens, and S. Djankov. 1997. "Privatization and Restructuring in Central and Eastern Europe: Evidence and Policy Options." World Bank Technical Paper 368. Washington, DC: World Bank.

Prasnikar, J. and J. Svejnar. 1991. "Workers Participation in Management vs. Social Ownership and Government Policies: Yugoslav Lessons for Transforming Socialist Economies." *Comparative Economic Studies* 33(4): 27–46.

Prasnikar, J., J. Svejnar, D. Mihlajek, and V. Prasnikar. 1994. "Behavior of Participatory Firms in Yugoslavia: Lessons for Transition Economies." *Review of Economics and Statistics* 76: 728–741.

Public Opinion Research Center. 1999. "Was It Worthwhile? The Czechs, Hungarians and Poles on the Changes of the Last Decade." http://www.cbos.pl/English/cbos_en.htm.

Rivers, D. and Q. H. Vuong. 1988. "Limited Information Estimators and Exogeneity Tests for Simultaneous Probit Models." *Journal of Econometrics* 39: 347–366.

Roland, G. 1994. "On the Speed and Sequencing of Privatization and Restructuring." *The Economic Journal* 104(426): 1158–1168.

——. 2000. *Transition and Economics: Politics, Markets and Firms.* Cambridge, MA: MIT Press.

——. 2001. "Ten Years After . . . Transition and Economics." *IMF Staff Papers* 48(Special Issue): 29–52.

Roland, G. and T. Verdier. 1999. "Transition and the Output Fall." *Economics of Transition* 7(1): 1–28.

Rollo, J. and A. Smith. 1992. "The Political Economy of Central European Trade with the European Community: Why So Sensitive?" Presented at Economic Policy: A European Forum, hosted by the Bank of England and Her Majesty's Treasury, October 15–16.

Sachs, J. 1992. "Privatization in Russia: Some Lessons from Eastern Europe." *American Economic Review, Papers and Proceedings* 82(2): 43–48.

Sachs, J., C. Zinnes, and Y. Eilat. 2000. "The Gains from Privatization in Transition Economies: Is Change of Ownership Enough?" CAER II Discussion Paper 63, Harvard Institute for International Development, Harvard University.

Saint-Paul, G. 1995. "The Pure Ricardian Theory of Privatization." DELTA Working Paper 36, Ecole Normale Supérieure, Paris.

Shirley, M. and P. Walsh. 2000. "Public Versus Private Ownership: The Current State of the Debate." Washington, DC: World Bank.

Shleifer, A. and R. W. Vishny. 1994. "Politicians and Firms." *Quarterly Journal of Economics* 46: 995–1025.

——. 1997. "A Survey of Corporate Governance." *Journal of Finance* 52(2): 737–783.

Smith, S., B. Cin, and M. Vodopivec. 1997. "Privatization Incidence, Ownership Forms, and Firm Performance: Evidence from Slovenia." *Journal of Comparative Economics* 25: 158–179.

Statistical Yearbook of the Czech Republic. 1991–1997. Prague: Center for Economic Research and Graduate Education.

Stiglitz, J. 1990. "Comment on 'Creating a Market Economy in Eastern Europe: The Case of Poland.'" *Brookings Papers on Economic Activity* 1990(1): 75–147.

——. 1999. "Whither Reform: Ten Years of the Transition." Presented at the Annual Bank Conference on Development Economics in Washington, DC, for the World Bank.

Svejnar, J. 1989. "A Framework for the Economic Transformation of Czechoslovakia." *PlanEcon Report* 5(52): 1–18.

——. 2002. "Transition Economies: Performance and Challenges." *Journal of Economic Perspectives* 16(1): 3–28.

Svejnar, J. and M. Singer. 1994. "Using Vouchers to Privatize an Economy: The Czech and Slovak Case." *Economics of Transition* 2: 43–64.

Tanzi, V. and G. Tsiboures. 2000. "Fiscal Reform over Ten Years of Transition." IMF Working Paper 113. Washington, DC: International Monetary Fund.

Temple, J. 1999. "The New Growth Evidence." *Journal of Economic Literature* 37(1): 112–156.

Vining, A. R. and A. E. Boardman. 1992. "Ownership Versus Competition Enterprise." *Public Choice* 73: 205–239.

White, H. 1982. "Maximum Likelihood Estimation of Misspecified Models." *Econometrica* 50: 1–25.

World Bank. 1994. *Averting the Old Age Crisis.* New York: Oxford University Press.

——. 1996. *World Development Report.* Washington, DC: World Bank.

——. 1999. *Czech Republic: Toward EU Accession.* Washington, DC: World Bank.

Zinnes C., Y. Eilat, and J. Sachs. 2001. "The Gains from Privatization in Transition Economies: Is 'Change of Ownership' Enough?" *IMF Staff Papers* 48 (Special Issue): 146–170.

CHAPTER 4

Privatization in Africa

What Has Happened? What Is to Be Done?

John Nellis

Consider the case of Guinea, one of the poorest countries in Africa and thus one of the poorest countries in the world. From independence in 1960 through the end of the 1980s, Guinea's state-owned enterprises (SOEs) in telecommunications, energy, and water provided consumers with an inadequate quantity of low-quality services. As of 1989, only 38% of Guineans had access to piped water, and almost none in rural areas. Those connected suffered frequent interruption of service. Water quality was poor and unhealthy; "waterborne diseases were the main cause of death for infants and there were periodic cholera epidemics" (Ménard and Clarke, 2002, 277). One plus: the price for the few connected customers was low: US$0.02 per cubic meter (m³) until 1986, and US$0.12 per m³ thereafter. But half or more of the water sent into the system vanished and was never billed. At this price and rate of loss, the national water company could not come near covering its operating costs, much less invest in badly needed maintenance and expansion. Donors made repeated attempts to work with the government to reform the national water company; these attempts failed to make a major or sustained difference.

In 1989, Guinea entered into a lease arrangement with a private provider to deliver water in the capital, Conakry, and 16 other towns. Under this scheme, government retained ownership of the assets, responsibility for setting policy and tariffs, and (with World Bank assistance) responsibility for marshalling investment finance and expanding the network. A private firm was selected to operate and maintain existing facilities and to bill and collect payments from customers. By agreement, the price per m³ of water at once more than doubled. This was still inadequate to cover operating costs, so a World Bank credit covered the difference between revenues and costs in the early years. This subsidy was to decline as either periodic rate increases or efficiency gains reduced the need.

Over the next seven years, major improvements took place. Connections increased from 12,000 to 23,000. The percentage of metered private customers rose from 5% to 93%, and to 100% for government customers. The percentage of the population with access to water rose from 38% to 47% (Brook Cowen, 1999, 1), and the pace of increase was greater than it had been under public ownership. Very importantly, water quality improved greatly.[1] Tariffs rose to levels covering variable costs, revenues of the water company rose by a factor of 10, and the World Bank subsidy ended. Sixty-four percent of customers billed paid their fees (Shirley and Ménard, 2002, 22), a modest rate compared to international norms, but much improved over past collection achievements. Compared to failed earlier attempts to reform the system without the involvement of the private sector, all this was impressive. But a number of major concerns remained.

First, by 1997 the price per m³ stood at US$0.83, a near seven-fold increase from 1989, and more than 40 times the 1986 price. The price was very high in comparison to most Organisation of Economic Co-operation and Development (OECD) countries, much less African neighbors,[2] and was considerably higher than in most other lease/concession arrangements in Asia and Latin America (where smaller increases had often provoked street protests). A cross-subsidy scheme allowed small-volume users to pay less than large users, but both the reduction in price per m³ and the monthly amount to which the lower price applied were smaller than in most other countries (Shirley and Ménard, 2002, 15). Post-privatization, an essential commodity had become less affordable.[3]

Second, while the physical network expanded, the rate of growth was less than anticipated. Unlike more recent leases and concessions around the world, this contract did not place investment responsibility in private hands, and it did not specify expansion and connection targets for the SOE that retained responsibility for enlarging the network. Third, the amount of unaccounted water remained well above 40%. Government customers did pay for service a bit more regularly than before, but many government offices remained in arrears to the provider—and the private company did not cut service to any central government unit, even though this was expressly permitted in its contract. Had water losses and billing and collection been more aggressively addressed, revenues would have increased, and prices might have fallen—but under the lease agreement the private provider had no overwhelming incentive to push for such improvements.

This was largely due to a fourth factor: The government was still very much involved in key parts of the water business, and its performance continued to be weak. The experienced private operator apparently had little difficulty persuading the inexperienced government regulators to accept price hikes. It may be that the private provider found it easier to negotiate tariff increases than to collect aggressively.[4] In any event, because all commercial risk was borne by the government, the private manager was free to select the path of least resistance, constrained only by the competence and dynamism of the government regulatory agency. The question then becomes: Did regulators[5] capture—for consumers—a reasonable share of the financial benefits arising from the efficiency gains produced post-lease? The answer depends on the "counterfactual": what would have happened had the contract not been let, had the public sector remained in control? As discussed below, careful students of the process conclude that private involvement produced superior results, despite the large price increases.

Thus, in sum, the lease produced gains, including gains to general consumers; but these were less than expected, and they came at a slow pace and quite a high cost.

AFRICAN PRIVATIZATION: THE RECORD TO DATE

The Guinea water story reflects in miniature Africa's struggle with privatization, particularly in infrastructure, where one finds the largest and most economically important SOEs. The general story is this: Poor service provision by loss-making public enterprises led first to reforms short of private sector involvement. These produced no, modest, or unsustainable improvements. Financial losses mounted. They led to further deterioration in service quantity and quality and increased burdens on the government budget. International Monetary Fund (IMF) involvement and surveillance led to a choking off of direct budgetary financing of SOEs. In most cases, the banking system, initially state-owned or dominated, then took on the task of financing the enterprises. Debts were incurred but not serviced. The banks rapidly accumulated a nonperforming portfolio and severe solvency problems. Financing/fiscal problems grew acute. These, and not efficiency concerns per se, became the principal driver of SOE reform. Typically, it was the IMF that highlighted the issue and insisted upon efforts to resolve it. In response, private sector management, financing, or ownership was proposed. The World Bank then became more directly involved in terms of reform/privatization design and assistance in implementation.

In many (probably most) African countries, the principal motivation for privatization has been to placate international financial institutions (IFIs) such as the IMF and the World Bank. African governments do increasingly recognize the SOE problem, and numerous African leaders and observers preach the gospel of financial discipline and market-oriented reform. Still, commitment to privatization as the best way to solve SOE problems has been neither widespread nor strong. Most African leaders and officials would prefer that the SOE problem be addressed by means other than ownership change.[6] A review of the scope and pace of African privatization supports this allegation.

On average, African states have privatized a smaller percentage—about 40%—of their SOEs than other regions, far less than Latin America and the transition economies.[7] Much of the African divestiture that has taken place has been of smaller, less valuable, often moribund manufacturing, industrial, and service concerns. In contrast, infrastructure privatization has lagged. Of the roughly 2,300 privatizations in sub-Saharan Africa in the period from 1991 to 2001,[8] only about 66 involved generally higher value, economically more important firms. An additional 92 transactions took place in transportation, some of which might have been classed as infrastructure. But even if one includes all the latter, less than 7% of sales has touched the upper-end infrastructure firms.

Moreover, activity has been concentrated in a very few countries: of the US$9 billion of African privatization revenue raised from 1991 to 2001,[9] a full third was generated by a handful of privatizations in South Africa. Another 33% came from sales in a group of four actively privatizing countries (Ghana, Nigeria, Zambia, and Côte d'Ivoire). Some 26 African countries, taken together, have privatized a scant US$0.7 billion of assets (see table 4.1 and figure 4.1).

Finally, African states have retained significant minority equity stakes in the comparatively few infrastructure privatizations they have concluded, holding back from the market an average of one-third of shares (see figure 4.2 and table 4.2). Governments claim that retained shares are weapons with which to protect the public interest against rascally or incompetent buyers. Moreover, they often hope to sell the retained shares later at a much higher price, after the new private partner has driven up value. Whether

TABLE 4.1 Privatization Record in Africa, 1991–2001

Country	Number of Transactions	Sale Value (US$ mn)	Share of Total SOEs Divested
Angola	57	6	—
Benin	28	49	38%
Burkina Faso	23	9	32%
Burundi	38	4	—
Cameroon	48	244	28%
Cape Verde	42	53	—
Central African Republic	18	—	50%
Chad	35	12	—
Congo (Brazzaville)	65	50	—
Congo (Kinshasa)	5	—	4%
Côte d'Ivoire	82	622	55%
Ethiopia	10	410	6%
Gabon	1	—	6%
Gambia	17	2.4	85%
Ghana	181	936.5	69%
Guinea	31	45	27%
Guinea Bissau	25	0.5	64%
Kenya	189	381	79%
Lesotho	10	6.5	20%
Madagascar	61	16.9	33%
Malawi	11	53.2	44%
Mali	59	67.4	92%
Mauritania	19	1.2	20%
Mozambique	474	135	39%
Níger	10	1.8	18%
Nigeria	30	893.5	6%
Rwanda	1	—	3%
São Tome and Principe	4	0.4	—
Senegal	39	415	23%
Sierra Leone	8	1.6	31%
South Africa	8	3,151	—
Sudan	32	—	—
Tanzania	199	287	53%
Togo	49	38	89%
Uganda	102	174	79%
Zambia	253	828	90%
Zimbabwe	6	217	10%
			Average:
Total	2,270	9,111.9	40%

Sources: This table is based on a compilation and updating of the databases conducted by Thierry Buchs, International Finance Corporation, 2002. They are drawn from the World Bank Africa Region Privatization Database (World Bank, 2002); World Development Indicators database, 1991–2000; International Monetary Fund Staff Country Reports, 1998–2002; and Campbell-White and Bhatia (1998), Table 1, Appendix A.

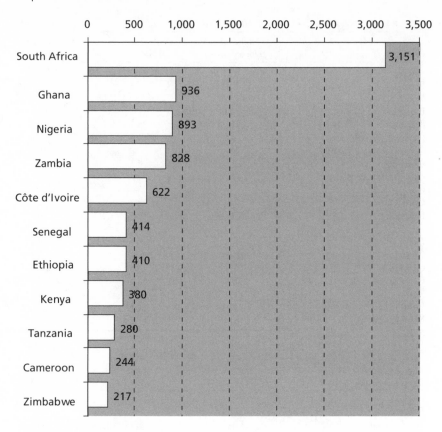

FIGURE 4.1   Countries in Which Total Transaction Values Exceeded US$200 million (cumulative, 1991–2001)

Sources: This figure is based on a compilation and updating of the databases conducted by Thierry Buchs, International Finance Corporation, 2002. They are drawn from the World Bank Africa Region Privatization Database (World Bank, 2002); World Development Indicators database, 1991–2000; International Monetary Fund Staff Country Reports, 1998–2002; and Campbell-White and Bhatia (1998), Table 1, Appendix A.

share retention actually achieves these goals is debatable. What is not in doubt is that continued government involvement and share retention reduces the number of bidders and therefore the price per share sold. The slow pace of sales, the reluctance to place the highest-potential assets on the market, the failure to sell all shares, poor business and legal environments, and the deficiencies of government regulation and administration—all combine to place African states in a dead heat with Middle Eastern and North African countries for the title of "region with the least foreign investment in infrastructure privatization" (see figure 4.3).

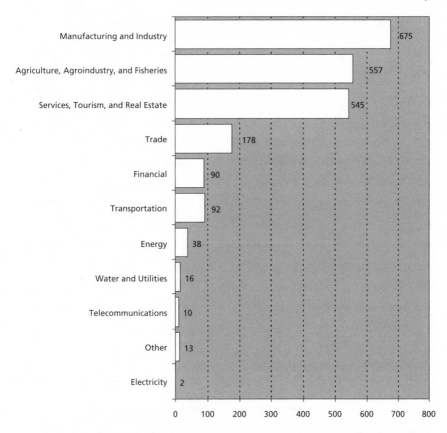

FIGURE 4.2   African Privatizations by Sector, 1991–2001

Sources: This figure is based on a compilation and updating of the data bases conducted by Thierry Buchs, International Finance Corporation, 2002. They are drawn from the World Bank Africa Region Privatization Database (World Bank, 2002); World Development Indicators database, 1991–2000; International Monetary Fund Staff Country Reports, 1998–2002; and Campbell-White and Bhatia (1998), Table 1, Appendix A.

CAUTION IS CORRECT?

Caution on ownership change could be the right policy for Africa. Here's the argument: Privatization outcomes are heavily affected by the institutional setting in which divestiture takes place. In their haste to correct the quality flaws and financial losses of SOEs, proponents of privatization pushed excessively for rapid ownership change while neglecting or insufficiently emphasizing the institutional foundations on which good privatization must be based. Experience such as Guinea's shows that privatization

TABLE 4.2   Government's Share of Equity Before and After Privatization

Sector	Average Government's Share of Equity	(%)
Manufacturing and Industry	Before privatization	79.7
	After privatization	7.9
Agriculture, Agroindustry, and Fisheries	Before privatization	79.5
	After privatization	1.6
Services, Tourism, and Real Estate	Before privatization	70.2
	After privatization	14.3
Trade	Before privatization	95.3
	After privatization	3.3
Transportation	Before privatization	97.6
	After privatization	4.9
Financial	Before privatization	86.7
	After privatization	8.2
Energy	Before privatization	88.3
	After privatization	46.5
Water	Before privatization	100
	After privatization	12.5
Electricity	Before privatization	100
	After privatization	33
Telecommunications	Before privatization	95.8
	After privatization	42.8
Other	Before privatization	63.3
	After privatization	10.2
Total average government's share of equity before privatization		89.1
Total average government's share of equity after privatization		10.3

Sources: This table is based on a compilation and updating of the databases conducted by Thierry Buchs, International Finance Corporation, 2002. They are drawn from the World Bank Africa Region Privatization Database (World Bank, 2002); World Development Indicators database, 1991–2000; International Monetary Fund Staff Country Reports, 1998–2002; and Campbell-White and Bhatia (1998), Table 1, Appendix A.

is more likely to result in increased efficiency and improved equity outcomes if it is embedded in a set of conceptually appropriate, functioning legal and economic institutions that support and guide market operations. These include the definition and protection of property rights; contract enforcement and commercial dispute settlement through lawful, peaceful means, or, more broadly, court decisions that are timely and based on the law, not payments; a degree of regulatory capacity; functioning bankruptcy/insolvency regimes; and a public administration that meets modicum standards of predictability, competence, and probity and thus lowers transaction costs. If these institutions are not in place and working, privatization will produce suboptimal, perhaps negative outcomes.

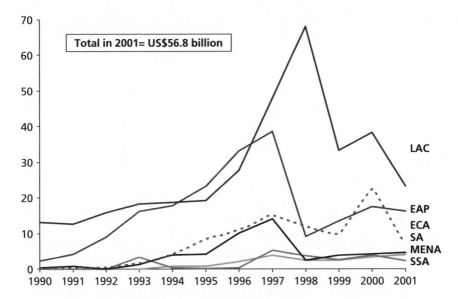

FIGURE 4.3   Investment in PPI projects by Region, 1990–2001

Source: World Bank, Private Provision of Infrastructure Database, 2002. The investment tabulated is that in network service industries only, but that is where the bulk of investment goes. LAC refers to Latin America-Caribbean countries; EAP, East Asia–Pacific; ECA, East Europe–Central Asia; SA, South Asia; MENA, Middle East–North Africa; SSA, sub-Saharan Africa.

This notion has risen rapidly to the status of conventional wisdom; indeed, it is getting difficult to find an analysis of privatization that does not attribute to institutional weaknesses any deviation from hoped-for results. But the concept is disturbingly vague and difficult to make sense of operationally. It is unclear as to precisely how these institutions come into being and attain a state of effectiveness. Nor is it clear just which ones are crucial in what particular circumstances, or in what sequence they should be introduced. And while most of these policies/institutions function under the control of the public sector, it is, again, not clear as to what governments, and those that assist them, can do to aid their emergence and enhance their capacity.

What *is* known? (1) There is a strong association between institutional density and capacity and positive results, in both efficiency and equity terms, of ownership change. (2) Low-income countries in general, and African countries in particular, rank low in terms of institutional density and capacity. (3) The creation and reinforcement of market-supporting institutions, while imperfectly understood, is certainly a slow process. Thus, if African governments are moving cautiously on privatization—particularly infrastructure privatization—in order to buy time to establish the needed institutional and regulatory frameworks, this could be a logical and positive step.

This is a large *if.* To date, it would appear that few African states have used the time gained through slow privatization to attack effectively the problem of deficient institutions—or if they have, the results are not yet visible. (On the contrary, as is shown below in the case of Zambia, delaying privatization has sometimes resulted in further financial and asset erosion.) Admittedly, results would be hard to assess: Practitioners possess little in the way of operational guidelines concerning the minimal level of institutional density or capacity a state should possess before considering ownership change.[10] And the standards by which to measure institutional effectiveness are embryonic and general. As Shirley (2003, 1) notes, "over time the development paradigm has shifted from 'get your prices right' to 'get your institutions right;' the latter instruction has proved as useless as the former."[11]

One reason for this is that inaction on SOE reform sometimes reflects not simply lack of expertise, resources, or institutional capacity, but rather intent, spurred by political hostility to privatization. As noted (see note 6), African intellectuals and officials have long been educated to view the public sector as the promoter and defender of indigenous interests, and to believe that privatization will empower and enrich foreigners. African trade unions and workers' representatives are generally opposed to privatization, fearing it will result in the loss of jobs or worsen terms of service.[12] Many African (and European, Asian, and Latin American) politicians and public officials reap material and prestige benefits from SOEs in the form of loans; gifts; transportation; housing; board memberships; future jobs for themselves; present jobs for friends, relatives, and supporters; procurement kickbacks; and much else. Domestic private sectors often have cozy supply relationships with SOEs that could be threatened by the arrival of more aggressive, quality-conscious, cost-cutting private owners. In short, there are many powerful groups in all African states that have material reasons to delay, dilute, or sabotage SOE reform, privatization in particular. Of course, they make their case not by complaining about potential harm to their material interests, but rather by pointing to perceived economic, financial, and social shortcomings of privatization. On what grounds do they make their case?

POST-PRIVATIZATION PERFORMANCE

Rigorous assessments of privatization are increasingly available in Latin American, transition, OECD, and Asian countries. Such studies are relatively rare in Africa[13]—though, as shown below, the few that exist generally present a positive picture of privatization's achievements, particularly in the manufacturing, industrial, and service sectors. First, the critics' indictment of privatization is presented; this is necessarily somewhat anecdotal in nature.

CON

To illustrate with a single important case, in 2002 officials in Zambia considered halting and perhaps reversing their privatization program—one of the most extensive in Africa in terms of number of transactions, proceeds generated, and percentage of SOE portfolio divested[14] (see table 4.1 and figure 4.1), and a program that in 1998 was hailed by the World Bank as "the most successful" in Africa (Campbell-White and Bhatia, 1998, 111). But four years later, many Zambians clearly perceived privatization as almost entirely negative, and they put pressure on government to rethink the policy. Privatization was alleged to have:

- Been imposed and micromanaged by the IFIs without sufficient attention to requisite policy or regulatory frameworks and with minimal involvement of Zambian citizens
- Resulted in the closure of many firms previously run by Zambians (there is particular resentment that many that continued or reopened are in the hands of foreigners, particularly South Africans)
- Added greatly to unemployment—and thus poverty and inequality—at a time when job opportunities are declining drastically
- Increased the incidence of corruption (there is widespread suspicion that the proceeds from sales have been unreported and misused)
- Benefited the rich, the foreign, the agile, and the politically well-connected (see Craig, 2002) at the expense of the poor, the domestic, the honest, and the unaffiliated—as illustrated by the allegation that new private owners extract subsidies and tax concessions from government

Zambians claim that the IFIs were originally uninterested in helping them deal with the negative social effects of privatization (severance packages, retraining schemes, monitoring contractual obligations of new owners), and that they only paid serious attention to such matters when they were expressly involved in a specific transaction; i.e., when the World Bank's private sector affiliate, the International Finance Corporation, was one of the investors/purchasers, or when an IMF condition mandated movement on the sale of a major firm.

The sentiments of Zambian opinion-makers toward liberalization in general, and privatization in particular, were neatly summarized in an editorial in *The Post* of Lusaka (November, 28, 2002):

> The hardships Zambians are going through are primarily a consequence of . . . neoliberalism and neoliberal globalization. . . . While it cannot be denied that corruption, extravagance and lack of priorities have considerably aggravated the situation, we shouldn't forget that these factors are a product of this whole system—they are inherent problems of these policies. These IMF and World Bank policies breed corruption, extravagance and lack of priorities in our leaders and indeed our people. . . . And despite having liberalized its markets, as dictated by the IMF and the World Bank, Zambia has still not started benefiting from it.
>
> What our country needs now is to think through its strategies and that primarily involves freeing itself from the IMF and World Bank indirect rule and start to direct the affairs of this country in the best interests of our people, and not the major shareholders of these institutions. Why should we privatize Zambia National Commercial Bank, Zesco Limited (electricity) and Zamtel (telecommunications) simply because the IMF and the World Bank want us to do so even when the great majority of Zambians are opposed to it because they believe it is not in their best interest? . . . The success of IMF and World Bank policies over any alternative model of social development is [more] a matter of propaganda than fact. If humans prevail, alternative policies to the IMF and World Bank's programs will be found and implemented. The main thing is to have a political leadership that has a clear understanding of today's neoliberal world and can stand firm.

This encapsulates the views, prevalent in Zambia then and now, and widespread in Africa as a whole, that privatization has been forced upon Zambia by the IFIs, has not produced the economic benefits it was supposed to deliver, has imposed substantial costs, and has increased the level of corruption. Are these allegations accurate?

PRO

In 2001, the Zambian Privatization Agency commissioned a study to assess the effects of privatization. It found that 235 of the 254 firms privatized since 1991 continued in operation at the time of the study, not a bad achievement given the very poor financial state of these enterprises prior to divestiture, and the dismal business environment prevailing in the country throughout the 1990s. In terms of numbers of sales, 57% of the buyers were Zambian citizens, and an additional 13% were joint ventures between Zambians and foreigners; the remaining 30% of sales were to foreigners (many of whom had been minority equity partners in SOEs and who held, and exercised, preemptive rights on the sales of shares). However, by value, Zambians accounted for just 5% of sales, joint ventures 83%, and totally foreign purchasers 12%. A scheme to "warehouse" a minority stake of shares in privatized firms and float them later to Zambian buyers has had minimal success. Some of the most visible firms, such as the breweries, went to South African owners (who have turned them into profitable ventures).

A prime rationale for privatization is the inability of government to access investment capital for renewal and expansion of SOEs. In the non-mining firms reviewed, post-privatization capital expenditures totaled more than US$400 million. Nineteen firms, or 7.5% of those privatized, closed following privatization, a fact much lamented in Zambia—though a 7.5% failure rate is less than small and medium business failure rates in most advanced industrial economies. Seven of the 19 firms subsequently resumed operations after being resold, and similar efforts were under way in an additional five—leaving only seven firms definitively closed.[15] A number of company closures sometimes cited as evidence of the failure of privatization were either firms that had always been private, or SOEs.

In the privatized non-mining firms, employment declined from 28,000 at the time of privatization[16] to 20,000 in 2001, a comparatively large percentage, but a small number in absolute terms. Most of the decline took place immediately following divestiture and was concentrated in a few large firms in agroindustry. Workforce expansions occurred in several firms.

There is less clarity and far more controversy about the fate of the 34,000 workers employed in the privatized mining sector. A highly publicized and troubling issue for the privatization program is that two large mines—Luanshya and Baluba—were sold to a bidder who agreed not to dismiss any of the 7,000 workers. The parent mining SOE, Zambia Consolidated Copper Mines (ZCCM),[17] had assessed that up to 3,000 of these workers would be redundant under any reasonable business plan and lacked the funds to make the required severance payments. It therefore accepted a bid based on the dubious premise that the entire workforce could be maintained. Shortly following transfer of title, the new owner dismissed 3,000 workers. Under Zambian law, private owners are responsible for termination benefits of workers dismissed after sale; in this case, the new owner failed to make the required payments. Subsequently, the firm went out of business entirely, and the residual 4,000 workers are now in the same boat as the previously laid off 3,000. Understandably, worker and public reaction has been severely critical.

Overall, it is clear that employment in the mining sector has decreased by at least 7,000 workers, or 20%. Assuming that the dismissal rate in the other affected mines was equal to that in the non-mining sector (28.5%), this would amount to an additional 7,700 layoffs and a total reduction of workers in the privatized mining sector of around 19,000. The fate of 10,000 of the remaining workers is in doubt, given the decision by Anglo-American, in January 2002, to pull out of the ZCCM copper mining operations it had purchased in 1999.

A digression is in order to sketch the sad story of copper in Zambia in the years 1993–2003. The highlights are a persistent and precipitous fall in world copper prices,[18] a deep and costly politicization of the management and employment/procurement practices of the firm while an SOE, and no investment in the sector for years prior to its sale—all this leading to Zambian production costs being among the highest in the world, and resulting in losses on average of US$15 million per month over the past five years of its existence as an SOE. Discussions to privatize the sector began in 1991, but despite supposedly powerful donor prodding nothing substantial was sold until 1999.[19] The first serious effort to sell came in 1996–1997. A fairly firm US$1 billion offer (counting promised investments) was on the table from a consortium of experienced copper firms. However, responsibility for the transaction was removed from the respected Zambian Privatization Agency and handed over to a team of mine man-

agers and former managers, many of whom had long opposed privatization. They rejected the offer, based on a book value calculation of the
assets, and asked for much more. The bidders walked away. Following
two years of further asset deterioration and large losses, the mines were
sold for much less than what had been offered in 1997. And no one seems
to know if there were any cash proceeds from the eventual sales,[20] or what
happened to them if they did exist (African Business, 2000).

Perhaps the counterfactual would have been worse? To repeat, the privatized firms, outside the then severely depressed copper sector, have done
quite well, almost certainly far better than they would have had they remained under government ownership—this in a time of severe economic
downturn in Zambia. In the mining sector, no one can defend the Luan-
shya/Baluba sale. Even the low-priced and subsequently canceled takeover
of the other ZCCM mines by Anglo-American has resulted in substantial
investments that the government would never have been able to make. One
can argue that perhaps these investments will serve as a foundation on
which a subsequent owner can make the venture profitable, though clearly
that was not the view of the highly experienced Anglo-American, which appears to have decided not to throw good money after bad. (The final irony
is that after two decades of declining and languishing prices, demand for
copper skyrocketed after 2003; prices rose by more than fivefold).

Overall, the argument that any reasonable counterfactual would have
resulted in inferior outcomes is fairly persuasive in the case of small and
medium firms producing tradable goods—but much less convincing when
large, relatively valuable firms are at issue. Certainly, the copper sector had
been grossly mismanaged under state ownership, but it is evident that the
privatization of the sector was poorly handled, both economically and socially. Zambians thus have legitimate reason to fear that privatizations of
major infrastructure firms could go wrong, given the nontransparent,
efficiency- and revenue-decreasing manner that large firms have been divested in the past. An anti-privatization argument of despair once made in
Russia may apply in the Zambian case: Retaining firms in state hands
means that any positive flow of resources generated will likely be largely si-
phoned off or wasted, depending on whether the managers and supervisors
are venal or incompetent (or both). But privatization may be worse, as the
lack of legal safeguards allows new owners to steal not simply the flow, but
the entire stock of the firm.[21]

Finally, a nagging doubt: is this problem "institutional" or "political" in nature, and what is the difference? In line with the emerging

conventional wisdom, institution building did precede ownership change in Zambia, as evidenced by the high marks given the personnel, policies, and procedures of the Zambian Privatization Agency and the relative lack of contentious sales carried out by this body. The major problem seems to have been the decision to remove the sales of the mining firms from the purview of the agency, a decision that was political in nature. Some would argue that poor or corrupt political decisions are themselves institutional shortcomings. This maintains the conceptual unity of the institutional argument, but at the cost of enlarging yet again an already too vast and unwieldy subject. And in practical terms, while one might make a case for retaining infrastructure firms in state hands pending the development of a modicum of regulatory capacity, the same can hardly be said for retention until the quality of sound political decision making reaches some acceptable level. The point is to reiterate unease with the institution-building argument and approach.

OTHER AFRICAN COUNTRIES

Is the Zambian case typical? Regarding the crucial issue of transparency, table 4.3 presents the type and incidence of privatization methods employed in Africa. While no method is guaranteed to be free of manipulation and corruption, some methods are more transparent than others. The sale of shares through a public floatation is generally thought to be about the most transparent sales approach, but it has rarely been applied in Africa (outside of Nigeria and South Africa) in part because of the thin or embryonic nature of capital markets in most countries. Other methods can be designed to be competitive and transparent, such as tenders. But the ultimate transparency of the tender method depends on the honesty and competence of its administrators to a greater extent than does stock issuing. One cannot systematically link the method applied to the size or importance of the relevant firm (though it is likely that only large firms were sold through public floatation).

BETTER NEWS

Summarizing other studies of African privatizations: Boubakri and Cosset (2002) looked at 16 privatizations on the continent of Africa (none in Zambia). Profitability rose and efficiency fell, both by slight percentages.

TABLE 4.3 Methods of Privatization, 1991–2001

Method of Divestiture	Number
Shares Sold on a Competitive Basis	728
Asset Sold on a Competitive Basis	454
Liquidation	386
Shares Sold to Existing Shareholders with Preemptive Rights	158
Lease	104
Direct Sale of Shares (i.e., noncompetitive)	94
Shares Sold Through Public Floatation	69
Not Specified	48
Restitution to Former Owner	47
Management Contract	42
Management/Employee Buyout	33
Direct Sale of Assets (i.e., noncompetitive)	29
Joint Venture	28
Free Transfer of Assets	12
Transfer to Trustee	11
Debt-Equity Swap	10
Concession	8
JV(D)	5
Lease/Management Contract	2
Merger	2
Total	2,270

Buchs (2003) estimates the countries where obviously less transparent methods have accounted for a significant minority of sales. The numbers are sufficiently large to raise concerns, though no firm conclusions can be drawn.

Neither of these shifts was statistically significant, but there was a significant increase in capital expenditures in the divested firms.[22]

Jones, Jammal, and Gokgur (1998) analyzed 81 privatizations in Côte d'Ivoire covering the electricity sector in infrastructure, with the rest operating in competitive or potentially competitive markets (in agriculture, agroindustries, and services). They found that (1) firms performed better after privatization; (2) they performed better than they would have had they remained under public ownership; and (3) privatization contributed positively to economic welfare, with annual net welfare benefits equivalent to about 25% of pre-divestiture sales. These significant benefits stemmed from increases in output, investment, labor productivity, and intermediate-input productivity.

Appiah-Kubi (2001) reviewed 212 privatizations in Ghana and reported positive results in terms of easing pressure on the balance of payments, increasing both allocative and x-efficiency, stimulating local capital markets, enhancing the inflow of foreign direct investment, obtaining widespread quality gains for consumers, and increasing employment and remuneration post sale (though increases in jobs after privatization had not yet matched the cuts in worker numbers made prior to divestiture). Andreasson (1998) assessed privatization's impact in Mozambique and Tanzania and found positive changes in operating and financial performance of the divested firms. In both countries, many commercial state firms had ceased operation before divestiture was contemplated; in both countries, three-fourths of such firms returned to productive activity following privatization. Substantial productivity gains were noted, due partly to reductions in the workforce, but also because of improved utilization of capacity. In most cases, investments, production, sales, and value added increased sharply post-sale. "The over-riding conclusion . . . is that performance of privatized companies has met and even surpassed expectations" (Andreasson, 1998, 10).

Temu and Due (1998) also reviewed Tanzania's privatization experience and examined in detail post-sale performance in a set of firms. Of the 158 firms divested through 1999, 136 (34% of the pre-privatization universe of 395 SOEs) had been sold, 115 closed or liquidated; an additional 24 firms had been leased, 8 placed under management contracts, and the rest were yet to be divested. By number, more than two-thirds of sales went to Tanzanian nationals; more than half of them "indigenous" or African buyers; the remainder, presumably, were Tanzanian citizens of Asian descent. South African firms (De Beers, South African Breweries, R. J. Reynolds Tobacco SA) featured prominently as purchasers of the larger value firms. In their study, Temu and Due documented the extremely poor physical and financial condition of Tanzanian manufacturing firms prior to privatization,[23] and the tortuous, lengthy negotiations—often lasting years—between potential buyers of even the most wasted assets and an endless line of officials; they termed it "privatization by exhaustion." They concluded that privatization "has increased government revenues, reduced subsidies to SOEs, and . . . forced firms to operate more efficiently" (339). In a second study (Due and Temu, 2002), they noted that employment levels in 16 privatized firms examined decreased by 48% (327).

In infrastructure, Wallsten (1999) econometrically examined the effects of privatization, competition enhancement, and regulation in telecommunications reform in 30 countries, half of them in Africa, the rest in Latin America. Enhanced competition produces the clearest, most positive effects. Ownership change by itself "does not appear to generate many benefits," but does so when combined with separate and independent regulation. These are summary conclusions not disaggregated by region. The data require careful interpretation in that "the finding that privatization is negatively correlated with the number of main lines . . . could arise because countries are more likely to privatize their incumbent telecom provider when service is poor" (Wallsten, 1999, 14). It may not be that privatization caused performance to weaken, as suggested by the regression, but rather that the weakest telecommunications firms were the ones to be privatized.

More positively, Ménard and Clarke (2002) conclude that despite the evident problems of private provision of water in Guinea, "all parties have benefited from reform . . . [as] increased coverage and improved quality more than compensated consumers for higher prices" (274).[24] A definitive judgment depends on what would have happened in the absence of private involvement: Ménard and Clarke argue that the situation would have been worse had water management remained in public hands. They reach even more upbeat conclusions concerning private provision of water in Abidjan, Côte d'Ivoire (Ménard and Clarke, 2002), where 30 years of private activity has resulted in very high levels of coverage despite rapid population growth, an excellent quality of water and service, and declining prices for all consumers. Areas of concern are the decline of competitive bidding, the likelihood that the average price per m³ could easily be even lower, and the fear that the flexible collaboration between government and private provider that lay at the heart of the Ivorian success in this venture will be destroyed by the political instability in the country since 1999.

WHAT IS TO BE DONE?

The first conclusion is that privatization of manufacturing, industrial, and service sectors, and especially the small and medium firms in these sectors, should proceed apace. The empirical record on the effects of privatization in Africa is not as dense and robust as it is in other regions. Still, accumulating evidence suggests that firms producing tradables do more for the shareholders, consumers, taxpayers, and economy in private hands they than ever did under public ownership. A surprising number of assets of this type remain in state hands in Africa; they should be divested without delay.

Utilities and infrastructure, banks, railroads, and the large natural resource producers are tougher cases. The dilemma is evident: retaining them in classic SOE form means more poor service and financial losses; privatizing them incorrectly can be economically and politically problematic. Wallsten's (1999) important conclusion[25] regarding telecommunications divestiture—that ownership change per se does not produce efficiency gains, but ownership change combined with separate and independent regulation does—must certainly apply to electricity, water, and sewerage sectors, particularly given the lack, compared to telecommunications, of technological change facilitating competition in these sectors.

Thus, the medium- to long-term solution is to create and reinforce the institutional mechanisms that guide and regulate sales and market operations. Institutional improvements are required if African markets are to attract and retain good investors to manage, finance, and own infrastructure services in ways that are beneficial to society while yielding a decent return on the capital and expertise expended. So, institution-building programs—to enact the policy framework for and build implementation capacity in sales, regulatory, and competition promotion agencies; to train the individual sellers and regulators; to empower and then isolate monitoring and enforcement agencies from political interference; to render contracts enforceable—would seem to be desirable. There is already much under way in these fields in Africa, most of it supported by the donor community. An examination of past initiatives to determine which were the more effective, why, and under what circumstances, with suggestions on how to replicate the successful, might be of use.

Should this be the main thrust of reform efforts? Perhaps not. First, as the Guinea water case indicates, some infrastructure privatizations, in even the least auspicious institutional settings, have produced results far superior to the SOEs that preceded them. It is unlikely that the benefits of holding off on the privatization until Guinean regulatory capacity was enhanced would outweigh the costs of poor SOE performance. Second, the long record of poor accomplishments in the area of institutional reform cannot be ignored. Nor can the ease with which substantive institutional achievements, such as the Zambian Privatization Agency, can be overturned or ignored at the drop of a political hat. Over the last few decades, donors and African governments have launched numerous institution-building, technical assistance, regulatory policy and capacity, and public sector management reform efforts—the positive and enduring results of which are hard to find. They are not invisible, but they are certainly modest and often ephemeral. On the reasoning that the impact of present and future institution-building efforts will resemble those of the past, and noting that even in the rare instances where positive institutional change has been effected it has taken ages to produce, I conclude that interim and innovative measures are needed to advance private participation in infrastructure provision.

Some possibilities:

1. *Outsource institutional provision:* for example, by contracting regulatory conception and monitoring activities from skilled outsiders. This was successfully carried out (prior to the escalation of violence) in the case of the Palestinian Water Authority in Gaza, in a situation of extraordinary institutional and political difficulty.

In 1996, a private firm was awarded a four-year management contract to handle water and sanitation services. Payment was in two parts: a set fee, and a bonus payment based on the achievement of stipulated performance targets. The provider agreed to submit periodic performance reports on which the additional payment would be based. The Palestinian Authority lacked the capacity to monitor the contract and especially the performance reports of the private provider.

The solution, funded by donors, was to hire Deloitte and Touche (D&T), Norway, to assess the technical and financial performance of the private provider. Every six months D&T reviewed the provider's performance reports, verified their accuracy, and confirmed or disputed the performance score. By 1998, water service had improved considerably (consumption and revenues way up, system losses way down, water quality vastly improved). Outsourcing of regulation reportedly worked well; in its first report, the private provider claimed a performance payment of US$498,000, but the D&T auditors disputed several results, and the amount was lowered to US$444,000 (Saghir, Sherwood, and Macoun, 1999).

2. A variation on this theme is: *Use private firms to carry out administrative functions that impede investment and privatization and harm the general business environment.* For example, British Crown Agents have been contracted to handle procurement on a range of government contracts in a number of low-income countries, including Bolivia and Mozambique. This should speed the contracting process and save money by lowering transaction costs and side payments.[26]

3. *Promote offshore commercial arbitration mechanisms:* for example, several small island states in the Caribbean use British courts to arbitrate contractual disputes between governments and private providers.

4. *Use respected nongovernmental organizations, such as Transparency International, to vet transactions and certify the probity of the sales process:* as has been done, for example, in a telecommunications license auction in Slovakia.

5. *Use IFI guarantees to give comfort to investors regarding regulatory and contractual risk.* For example, the World Bank offers investors partial risk guarantees insuring against sovereign, political, and regulatory risks, e.g., state failure to meet payment obligations, disallowance of stipulated tariff hikes, expropriation, legal changes with adverse material effects on the investor, availability and convertibility of foreign exchange, and so on. Partial risk guarantees in Côte d'Ivoire and Uganda infrastructure privatizations have helped to mobilize financing and cofinancing, lengthened maturities far beyond prevailing market terms, and significantly reduced interest spreads. Because the guarantee backstops only the contractual agreements states make with investors, governments incur no additional contingent liabilities.[27] Fees for the guarantee are born by the investors (Gupta et al., 2002).

6. *Encourage the use of regional exchanges* to address the problem of small or deficient equity markets.

Finally, the external private sector might assist by offering guidelines on transparent procedures on the part of investors in privatization transactions or, more simply, by subscribing to, endorsing, and helping to promulgate the promising "Business Principles for Countering Bribery" initiative of Transparency International.[28]

Outsourcing and the reliance on such external measures could, indeed should, produce positive effects. But they will be politically sensitive or outright unacceptable to many in Africa, who are likely to regard them as further infringements of sovereignty or further suggestions of African incompetence. Even if accepted, they are at best temporary, stopgap measures. The real answer lies in the internal evolution of the institutional and political frameworks, a process—to hammer home the point—that is not well understood but is, at the very least, time consuming. Donors can cajole and help, as they have done in Guinea, Gaza, and elsewhere, but their effectiveness is less than the eternally optimistic statements they issue. The African privatization dilemma, at least for the largest and higher potential firms, is unresolved.

NOTES

Acknowledgments: Helpful comments on earlier drafts were received from Nancy Birdsall, Guy Pfeffermann, Mary Shirley, Mike Stevens, Nicolas Van de Walle, and John Williamson. Particular thanks are due to Thierry Buchs, formerly of the International Fiance Corporation (IFC) and now at the Swiss State Secretariat for Economic Affairs, who compiled the data found in the tables. An earlier version of this chapter appeared in 2003 as Working Paper No. 25 of the Center for Global Development, Washington, D.C.

1. Improving water quality can have a large social impact. In Argentina, improvements in water quality in the 30% of municipalities with privatized provision led to declines in infant mortality, from water borne diseases alone, by 5% to 9%, versus areas where water continued to be supplied by publicly operated firms. The poorer the area, the greater the impact; poorest neighborhoods saw declines in infant mortality of up to 24%. See Galiani, Gertler, and Schargrodsky (2002).

2. In Abidjan in the neighboring Côte d'Ivoire, the privatized water company offered an average price in 1997 of US$0.54 per m³.

3. Less affordable for some; the distributional impact of the price increase is unclear. Most poor people in Guinea were not and still are not hooked up to the water network; those connected are probably from the middle- and upper-income strata. A price rise for these consumers, even substantial, may have a limited direct effect on either inequality or poverty. But it is also quite likely that increased prices in the formal water network have been passed on to many poor consumers, at least in urban areas, who often get their water from vendors (whose prices are always much higher per unit than from a formal connection to the network).

4. The private provider would argue, with justification, that the high price was legitimate given government's inability to expand the network as expected and to permit service termination to customers in arrears—i.e., to hold up its side of the bargain—and the reluctance of local courts to allow the water firm to sanction customers who failed to pay.

5. In Guinea, regulation of the contract was placed in the hands of the "rump" SOE that had formerly managed the water supply, not in a new, separate, legally defined and empowered regulatory body.

6. Temu and Due's description of Tanzanian reaction to the very idea of privatization applies in a number of other African states: "The concept of a centralized economy had been well taught and well learned. The government feared losing its commanding heights; the people feared the loss of the enterprises their hard-earned taxes had supported. Those fearful of private enterprise saw the new owners dismantling the parastatals and cashing in on the rewards. Even supporters of privatization saw parastatal managers stripping the firms and cashing in whatever was saleable" (1998, 333).

7. And if one removes from the list of 29 countries (for which one can estimate the percentage of the SOE portfolio divested) the six leaders in terms of numbers of firms sold—Gambia, Ghana, Kenya, Mali, Togo, and Zambia—the fraction of SOE stock privatized falls to about one-fourth. Thirteen of these 29 countries have privatized less than 30% of their SOE portfolios; only six have divested more than 75%.

8. Note that most of the 2,300 sales were completed by 1997; since then, in line with the worldwide decline in investor interest in emerging markets, the number of privatizations in Africa has fallen below 100 per year.

9. In contrast, privatization revenues in Italy alone, in the period 1990–2001, totaled US$112 billion, and even New Zealand—ranking tenth on an OECD list of privatizing states and with a population of less than 4 million—generated more from privatization in this period than did all 37 African countries (Mahboobi, 2002, 46). Moreover, African privatization revenues may be significantly overestimated; in a number of countries, buyers have failed to make payment on transactions already recorded as complete.

10. A step in this direction, for one important sector at least, is found in Newbery. He lists the policy, regulatory, and institutional requisites for electricity privatization to be effective. In their absence "reform of the . . . state-owned ESI [electricity sector industry] to improve autonomy, accountability, and financial viability, may be the only option. The fact that such reforms have failed in the past does not make it wise to encourage irreversible reforms of unproven worth, and privatisation in unpropitious circumstances may be even more costly than the unsatisfactory status quo" (2001, 43–44). No African case is discussed in Newbery's paper. See also Sachs, Zinnes, and Eilat (2000), who argue that in transition states, at least, ownership change must be accompanied by a threshold level of what they termed "agency-related" institutional reforms of the type listed above. If this modicum level of contracting and incentive reforms is not present, then ownership change may produce no or even negative effects. Conversely, institutional change by itself is also insufficient to generate economic performance improvements "unless enough change-of-title privatization has already occurred" (54).

11. Rodrik, Subramanian, and Trebbi (2002) argue that "the quality of institutions 'trumps' everything else" in explaining economic development outcomes. But they note that the argument is at such a high level of abstraction as to provide little or no guidance to policy makers.

12. At the time of this writing, among many examples that could be given, COSATU—the trade union organization in South Africa—has recently held public demonstrations to protest all past and planned privatizations, and the Zambian trade union congress has held protest marches and called on government to rescind its decision to privatize the Zambian National Commercial Bank, and to halt preparations for privatization in the electricity and telecommunications sectors.

13. "Monitoring and evaluation have largely been ignored; hence the paucity of data on—and the difficulty of judging—the progress and impact of privatization to date" (Campbell-White and Bhatia, 1998, 125).

14. Though in value terms, many of the firms sold (outside the copper sector) have been small; the big companies are only now being prepared for sale.

15. Three of the closed firms had long been nonoperational prior to sale.

16. It is likely that there had been reductions in employee numbers prior to privatization as part of reforms or in preparation for sale. In many countries around the world, the largest layoffs come well before a change of ownership. Thus, comparing

employee numbers at the moment of privatization to some later point may underestimate the downsizing that occurs.

17. Itself subsequently privatized.

18. Copper traded at close to US$7,000 a ton in 1966 and averaged above US$3,000 a ton until the mid-1990s; prices fell to between US$1,450 and US$1,600 a ton in the early 2000s–before bouncing back to over US$7,000 a ton in 2006.

19. The IFIs cannot win; they are blamed both for rushing the sale *and* delaying it. When asked why the sale took so long, a Zambian mining official said that it was the fault of the donors; their pressure on government to sell led bidders to "sit and wait until they feel the price is right" (African Business, 2000, 2).

20. It is conceivable that there were no proceeds from these transactions. The costs of financial clean-up and severance payments (even where they were correctly handled) might have matched or exceeded all revenues. But in the absence of a proper accounting, the public is given license to speculate that not only these transactions were corrupt, but all others as well. (The IMF calculates, for 18 privatizing countries, that gross proceeds amount, on average, to 2% of GDP, while net proceeds [gross minus costs of advisers, financial clean-up, and worker dismissals] amount to half this number.)

21. A similar argument was advanced in Kenya in January 2000; several opinion makers interviewed said they deplored the inefficiencies and rampant corruption in the major SOEs, but feared that privatization would only enlarge and entrench theft and mismanagement.

22. The Boubakri-Cosset (2002) findings are of limited utility to this study because 10 of the 16 transactions analyzed took place in Morocco and Tunisia, not in sub-Saharan Africa.

23. For example, the Morogoro Shoe Company, built—with IFI assistance—to produce 4 million shoes annually, 80% for export, never reached more than 4% of installed capacity.

24. Recent studies of privatization of infrastructure in Latin America also conclude that the benefits of increased access to these services post-sale outweigh the costs imposed on consumers by price increases (McKenzie and Mookherjee, 2002).

25. Mirroring the conclusion of Sachs, Zinnes, and Eilat (2000).

26. There are no panaceas. A Swiss firm (SGS Holdings) contracted to handle some aspects of the corruption-ridden customs service in Pakistan is alleged to have bribed government officials in return for the contract, thus tainting the idea of outsourcing.

27. There is a cost in that the amount available for lending from the World Bank (or International Development Association) to the country is reduced by the amount guaranteed. That is, the sum guaranteed is nominally recorded as a World Bank loan. The country pays no fee and makes no payments (unless the guarantee is called and the World Bank has had to pay the investor).

28. Launched in December 2002 with the assistance of a number of private firms including General Electric, Shell International, and Rio Tinto, the principles "provide a framework for good business practices and risk management strategies for

countering bribery." The summary document lists the areas where bribery and corruption are most prevalent in business operations—outright bribes, political contributions, charitable contributions and sponsorships, facilitation payments, gifts, hospitality, and expenses—and states clearly the actions that participating firms will eschew (Transparency International, 2002).

REFERENCES

African Business. 2000. "ZCCM: A Tale of Heartbreak and Tears." http://dsapce. dial.pipex.com/town/ terrace/lf141/ab/feboo/abmno201.htm.

Andreasson, B. 1998. "Privatization in Sub-Saharan Africa: Has It Worked and What Lessons Can Be Learnt?" Gothenburg, Sweden: Swedish Development Advisers. http://www.swedevelop.com.

Appiah-Kubi, K. 2001. "State-Owned Enterprises and Privatization in Ghana." *Journal of Modern African Studies* 39(2): 197–229.

Boubakri, N. and J. Cosset. 2002. "Does Privatization Meet the Expectations? Evidence from African Countries." Draft paper.

Brook Cowen, P. 1999. "Lessons from the Guinea Water Lease: Public Policy for the Private Sector." Note 78. Washington, DC: World Bank.

Buchs, T. 2003. "Privatization in Sub-Saharan Africa: Some Lessons from Experiences to Date." International Finance Corporation, mimeo.

Campbell-White, O. and A. Bhatia. 1998. *Privatization in Africa*. Washington, DC: World Bank.

Craig, J. 2002. "Privatisation and Indigenous Ownership: Evidence from Africa." Centre on Regulation and Competition Working Paper 13, University of Manchester.

Davis, J., et al. 2000. "Fiscal and Macroeconomic Effects of Privatization." IMF Occasional Paper 194. Washington, DC: International Monetary Fund.

Due, J. and A. Temu. 2002. "Changes in Employment by Gender and Business Organization in Newly Privatized Companies in Tanzania." *Canadian Journal of Development Studies* 23(2): 317–333.

Galiani, S., P. Gertler, and E. Schargrodsky. 2002. "Water for Life: The Impact of the Privatization of Water Services on Child Mortality." Draft paper.

Gupta, P., R. Lamech, F. Mazhar, and J. Wright. 2002. "Mitigating Regulatory Risk for Distribution Privatization—The World Bank Partial Risk Guarantee." Energy and Mining Sector Board Discussion Paper 5. Washington, DC: World Bank.

Jones, L., Y. Jammal, and N. Gokgur. 1998. "Impact of Privatization in Côte d'Ivoire." Draft Final Report, Boston Institute for Developing Economies, Boston University.

Kayizzi-Mugwera, S. 2002. "Privatization in Sub-Saharan Africa: Factors Affecting Implementation." WIDER Discussion Paper 12, United Nations University.

Mahboobi, L. 2002. "Recent Privatisation Trends in OECD Countries." *Financial Market Trend (OECD)* 82: 43–58.

McKenzie, D. and D. Mookherjee. 2002. "Distributive Impact of Privatization in Latin America: An Overview of Evidence from Four Countries." Unpublished draft paper commissioned by Inter-American Development Bank.

Ménard, C. and G. Clarke. 2002. "A Transitory Regime: Water Supply in Conakry, Guinea." In *Thirsting for Efficiency: The Economics and Politics of Urban Water System Reform*, ed. Mary Shirley, 273–316. Washington, DC: World Bank.

Newbery, D. 2001. "Issues and Options for Restructuring the Electricity Sector Industry." Unpublished draft paper, Department of Applied Economics, Cambridge University.

Rodrik, D., A. Subramanian, and F. Trebbi. 2002. "Institutions Rule: The Primacy of Institutions over Integration and Geography in Economic Development." IMF Working Paper 189. Washington, DC: International Monetary Fund.

Sachs, J., C. Zinnes, and Y. Eilat. 2000. "The Gains from Privatization in Transition Economies: Is 'Change of Ownership' Enough?" CAER II Discussion Paper 63, Harvard Institute for International Development, Harvard University.

Saghir, J., E. Sherwood, and A. Macoun. 1999. "Management Contracts in Water and Sanitation—Gaza's Experience." Viewpoint Note 177. Washington, DC: World Bank.

Shirley, M. 2003. "Institutions and Development: A Statement of the Problem." Unpublished draft paper, Ronald Coase Institute.

Shirley, M. and C. Ménard. 2002. "Cities Awash: A Synthesis of the Country Cases." In *Thirsting for Efficiency: The Economics and Politics of Urban Water System Reform*, ed. Mary Shirley, 1–41. Washington, DC: World Bank.

Temu, A. and J. Due. 1998. "The Success of Newly Privatized Companies: New Evidence from Tanzania." *Canadian Journal of Development Studies* 19(2): 315–341.

Transparency International. 2002. "Business Principles for Countering Bribery." http://www.transparency.org/building_coalitions/private_sector/business_principles.html#countering.

Wallsten, S. 1999. "An Empirical Analysis of Competition, Privatization and Regulation in Africa and Latin America." World Bank Working Paper 2136. Washington, DC: World Bank.

World Bank. 2002. *Private Participation in Infrastructure Database.* Washington, DC: World Bank, Private Sector Advisory Services.

CHAPTER 5

Privatization in Latin America

The Good, the Ugly, and the Unfair

Antonio Estache and Lourdes Trujillo

Most casual observers of reform processes in Latin America are likely to quote privatization as one of the pillars of the 1990s reforms in that region. In fact, Latin America has over 30 years of experience with large-scale privatization. It started in 1974 with Chile.[1] Mexico and Jamaica followed at some distance when they launched the first phase of their own major privatization programs in the early 1980s.[2] The clearer image of a privatizing Latin America actually dates from the significant effort in Mexico by the Salinas administration in 1988 and from the widely publicized Argentinean reforms started in 1989 by the Menem administration. Bolivia, Brazil, Colombia, El Salvador, Guatemala, Nicaragua, and Panama later followed the same path during the 1990s, contributing to build the image of a privatizing Latin America.

The privatization of agricultural, fishing, manufacturing, oil, gas, and mining industries; public and social services; and banks, insurance, and other services resulted in the transfer to private operators or the closure of about 1,600 public companies in the region. The biggest bang may have been in Mexico, where the number of public enterprises shrank from 1,155 to 219 between 1988 and 1994. But the changes were also quite dramatic in the rest of the region. Argentina privatized 115 enterprises between 1990 and 1994; Brazil transferred 119 firms between 1991 and 2001; Jamaica privatized over 200 companies during the 1990s; and Nicaragua eliminated 343 between 1991 and 1998.

The short-term cash flows associated with the privatization transactions were important. The policy generated about US$175 billion in income for the region between 1990 and 1999. Almost 60% of this revenue was generated by the privatization of infrastructure services and over 10% by the privatization of financial services. But the total revenue was quite concentrated among a few countries. Indeed, about 95% of the 1990s proceeds from privatization accrued to six countries: Brazil (40%), Argentina (26%), Mexico (17%), Peru (5%), Colombia (3.5%), and Venezuela (3.5%).[3] The smaller countries generated much less revenue in dollar terms. However, while not significant for the region, for some of them, the revenue payoffs were important in relation to the size of their economy. For instance, while the average proceeds from privatization represented about 2.7% of GDP, for Bolivia and Panama this income was equivalent to over 10% of their GDP.

To get a better sense of the actual importance of the policy changes behind those flows, consider the index of progress in the implementation of privatization policies proposed by Panizza and Lora (2002).[4] The index measures on a scale of 0 to 1 the privatization effort. This effort is itself measured as the cumulative value of the sales and transfers of companies, starting in 1986, as a proportion of GDP in any given year.[5] According to this index and for a sample of 17 Latin American countries, Bolivia made the most of the policy and reached an index of 0.90. The next best performers were Peru, Brazil, Argentina, and El Salvador, with indices ranging from 0.65 to 0.35.

The diversity in performance across countries illustrated by this index also makes it quite clear that privatization as a policy choice did not spread throughout the region, contrary to what is sometimes argued by casual observers. Uruguay, Paraguay, Costa Rica, Honduras, Ecuador, and many of the small Caribbean countries, for instance, have indices well below 0.05 as they have not followed the privatization wave—in a few cases as a result of referenda—and have generated very little public revenue from this policy.[6]

Even if this policy had not been adopted with equal enthusiasm by all countries, it is useful to take stock of what had been achieved at a time privatization is being rejected by some of the countries that were once its champions. The recent policy reversals or moderations in Argentina, Bolivia, Brazil, Peru, and Venezuela have indeed caught the popular attention as much as the privatization efforts had done during the 1990s. The discussions in the media and some policy circles are, however, not always based on fact. Indeed, emotions tend to rule the debate on privatization in the region. Surveys, such as the one published by Latinbarometro, forcefully demonstrate the growing sense of discomfort with this policy with an almost steady decline in support since 1998.[7] As of 2003, negative views of privatization ranged from 53% in Honduras to 83% in

Argentina. On average for the region, two out of three people had a negative view.

The change in support for this policy has generated a large number of studies since 2000 intended to separate facts from emotions to try to explain the increasing concern with this policy among the population, and hence the politicians.[8] This chapter summarizes briefly the main lessons from these studies of the Latin American privatization experience. Because the specifics of privatization are much less homogenous than often believed outside of the region, the various country experiences provide many insights on what has been learned over the last 15 years or so as to what works and what does not work with this policy instrument. In particular, this experience shows that it is important to distinguish between the privatization of public services and other industries and services.

The chapter is organized as follows. The first section provides a brief overview of the initial conditions that were used to justify the decision to privatize in every country and the main forms that privatization took in each country. The second section looks at some of the main achievements of these reforms, including the effects on prices, quality, investments, employment, financial autonomy, and public finances. The third section focuses on the things that did not work out the way they were expected to work at the time reforms were designed, including the distributional consequences, competition policy failures, and some important institutional and governance issues.

WHY AND HOW DID COUNTRIES "PRIVATIZE" TO BEGIN WITH?

Because the history of privatization has so often been rewritten for ideological reasons, it may be useful to review some of the basic facts on the initial reasons at the beginning of the reform processes within the countries. The original motivation and expectation of reform can indeed be quite important in assessing the actual evolution of the impact of the policy, as compared to the perceptions of this impact and the evolution of these perceptions. The original motivation can also come in handy in understanding the interactions between objectives, privatization forms, and additional complementary policies that have been or should have been taken to fine-tune implementation mistakes. It can finally smooth the learning process that comes from the "doing" rather than simply from an academic assessment of the good and the bad of any reform.

The review of the country-specific histories is important because, it is sometimes argued (as in Brune and Barlett, 2000), that diffusion (i.e., "copycatting") explains privatization better than domestic, political, and economic considerations.[9] In other words, irrespective of what local political speeches may have been arguing over the last 15 or so years in the region, the main motive, according to these authors, may have been a less rational response to local concerns. Without questioning the validity of this result, it seems difficult to doubt that in many of the countries, significant efforts were allocated to implement reforms that matched local circumstances, local political feasibility constraints, and what were perceived to be local concerns.

The privatization form has to recognize that countries differ in market size, in level of poverty, in ability to bargain with multilateral and commercial banks, in level of democracy, or in level of corruption. The details of the implementation of the policies seem to show that governments at the time did understand this quite well. However, before getting into the specific motivations as argued by each reforming government, it may be useful to point to an important historical detail. It is sometimes forgotten that Chile's experience, and to some extent Mexico's experience, predate the British experience. Indeed, Thatcher's programs started later in the 1970s and accelerated only after 1983. These could not possibly be copycat experiences, and this is why this review starts with these cases studies.

CHILE

Chile's privatization experience is in fact a series of privatization waves.[10] The first wave was between 1974 and 1978 and focused on over 550 companies. It is notable that it excluded utilities but included companies that had been nationalized by the Allende administration. It was part of the adoption of the neoliberal view of the world carried out under the military regime of General Pinochet—this is what most people seem to remember from that experience. The reforms demanded stabilizing the economy and very restrictive fiscal policies. These very restrictive policies in turn demanded large revenues, and *generating revenue was hence the main objective of this first wave of privatization.* To achieve these revenue targets, the government offered controlling packages to investors and provided credit (through auctions often) to investors to ease to the constraints imposed by the underdeveloped Chilean capital market.[11]

The second wave of privatization took place between 1984 and 1990. It started with the "reprivatization" of many of the firms that did not perform well in the first privatization wave (mostly in the finance sector). An important component was the sale of the major infrastructure companies (about 30). For infrastructure services, this was done by transforming the firms into public companies and selling the shares gradually. These shares were tradable, and these companies were subject to standard commercial auditing procedures. The percentage of private owners increased in all companies quite progressively. For instance, from December 1986 to early 1990, the increase of the private ownership share in ENDESA, an electricity company, was from 30% to 72%. Institutional investors (such as pension funds) would eventually account for about 25% of the total stocks of privatized utilities, providing a good long-term commitment to the financing of the sector. Usually workers of the privatized would get between 5% and 10% of the shares to ensure their political support. In the case of the electricity and telecommunications privatization, a small percentage of former civil servants would acquire a large percentage of these shares; this later became a sore point. Because there was a major concern with the high degree of ownership concentration that resulted from the first privatization wave, the declared objective of this second wave of divestiture was *the increased distribution of ownership rather than the maximization of revenue.*

Under the Lagos administration, Chile entered its last wave of privatization with the residual utilities. The main concern of this latest wave has clearly been efficiency as revealed by the concern for the design of the regulatory regime and highly publicized and controversial debate on the issue.[12] This concern is in fact also quite present in the Bachelet administration that took over from the Lagos administration in 2006.

MEXICO

Mexico's experience with privatization is just as important historically as it is contemporaneous to British reforms, and along with Jamaica it signals the first set of privatization reforms in the 1980s in the region. It is particularly interesting because it involves the sale of an exceptionally large number of firms and was part of the first massive reform of the public sector after the debt crisis. The reforms were quite encompassing sectorally and spread over almost all sectors, with the notable exception of utilities, as was the case under the first wave of reform in Chile. However, the process was slow as the need to build political support proved to be a demanding task. Started by the De la Madrid administration in the early 1980s, most implementation did not take place before 1988 and ended in 1994 under the Salinas administration. While the search for efficiency was the official motivation, many saw in the massive effort an attempt to create an irreversible change in the role of the public sector in the economy (Ramirez, 1994). The Zedillo administration continued the push but was less successful—partly because the assets put on the market were less attractive, and partly because in some of the sectors the government only offered minority shares, as in the case of the Morelos petrochemical complex, which were were matters of concern for potential bidders.[13]

The most publicized impact of this latest wave of privatization was achieved in the transportation sector when airport, port, and railway infrastructures were successfully restructured and concessioned under wide media coverage. The experience in the road sector was less successful and required a major restructuring that started just before the Fox administration took over. Its implementation has been very gradual, and the outcome is not yet obvious. The announced privatization of the crown jewel, the oil sector, is regularly on the agenda, and from its sheer market potential, it should be commercially successful if implemented at some point. The sector has been a public monopoly since 1938 and is likely to be a major source of political argument under any administration. A similar concern applies to the power sector. The debate is still very much alive and was one of the hot issues during the 2006 election.

ARGENTINA

Privatization was a key component of the Argentinean stabilization and reform program and part of the push for a new development model.[14] It was in fact being prepared as part of an effort to reform the state under the Alfonsin administration, but it really took off under the Menem administration. It is quite remarkable that 50% of the US$23 billion realized between 1990 and 1997 was used to retire public debt, although in some cases, the government picked up new debt when it took over the residual debt accrued by some of the public enterprises it was privatizing.

In spite of the unhappiness of the Argentinean Left, which had supported Menem in his 1989 election, privatization gained popular support thanks to very effective marketing of the reforms by his administration, including the distribution of shares to employees as part of the privatization of some of the infrastructure services. In contrast to the experiences of Chile and Mexico, the core of the program was, indeed, the privatization of public services and in particular infrastructure services. Over 60 contracts were signed by the national government alone. The relative importance of this sector in the privatization agenda reflected the fact that the fiscal crisis impeded the historical subsidy levels in the sector, and hence rationing of service and quality were starting to become a major issue. But for these sectors, privatization was in name only, because most of the services were in fact concessioned, that is, leased for a specific duration with specific levels of services and investment obligation specified in contracts. In many cases, workers also received a percentage of the income generated by the reform process. This concessioning approach became the model for the region. In Argentina, the commitment to the private sector went beyond the contract, but also included the signature of international treaties with the governments of the main investors (e.g., Spain, Italy, and France) as a way to demonstrate the political commitment to the reforms.

In the other sectors, asset sales took place in a wide range of activities. The most important was the privatization of the state oil company YPF, which was a major success and had a major demonstration effect in the region for the sector. But somewhat surprisingly, it was when the Menem administration put market assets on sale such as Argentina's share of the Iguazu Falls—Brazil owns the other share of the zoo—that strong popular reactions against privatization policy started to grow. This unhappiness with the policy accelerated with the recession that resulted from the credit crunch after the Tequila and Asian crisis. There was also a major incident in which parts of Buenos Aires went without electricity for up to 10 days. The De la Rua administration had a difficult relationship with the concessionaires, and as the 2002 crisis exploded, the privatization of the public services become a major headline in the local press and among opinion makers, ending the initial support that it had enjoyed at the beginning of the reform process.

The Kirchner administration has revisited the public service concessioning programs early on. Many of the contracts of the 1990s have de facto been cancelled or restructured. New local actors, some public but many private, are now running many of the services that were under the management of large foreign operators until the 2002 crisis, implying a clear sense of pragmatism in the interactions of this government with the private sector.

BOLIVIA

Faced with the prospect of a complete economic collapse, in 1986 Bolivia became the second country in the region (after Chile), and the first democracy, to implement economic shock therapy under an International Monetary Fund structural adjustment program. In that context, the privatization process formally started in 1992 with a law that laid out some of the groundwork for the changes to come. Broader structural reforms, however, were left to the administration that took office in 1993. The reforms concentrated on infrastructure and banking. The specific objectives were to attract foreign investment, increase competition and efficiency, and strengthen public finances. Privatization was one of the four major components of the reforms; the others were modernization of the legal framework, establishment of independent regulatory systems, and restructuring of the relevant ministries. The privatization was primarily through a new approach called "capitalization," which generated 80% of the US$2 billion revenues from privatization. This approach allowed strategic investors, selected through a public competitive bidding process, to obtain a 50% controlling stake in the enterprise. However, instead of purchasing existing shares from the Government of Bolivia, the winner invests the bid amount in the enterprise as an increase in capital within a fixed period of time. This approach was used in cases where substantial additional investment was desired, as it ensured new resources. Concessions or simple sales were used in other cases.

Politically, the approach also had strong appeal because the government was not actually selling its assets, but rather was inviting the private sector to make new investments, and because the population would share directly in the eventual profits of the companies. The main drawback from a macro stabilization viewpoint was that the resources were not going to the treasury. However, at the time, the government saw this as a benefit because it was trying to minimize the risk of additional revenues that could lead to an unsustainable expansion in expenditures. The privatization efforts of the residual public services slowed down significantly after the widely publicized incidents in Cochabamba, in 2000, where a water concession turned sour.[15]

As Kirchner has done in Argentina, the Morales administration has renegotiated many of the contracts, including a very widely publicized reversal of the privatization of hydrocarbons implemented in 1996 by then-president Sanchez de Lozada. For all practical purposes, many of the privatizations implemented a few years earlier are for now on hold.

The Brazilian privatization program begun in 1991 under the Collor administration was continued by the Cardoso government, and ended up being one of the largest worldwide in dollar terms, outside of the programs adopted in Eastern Europe. It worked quite well until 1998 when it slowed down as the economy turned sluggish. The program has now been placed on hold by the Lula administration. Between 1991 and 2002, it transferred over 120 companies to the private sector. An interesting feature is that many companies were not transferred with majority stakes, but under minority stakes—that is without management control—suggesting that the size of this market is large enough to get investors interested to take part even without control.

Implementation was simultaneous at the national and subnational level, particularly in São Paulo. In both cases, the main purposes were to generate revenue and cut outstanding public debt. The transactions resulted in over US$100 billion of net revenue. The privatization of infrastructure services, mostly telecommunications, roads, railways, and electricity, generated almost three-quarters of the income. The other companies included many research institutes, councils, and other professional organizations that had historically been organized as autonomous public companies and had been restructured during the 1980s. While in dollar terms this was a very significant privatization experience, in terms of its impact on the structure of the economy, the real impact remains unclear. Some of the historical industrial champions of the country are now in private hands, as are important sectors such as telecommunications and railways. However, there are still many sectors for which liberalization and competition are much more important concerns for the government and where the public sector continues to be the major player. This includes ports, the oil industry, and many components of the energy industry and of the financial sector.[16]

Lula's administration has been much less enthusiastic about the privatization option than the Cardozo administration, but has not imposed any significant policy reversals. Lula's team has publicly acknowledged the successes of many of the privatizations and has made it clear that it will not renationalize companies that were sold. They are unlikely to implement more, however. The new policy is to champion public-private partnerships rather than to sell assets.

COLOMBIA

The decision to privatize in Colombia was actively considered as early as 1986 when the government started to work on the divestiture program of the former Instituto de Fomento Industrial, which covered a large share of the manufacturing capacity of the country and had historically been the engine behind the industrialization process of the country. At that time, the privatization policy was essentially viewed as an instrument to promote efficiency. The implementation of the program accelerated as part of a liberalization program initiated in the early 1990s, but at that point, its revenue effect became a major concern of the government, along with the desire to attract foreign private investment. The agenda was modest because historically the size of the state had been relatively modest for the region. However, the revenue objectives were important for the government and contributed significantly to the 1994–1998 stabilization program.

Concession and sales contracts were the main instruments used, and the constitution and legal systems were changed to facilitate their usage. Concession contracts were intended to be used mainly for public services. Between 1993 and 1998, 35 concession contracts had been signed, most of them for roads, gas pipelines, and telecommunications services. In spite of needs in over 1,400 municipalities, few contracts were signed in the water and sanitation sector. As for the other sectors and local, regional, and the national governments, during the same period, only 25 transactions took place in which shares were sold to private investors. Most of the deals took place in the manufacturing and mining sectors. Overall, the achievements of the 1990s have been relatively modest, and since then support for the program has been subject to major swings. Most of the effort has been and continues to be on the restructuring of sectors to promote competition wherever possible.[17]

The short-term future looks much more pro-privatization than in many of the other countries of the region. President Alvaro Uribe indeed introduced a plethora of neoliberal reforms since assuming office in 2002, including an interest in scaling up the privatization efforts. In addition, the Uribe government has budgeted for the privatization of more than 280 government-owned enterprises, including partially privatizing the state-owned oil company Ecopetrol.

JAMAICA

The privatization experience in Jamaica is really the tale of the reversal of a nationalization policy carried out between 1972 and 1979 by the Manley government. During the Manley tenure, this government had created 185 public companies covering all infrastructure and most banking and tourism services. As in many countries in the Caribbean, this nationalization policy was a rejection of private multinationals. This rejection was reversed after the 1981 election of Seaga, who campaigned for the return of private capital in the country. In other words, privatization was initially adopted on ideological grounds. It was not until 1985, however, that the privatization program took off seriously. The catalyst was an emerging fiscal crisis for which revenue was needed, and the program started with the offering of public shares in a major bank.

In a surprising turn of events, Manley, the father of nationalization 20 years earlier, was elected again in 1991 and decided to extend the privatization experience. The main objective was now to reduce the size of the state and promote full-scale liberalization to improve efficiency in the economy. The main policy action on the privatization front was a further decrease in the government shares combined with an increase in the share of employees in ownership to over 10%. After that stage, the government was only a minority owner in most companies. In phase 3, the government sold its residual shares through a local investment syndicate.

Within 10 years, Jamaica had privatized 201 companies across all economic sectors. By 2000, considerable progress had been made across the board, in particular in the financial sector. Four state-owned banks and a number of smaller entities were merged into the Union Bank, and restructuring of the National Commercial Bank continued with both banks being prepared for privatization. Following some setbacks—when some privatized entities reverted to public ownership or continued needing government subsidies—privatization has generally enjoyed strong support until very recently.[18]

NICARAGUA

Privatization in Nicaragua took place in a very different context, somewhat similar to the Chilean context when it reversed the Allende nationalizations. The election of Chamorro was a rejection of the socialist model, which in turn resulted in the first phase of privatizations between 1991 and 1996. Privatizations included a wide range of very different sectors across the production line, from agriculture to services, including banking but excluding utilities. Infrastructure privatizations were at the core of a second wave of privatization started in 1995, during which electricity and telecommunications were restructured and their services concessioned. Between 1995 and 2002, this wave generated close to 5% of GDP in revenues, and residual reforms are still under way.[19]

The main criticism of the first phase was a lack of transparency regarding the fiscal payoffs from privatization; these were quite important given that they reached 2.5% of GDP every year during much of the initial reform phase. Some of these revenues were used to wipe out the commercial debt of the privatized companies, but the rest went into complex budgetary accounting settlements. In recent years, privatization efforts have significantly cooled down and include a very intense public debate on the privatization of the water sector. The newly elected president, Daniel Ortega, has stated, however, that he would maintain the economic policies enacted since the end of his first term as president in 1990, including the privatization of formerly state-owned businesses.

PANAMA

Started in 1992, the privatization program in Panama has largely been concluded. It cut across sectors and started with the sale of a state cement company and a state-owned fruit company. Within four years, the government had awarded concessions for private toll roads, cellular phone service, railway services, and ports. Intel, the Panamanian telephone company, was partially (49%) sold in mid 1997 and is now being managed by the British firm Cable and Wireless. Government-owned casinos and race tracks were privatized in 1998. The power company was restructured and converted into eight companies, which were partially sold to the private sector in August 1998. Four American companies participated, including Enron, Coastal, AES, and Constellation. Two sugar mills were privatized in 1998 to local groups with some Colombian participation. Pending announced privatizations include a large convention center and the international airport. Water privatization was halted in 1998 after violent protests and appears unlikely to proceed under the current government.

Although there had been substantial new foreign investment in recent years, most of it resulting from privatization, the implementation of the policy slowed dramatically in 2000 as opportunities and enthusiasm for further privatization dwindled. Instances of questionable government practices have soured some large international firms on doing business in Panama. These include past bidding procedures, contract obligations, project security, and a slow and imperfect judicial system.

The position toward the private sector is unlikely to change much in the foreseeable future, but processes and social concerns are taking a much higher profile as in many other parts of the region. President Torrijos was elected in 2004 on a platform that included a commitment to increase transparency and to address the social concerns associated with the privatization of the public services, most importantly water, which has been associated with very strong protest from a significant part of the population.[20]

PERU

After its worst macroeconomic crisis, Peru launched, as part of a macroeconomic adjustment program, the reform of its public enterprises under the Fujimori administration. The sector covered all activities from agriculture, mining, industry, and public services to banking and was widely viewed as unfocused, costly, and inefficient. The design of the program was intended to attract foreign private investors to the extent possible. Most of the privatization took the form of sales with about 5% of the revenue generated through concessions and a few capitalizations deals. The program was initially modest and focused on 23 companies that were all sold within the first two years. The peak of the program was during the 1994–1996 period, when 64 more companies were privatized, including the telecommunications and energy companies. In 1998, the program started to cover the transportation sector and enjoyed mixed success. In its first decade, with the privatization of about 150 firms, the program generated about US$8.9 billion in revenue and investment commitments of over US$7 billion. Over 80% of the revenue was generated by telecommunications, electricity, and mining. While the telecommunications and banking sectors have in fact been fully privatized, the main residual assets of the government that have not yet transferred to the private sector are in infrastructure and agriculture.[21]

The acceleration of the privatization of these residual companies was part of the initial agenda of the Toledo administration to generate enough revenue to cover a growing deficit problem. Instead, the program slowed down significantly, and in electricity, the government was in fact forced to reverse the privatization of two companies in 2002. Alan Garcia, elected president in 2006, is likely to have to address the pressure of a changing public opinion in the region, including a strong resistance to further privatization, in particular in politically sensitive sectors such as the water sector.

SUMMING UP

This overview of selected country experiences suggests that:

- Privatization has been used to address multiple objectives
- Privatization is a much too generic word that hides a multiplicity of concepts and instruments
- The privatization of infrastructure services should be addressed as a separate category

These three lessons are reviewed next in some detail.

THE OBJECTIVES

The brief overview of country experiences shows that there were many different objectives to the reforms. There are certainly many ways of categorizing these objectives, whether explicit or implicit; one way is to classify them into the following seven types:

1. *Ideology*, a conscious attempt to redefine the boundaries of the role of the state in the economy; this was clearly the case in Mexico, Jamaica, Nicaragua, and Chile.

2. *Fiscal pragmatism*, or the decision to rely on the sale or lease of public assets to contribute to the fiscal effort needed to implement a stabilization program. This was the case in the first wave of privatization in most countries and was a strong motivation for privatizing the transportation sector, which historically has imposed a heavy burden on the public sector—most obviously in Argentina, Panama, and Peru, but also in Chile and at least implicitly in almost all cases.

3. *The improvement of the performance* of a sector through changes in incentives and a focus on the commercial objectives only, rather than on the multiple objectives typically assigned to the managers of public enterprise. This may have been the dominant motivation in many of the

privatizations in Brazil, Chile, Colombia, and the second stages of reform in Jamaica; this is one of the reasons why restructuring to facilitate competition in and for the market is often the first stage of any privatization.

4. *Increasing the access to private financing* was a major consideration in the reform of major public service in all countries.

5. *The dissemination of ownership* of productive assets in the economy, to push intra-market competition, was quite clearly the case in Brazil, Chile, and Colombia.

6. *The development of the local capital market*, as in the case of Bolivia in particular, but also in many of the other countries such as Argentina, Bolivia, Chile, Jamaica, and Nicaragua, where workers were given shares of the companies privatized.

7. *The restitution of recently nationalized assets* as in the case of Chile and Nicaragua at the end of the Allende and Sandinista governments, respectively.[22]

Whether these objectives were explicit or implicit is not all that important. As we will discuss later, the weight assigned to the various objectives was probably a more important determinant of the outcomes.

ONE-SIZE PRIVATIZATION DOES NOT FIT ALL

No two countries in the region have followed exactly the same model, in spite of the fact that advice and consulting on privatization and restructuring by former government officials have become major export products for Argentina and Chile! The differences in initial conditions contribute to an explanation of the choices—Argentina, Bolivia, and Peru were in the midst of macro crises and had little bargaining power. This was not the case for Brazil or Mexico, which worked at their own speed and enjoyed strong bargaining power. The differences across countries in the weight assigned to each goal also drove the differences in approaches to privatization.

The categorization of the approach to privatization is itself a challenge. There are indeed many ways in which the term *privatization* has been used in Latin America. One way is to classify privatization is into the following five different approaches:

1. *Full sale/divestiture*: This is when the public sector gives up all control and ownership. In Latin America, it has been most common in competitive industries such as telecommunications or power generation for

infrastructure, most agricultural and fisheries sectors, and service sectors such as insurance and banking; Mexico provides a large sample of privatizations that followed this model.

2. *Sale of majority or minority shares*: This approach allows the government to retain a certain level of control, to share the gains or losses achieved by the private operators, and to follow a gradual approach in the implementation of the reform; this control can vary on a wide scale.

3. *Lease/concession*: This is now the most common approach for infrastructure services and has the main political advantage of allowing the government to retain the legal ownership of the assets; the relationship with the private sector is through a contract that specifies the rights and obligations of all parties involved; Argentina is widely perceived to be the poster child of this approach, but concession contracts are widely used across countries in the region for infrastructure privatizations.

4. *Capitalization and other forms of development of the capital market*: This approach allows the government to catalyze the development or expansion of a capital market that in many of the countries has proven (and continues) to be one of the major impediments to sustained growth. This is particularly the case for sectors requiring long-term investment with politically difficult pricing options, as in the case of public services. Voucher programs and the allocation of shares to employees were widely viewed as a potentially important buy-in for the unions into a new, more capitalist development model, but their effectiveness was modest at best.

5. *Restitution:* This approach was, for obvious reasons, specific to the few countries in which political changes had resulted in large nationalization programs. The form of restitution did, however, vary across countries and generally matched the more standard privatization program.

WHY IS INFRASTRUCTURE PRIVATIZATION SPECIAL?

The country surveys show that infrastructure services tend to be taken into consideration in a particular way. The countries that implemented privatization in a state of crisis (e.g., Argentina, Bolivia, and Peru) had placed the privatization of infrastructure at the core of their initial reform waves, while the countries in a position of strength took their time (e.g., Brazil, Chile, and Mexico). This gives a sense that infrastructure is politically special and that when governments have the choice, they seem to prefer to leave it for last, but that when they have a major concern, the fiscal burden imposed by the sector leaves them with little choice and forces them to take on the public pressure associated with the privatization of public services.

The perception that infrastructure is special and especially politically difficult is indeed widespread. Many users feel entitled to the key public services. Water is widely recognized as a necessity; electricity and public transportation are about to reach that status; and it seems that cell phones are close to being in the same category for the new generation of users. The idea of passing on control to the private sector of these basic necessities is typically a source of concern when the control is combined with a right to recover costs to minimize the subsidy requirements. This is why even if the de facto control of the sector of many public services was often shifted to the private sector as part of the reform process, the adoption of concession contracts by reforming governments was so popular for this sector. It allowed governments to manage the political perception of the privatization process, at least initially (see table 5.1).

Assets were not sold, but leased, and in many cases were expected to generate revenue for the government. The only infrastructure sectors where privatizations with ownership change took place were in the telecommunications and power generation sectors. These were major sources of revenue during the 1990s. For most infrastructure services, however, the most notable fact was not necessarily the revenue generated or the reduction in the associated fiscal cost, but rather the fact that privatization was taking place in the context of a major restructuring aimed at promoting competition. For many, this was the main signal of a commitment to the neoliberal policies now questioned in the region.

This questioning, however, is not happening in a neutral context. Over the last few years, in particular after a series of international crisis hurt the region, unemployment has returned and poverty levels have increased. A few major crisis such as power outages and water rationing problems—

TABLE 5.1 Relative Importance of Concessions Contracts in Infrastructure Privatization in Latin America, 1990–2000

Sector	Concession as a % of Total Infrastructure Privatization Projects
Water	89%
Transportation	97.5%
Energy	54.4%
Telecommunications	0.5%
Total	65.5%

Source: World Bank, Private Provision of Infrastructure Database.

due more to climatic condition than to the privatization policy—is modifying the perception of a large share of the population about the benefits of such reform. Infrastructure concessions are now widely viewed as equivalent to any other type of privatization and hence as questionable in this changing environment. Indeed, as the economic and social situation of many households deteriorated, and as many were finding it difficult to pay their bills, their interface with the private operators ended up being similar to interactions with car dealers or bankers. This was in sharp contrast with the treatment they had received from the public operators of public services when nonrecovery of bills would simply be transformed into new demands for subsidies or transfers from the public sector accounts.

In sum, infrastructure is special because it seems to be at the core of changing perceptions on the desirability of reform. Failures in this sector will drive the overall perception, and it is thus crucial, to the extent possible, to distinguish between the effectiveness of privatization in infrastructure sectors and privatization in other sectors. Drawing general conclusions from analysis of privatization while ignoring the political, social, and economic characteristics of infrastructures and the associated services would be misleading. This can be clearly seen in Checchi, Florio, and Carrera (2005), who find that disagreement with privatization is most likely when the policy involved a high proportion of public services as water and electricity.[23]

HOW EFFECTIVELY DID PRIVATIZATIONS POLICIES MEET THEIR OBJECTIVES?

Ignoring for now the ideology motive for privatization, it seems useful to assess the extent to which the objectives have been met. This should give a clear sense of the good achieved by that policy—although this obviously does not apply to the ideological goal. This section offers a review of these achievements relying on a large body of recent literature.[24] Whenever possible the discussion points to the differences in achievement between infrastructure privatizations and others because they seem to shape some of the negative perceptions of privatization in the region. The review focuses on fiscal, performance, and quality effects of the reforms.

In terms of the fiscal objectives associated with stabilization programs, they seem to have prevailed as one of the most important, if not the most important, objective, and the immediate—i.e., the short-term—impact of reform was quite positive. In the 1990s, in 18 Latin American states, accumulated privatization revenues averaged a sizable 6% of GDP (Inter-American Development Bank, 2002); additionally, debt restructuring allowed reductions in interest rate charges and debt amortization schedules. In contrast to other regions (again, outside the countries of the Organisation for Economic Co-operation and Development), over half of all Latin American privatizations have been high-value infrastructure or utility firms. From 1990 to 2005, private investment in infrastructure alone in Latin America totaled US$416 billion, almost double the investment achieved by the attractive East Asia-Pacific region. These sorts of figures had to look good in the books in the short run.

But this is only part of the fiscal story. The cross-country studies generally ignore the fact that fiscal gains come in two forms: a stock effect and a flow effect. The numbers usually quoted give a sense of the stock effect (this is what the gains from the sale or the lease tend to pick up). However, there is also a flow effect (the demand for operational or capital subsidies), which can and does change over time with demand, with renegotiations, and with financial restructurings aimed at assisting the poorest performers. What appears to be an initial gain from the stock effect can easily become a loss from the accumulation of negative fiscal flows effects. Renegotiations of concession contracts throughout the region are generating a risk of a major shift of investment responsibilities back toward the public sector, which would thus offset the initial gains. This observation is particularly important in the context of infrastructure services, where contracts renegotiation often leads to reduction in private sector commitment to investment and increases in government commitments to subsidies.

In terms of the impact on the performance of the privatized firms, in general, the success is quite difficult to deny in general terms. The most analytically rigorous studies of Argentina, Chile, Colombia, Mexico, and Peru—many done by Latin American academics—show that the performance of the privatized companies has improved in terms of profitability (measured as return on sales), operational efficiency (measured as sales per workers), and output.[25] As compared to the pre-privatization situation, profitability across the board increased as follows: 61% in Mexico, 51% in Argentina, 41% in Peru, 10% in Colombia, 8% in Brazil and Chile, and 5.3% in Bolivia (although in this case, it was measured for a smaller sample). These results are of course impressive, but it is unfortunate that the studies do not distinguish between regulated and competitive sectors.

The only study to do so systematically is for Chile, making the case for additional analysis of this difference across countries.[26] Indeed, the study finds that for competitive firms, there are no major changes in efficiency as a result of major restructuring programs. Most of the gains in profitability from privatization are in fact due to improvement in the regulated sectors that mostly cover the infrastructure services.[27]

The discussion of the operational gains, measured in terms of sales per worker, is somewhat complex. Indeed, it is often argued that the main efficiency gains from privatization come from the resulting reduction in employment. Could it be that the 88%, 92%, and 112% gains achieved by Chile, Mexico, and Peru respectively are mostly due to job losses in those sectors? The fact that the output of the privatized firms increased in these countries by 25%, 53%, and 25% respectively suggests that not all gains must have come from cutting employment, although it is hard to deny the employment reductions in the short run. In Argentina, for instance, employment decreased by 40% in the privatized firms.

One dimension often omitted from the discussions on the literature and in public policy debates is the impact of the reforms on the quality of the goods and services provided.[28] In many cases, and in particular in the case of infrastructure, privatization was associated not only with improvements in production, allocation, and technological efficiency, but also with major improvements in the quality of service offered.[29] Few today seem to remember the five- to ten-year waiting period to get a residential and sometimes a commercial phone, the interminable delays in obtaining repairs and services, and the high costs of bribes paid to utility officials to jump the line and obtain—and maintain—connections. In many of these countries, few remember that the lack of safety and reliability of public transportation strongly contributed to the increase in the use of private transportation modes. It is in that context that many of the reforms were initially welcomed except by the public sector workers (and their families) who lost jobs and often associated privileges; jobs and privileges that were financed by taxes paid by the contemporary population, or bonds currently being repaid by the following generation.

In sum, it seems that the standards applied to assess the effects of reform today are significantly higher than the standards used to gauge delivery systems people were living with at the beginning of the 1990s in Latin America. This may be one of the reasons why the conclusions that emerge from these quantitative results, even if they point to some potential problems, are in sharp contrast with the unhappiness with the effects of privatization expressed in surveys of impressions. The issues raised in the next section contribute to solving part of the puzzle.

SO, WHAT ARE THE REALLY UGLY FACTS ASSOCIATED WITH PRIVATIZATION?

Many issues that have emerged from this experience deserve being highlighted in this overview. The rest of this section is a brief annotated list of these problems and supporting bibliographical references.

THE CONTINUED AND GROWING FISCAL COST PROBLEMS

Many, if not most, observers of the reforms would argue that fiscal objectives were dominant in most countries. Any failure on this count would then be a major setback for the policy makers who implemented them. However, most of the literature has focused on the stock problem, which seems to have been reasonably well addressed by the reforms. When adding the flow problem alluded to earlier, the picture is not as clearly positive. There is indeed increasing anecdotal and analytical evidence that the flow problem has not been solved. Campos et al. (2003) showed that for the infrastructure sector over the long run, Latin America's private participation in the utilities sectors tended to reduce the demand for recurrent subsidies and increased public investment in the sector. The exact opposite was found for privatization of transportation: private investment in transportation crowds out public investment but requires a commitment to operational subsidies. In other words, privatizations have been associated with increases in either recurrent or investment public expenditures overtime. The net effect of the stock and the flow effects are an empirical matter that needs to be assessed at the country level. This analysis is overdue.

THE OBSERVED RATES OF RETURN

In countries where privatization took place in noncompetitive activities, a fairer assessment of the performance would also monitor the match between the cost of capital and the rate of return. Privatizations were not intended to create or re-create rents for private operators. In a recent paper on the infrastructure sector, Sirtaine et al. (2005) show that, depending on how costs are classified, as revenue or as costs, the rate of return on capital can vary from 9% to 33% in any given sector. Considering that the cost of capital varied between 15% and 25% for most sectors of most of the countries, it is clearly not very easy to assess how much the regulatory regime mattered and how big a rent was actually created by the reform process.

THE UNDERESTIMATION OF REGULATION OF THE RESIDUAL PUBLIC SERVICES MONOPOLIES

This is related to the rate of return discussion and is particularly important for infrastructure services. A key reason for infrastructure privatization's lack of popularity is a feeling that the documented efficiency gains achieved by privatization have not been distributed fairly. Estache (2004) shows for Argentina that the major efficiency gains have not been shared with the users as expected in many of the key sectors. This is to a large extent the responsibility of the regulators or of the design of the processes firms have to follow. The principal distributional mandate of regulators is to assess the cost reductions achieved by the operators and to pass on some—a fair proportion—of these gains to the consumers as part of the scheduled tariff revisions processes. In too many countries, the regulators may be too weak (that is, captured by politicians and/or operators) or may simply be incompetent to deliver on this mandate. The basic efficiency gains that should eventually be shared have typically not been measured by the regulators and hence seldom redistributed.[30] In sum, regulators are crucial players in determining the perception of the equity of privatization because they largely determine the extent to which the poor get their fair share of the gains from reform (if they are working with proper legislation).

Chisari, Estache, and Romero (1999) document the regressive consequences of poor regulation in the context of privatization and regulation of energy, telecommunications, and water sectors in Argentina. The analysis separates the benefits of privatization per se from the benefits of effective regulation. The finding is that privatization yielded operational gains in the infrastructure sectors equivalent to 0.9% of GDP, or 41% of the average expenditure on utility services. Effective regulation added gains worth 0.35% of GDP, or 16% of the average expenditure on utility services. Higher-income households gained more in absolute terms than did lower-income households, but the benefits of effective regulation as a proportion of existing expenditures on utility services were highest for the lowest-income quintiles. This is because regulation acts as a mechanism for transferring rents from the owners of capital to the consumers of the service. Overall, according to the simulations, income inequality drops significantly if regulation is effective.

THE PAINFUL EMPLOYMENT AND WAGE EFFECTS

What seems to stick to the memories of people is that they lost their jobs as part of the privatization process. In many cases, the number of people who lost their jobs was significant at the company level (as high as 70%). This number, however, seldom represented more than 2% of the total labor force in each country—with the exception maybe of Nicaragua, where the adjustment was quite dramatic. Moreover, over time, employment recovered in many of these industries. Chong and López-de-Silanes (2004) show that for a large sample of Latin American firms, 44% of the firms that fired workers before privatization rehired the same workers about 18 months later. In Peru in the telecommunications sector (Torero, 2002), or in Mexico in the port sector (Estache, Foster, and Wodon, 2002), the evidence is quite strong that with increased demand private operators recruited heavily. What this suggests is that while job losses are a problem in the short run, in the medium term, they are driven by macroeconomic conditions and not privatization. For instance, in Argentina, a recent paper by Benitez, Chisari, and Estache (2003) shows that credit rationing following the Tequila and Asian crisis could be blamed for most of the increase in the unemployment between 1994 and 2000. These types of analyses are, however, largely ignored by the media-driven debate.

THE MISMANAGEMENT OF THE SOCIAL COSTS OF REFORM

McKenzie and Mookherjee (2003) suggest that in spite of what is widely argued regarding privatization in Latin America, there is no clear pattern in the direction of price changes. In fact, prices went down 50% in five country studies conducted (Argentina, Bolivia, Mexico, Nicaragua, and Peru). Moreover, the studies point out that when prices rose, this negative effect was offset by a corresponding increase in access to goods and services previously not available. An almost simultaneous research project, managed by Ugaz and Waddams Price (2003), on the social impacts of the reforms shows that in many cases the price increases were most painful for the poorest and that this was often mismanaged by the authorities; tariff rebalancing and reforms aimed at improving efficiency resulted in regressive tariff structures.

One of the most highly publicized cases was the Cochabamba water concession in Bolivia (where 70% of the people live below the poverty line). Because this case may have catalyzed many of the massive rejections for large private operators in the region, it is important to understand its underpinnings. The social and hence political problems began when subsidies were eliminated and the price of water was tripled in January 2000. This hurt the utility's existing customers, but also peasants (largely Quechua Indians) who would have to pay for water that previously had been available free of charge. The price increases in Cochabamba were partly due to improved cost recovery through reductions in subsidies, but they were also necessary to pay for a US$300 million project involving the construction of a dam, a tunnel, and water purification plants that would boost water supplies to the Cochabamba area. Soon after the April 2000 protests, Bechtel, the private operator, pulled out of Bolivia, and the government of Bolivia repealed its water privatization legislation. Following the departure of International Water, the management of SEMAPA, the local municipal water company, was turned over to its employees and the citizens of Cochabamba. Bechtel has since sued the government of Bolivia, asking to be reimbursed for the approximately US$25 million in investments it had made prior to date. Water privatization efforts have never been the same since then in Latin America or elsewhere in the developing world.

THE INCREASED REGRESSIVE TAXATION OF PRIVATIZED SERVICES

An underestimated source of unfairly distributed outcomes from reform is the transformation of the public service sector into a major source of tax revenue for all government levels. When they were operated by the public sector, infrastructure services sometimes generated large revenue volumes for the government level responsible for the operation of the service (even though this was often not enough to cover all costs). After privatization, at least in the case of utilities—but not always in transportation—it seems that these sectors are becoming net "cash cows" for the government at all levels. In Argentina, for instance, utilities generate about 1% of tax revenue for all levels of government, mostly from a 35% income tax and a 21%

value-added tax passed on to consumers. But the effective tax rate paid by users is typically much larger than 21% because of municipal and provincial taxes. The indirect taxes on telecommunications and electricity can add up to over 55% of the cost of service in some large municipalities. This is why when assessing the impact of reform on tariffs, it is quite important to look at the evolution of tariffs with and without taxes. This is also important in undertaking international tariff comparisons for similar services because tax burdens vary across countries. The failure to distinguish between the evolution of tariffs with and without taxes distorts the assessments of the effects of reform. The experience suggests that there are an increasing number of situations where private operators are effectively sharing achieved efficiency gains with the government rather with the users. This may be appropriate, but not when done through a regressive tax system.

THE HIGH RATES AND HIGH PROFILES OF RENEGOTIATION

One of the most surprising events associated with privatization was the commonality of renegotiations of contracts in the public service sector. Table 5.2 shows that one in three contracts were renegotiated in Latin America and that rate goes as high as one in two for the transportation sector and three in four for the water sector. Renegotiations took place on average 2.19 years after the award of the contract; this average is for concessions granted for about 20 to 30 years that had a 5-year period for a tariff review (for concessions granted under a price cap regime). Essentially, in two out of every three contracts, the change is requested by the operator. This is a significant proportion, which raises many questions on the consistency of the government over time to the commitments made when reforms were initiated. In many instances, the renegotiations result in higher tariffs, lower investments, and/or lower service quality. Whether a renegotiation is justified is not that important from the viewpoint of the public; the main concern is that the revision tends to affect the users or the taxpayers.[31]

THE ILLUSION OF COMPETITION FOR THE MARKET

To some extent, the fact that governments are forced to get into renegotiations is the result of the fact that there were often few bidders when they auctioned the businesses. This points to the failure of efforts to achieve

TABLE 5.2   Incidence of Renegotiated Concession Contracts According to Sectors and Characteristics

All Infrastructure Sectors (%)	Transportation (%)	Water (%)
30	54.7	74.4

Source: Guasch (2004).

competition for markets where simply opening up competition in the market was not possible. If competition for the market is to be effective, the number of bidders participating in every auction should be significant, and the nature of the bids should be such that there is no concern about risks of collusion. If there are not enough local bidders, opening the doors to foreign bidders can only help. One of the failures of reforms was that this competition was seldom as effective as expected. In many cases, there were many fewer bidders than expected. This is particularly true for the privatization of infrastructure services. The evidence available suggests that competition for the market is not working well in most developing countries and that increased trade in services may be helping, but not much. Typically the number of serious bidders for a concession or a greenfield project in the infrastructure sector is not much higher than two or three; there are some examples with more players, but this is not the norm. Technically, this is competition, of course, but not impressively strong competition. Moreover, in many cases, the new foreign players are associated with the local players who enjoyed most of the procurement contracts awarded by these companies when they were public.

THE HIGH CONCENTRATION OF PLAYERS IN SOME MARKETS

Part of the explanation for the limited number of bidders is the limited number of players (as discussed in Benitez and Estache, 2005), at least in some of the markets. In the transportation sector, where the construction component continues to be important for roads, ports, and airports at least, companies such as Dragados (Spain), EGIS Projects or Bouygues (France), Macquaries (Australia), and Bechtel introduce competition in many parts of the world. This does not seem to be enough to ensure that every auction attracts the interest of many bidders. The major railway and port contracts around the world are shared by fewer than 10 companies; the power and telecommunications markets have a somewhat larger number of players but not many more. The extreme example in supply concentration is the international sanitation privatization business (water, sanitation, and solid waste). Between 1990 and 1997, out of 58 projects involving about US$25 billion in investment and covered by the PPI database, 28 were awarded to Suez-Lyonnaise des Eaux, 13 to Vivendi, six to Aguas de Barcelona, six to Thames Water, and five to SAUR International. This suggests five major players on the supply side. Even when there are significant opportunities for competition, market concentration continues to be strong. For instance, there are close to 100 significant independent power companies that can compete to become independent power producers. However, the top eight (AES, National Power, Southern Energy, Edison Mission Energy, Tractebel, Sithe Energies, NRG Energy, and Enron International) concentrate over 50% of their equity in projects. Similar observations hold in the other sectors. There are not that many foreign banks and insurance companies in Latin America, nor are there that many active players in the mining and oil sectors. Ultimately, this raises local frustration with the perception that the governments are being sold out to "bad" multinational companies, while in practice, it raises supra-national competition issues that cannot be dealt with individually by national governments.

In sum, this section suggests that lingering problems are associated with the use of privatization as a policy instrument in Latin America. However, many of the flaws and problems that have been blamed on privatization have very little to do with privatization. They reflect poor preparation of deals and misunderstanding of key social, economic, and political constraints that have to be addressed as part of any reform and that may be underestimated by the privatization teams, in particular those working on infrastructure deals.

Latin America's privatization seems to have delivered a lot more good than is currently recognized by critics. Overall, the evidence is quite strong, although not always as strong as the most dogmatic partisans of privatization keep arguing. The degree of success has varied quite significantly across sectors and across countries. So have the number of ugly facts that deserve consideration in this assessment of the Latin American privatization experience.

The main differentiation of performance is probably between the privatization of competitive and noncompetitive activities. While the privatization of competitive industries has gone relatively well in the region, privatization has not enjoyed the same success with noncompetitive activities. The regulation of noncompetitive activities has indeed proven to be a major challenge for most reforming governments. Whether voluntarily or not, the experience of infrastructure privatization shows that for many of the regulated firms, the rates of return have often tended to be much larger than the cost of capital their operators or owners were facing in most sectors. Moreover, the major efficiency gains achieved from privatization have been slow to trickle down to users. When users are foreigners, because the output is exported and demand is inelastic, there is no local complaining, particularly because part of the rent will often stay in the country through royalties or tax contributions. When the noncompetitive industries in question cover the public services for which demand is not very elastic and that many people consider an entitlement, the diagnosis is different and the perception of ugliness increases. In spite of the major improvements in service quality and access often achieved, the failure to pass efficiency gains through tariff cuts, in light of the often high rates of returns in regulated sectors, has been a source of conflict between users and operators.

The main problem across the region has been the weaknesses of competition and regulatory institutions put in place as part of the reforms. The commitment to strong agencies has been the exception rather than the rule, and in general competition agencies have proven to be much more effective than the regulatory agencies. This has been and continues to be an issue. Ultimately, the governments have either failed to understand that bad regulation is just as regressive as the indirect specific taxes that all government levels have been imposing on regulated services, or they have implicitly decided to collude with the operators because the higher profits also mean higher tax revenue. Because consultation processes have tended to be just as weak as regulatory processes, the voices of the users have seldom been heard in the decision-making process.

While the ultimate assessment of the effectiveness of privatization needs to balance the good and the ugly, it is important to recognize that assessments can also be unfair in that they ignore the relative importance of many factors that have little or nothing to do with privatization as a policy. In many instances, the privatizations were only one of many policy changes taking place. Various international financial crises quite dramatically hurt the investment opportunities for many of the new operators. Local banking reforms that did not always work out contributed to the problem. Nonexistent, nonperforming, or only nascent safety nets contributed to the pain of adjustments associated with short-term employment reductions and price increases. Decentralization also often allowed subnational governments to offset some of the benefits to users of the reform achieved by the national governments—e.g., offsetting price reductions with local tax increases. Finally, in many countries, politicians involved in the reforms are now being accused of corruption and of accruing private benefits from the reforms. These emerging corruption cases are the result of flawed consultation processes. Corruption is also a key reason for the rejection of a policy that many people assess on the basis of associated processes rather than on the basis of outcomes.[32] Full-scale assessments need to isolate these factors if they have any claim at being fair. Only then will the analysts be able to come up with a true sense of the good and the ugly associated with the privatization policy in the region.

NOTES

The views expressed here are however our own and should not be attributed to any of the institutions with which we are affiliated. This chapter builds on Estache and Trujillo (2004).

1. From a historical viewpoint, in some of the sectors, this is a return of the assets to the private sector at the end of a century that saw the nationalization of many of the companies started by private investors at the end of the last century and at the beginning of this century. This is particularly true for public services. Most railways and power and water companies were in fact private companies during most of the first half of the twentieth century in the region.

2. Note that Thatcher's programs started later in the 1970s and accelerated only after 1983, implying that Chile's and Mexico's policy choices were not influenced by the British experience.

3. Chile's main revenue was collected between 1974 and 1985 during its first two privatization waves. Note that the Chilean experience is unusual in many ways because the first wave consisted of a return to the original private owners of 377 firms that had been nationalized or acquired by the Allende administration (see Fisher, Gutierrez, and Serra, 2003).

4. This index is one of several they use to track down the key components of the 1990s structural adjustment programs. Others include trade liberalization, tax reform, and financial reform.

5. This index is useful but somewhat misleading. First, countries do not get credit for reforms undertaken before 1986. This means that the index does not provide a good approximation for Chile, for instance, and probably represents an underestimation of the privatization performance measure as suggested by Panizza and Lora (2004). Second, it does not normalize for the initial conditions. Not all states had the same initial level of involvement in the economy to begin with. The same privatization revenue may thus represent very different reform effort levels for two countries with

very different initial conditions. Third, it does not normalize for asset values and hence ignores any undervaluation or overvaluation that may have taken place at the beginning of the process. Finally, it does not correct for any changes in the asset value or the payment to or from the government that may have resulted from a renegotiation.

6. Note that in each of these countries, there are ongoing privatization programs under discussion. In Uruguay, for instance, there are now private operators in transportation and in the water sector, although the bulk of the services remain under the control of the public sector.

7. These surveys are in sharp contrast with the strong endorsement by the politicians as well as the majority of the population documented in a 1995 survey reported at a UN conference. See United Nations (1999).

8. See, for instance, Boix (2005), Bonnet et al. (2006), Checchi, Florio, and Carrera (2005), Graham and Felton (2005), and Martimort and Straub (2006).

9. It is also often argued that the pressure exerted by multilateral donor agencies is a driving force, but this is also rejected by many econometric studies. For an example and a brief survey of the econometric literature, see Meseguer (2003).

10. For more details, see, for instance, Luders (1991) or Galetovic and Sanhieza (2002).

11. Although there were cases in which the government simply returned the assets to their previous owners, illustrating the market-oriented economy.

12. Galetovic and Sanhieza (2002).

13. See La Porta and López-de-Silanes (1999) and Ramirez (1994) for more details on Mexico.

14. See Estache (2004) for a much more detailed discussion of the Argentinean experience.

15. See Barja and Urquiola (2003) for a much more detailed discussion of the Bolivian experience.

16. See Macedo (2000) and Pinheiro (1996) for a more detailed discussion on Brazil.

17. For a detailed discussion of this experience, see Combo and Ramirez (2002).

18. For more details on the Jamaican experience, see Paredes (2003).

19. For a detailed discussion of the Nicaragua experience, see Freije and Rivas (2002).

20. For more details, see the Web site of the government of Panama (http://www .state.gov/e/eb/ifd/2005/42100.htm).

21. See Torero and Pasco-Font (2003) for a detailed discussion of the reforms in Peru.

22. For an interesting discussion of the trade-offs between ideology and pragmatism, see Manzetti (1999).

23. They also find a strong negative when the respondent is poor and privatization was large and quick. High inequality of incomes also mattered.

24. Chong and López-de-Silanes (2004) offer a useful overview for a large sample of countries but fail to distinguish between the privatization of infrastructure activities and others. Andres, Foster, and Guasch (2005) offer an overview of the empirical

evidence on the effect of privatization in infrastructure, offering important refinements of the conclusions drawn by Chong and López-de-Silanes.

25. Inter-American Development Bank (2002).

26. Fisher, Gutierrez, and Serra (2003).

27. According to the study (see note 26), the gains are due to improvements in operational efficiency stimulated by effective regulatory regimes. This conclusion is, however, not unanimous in Chile, but the surrounding debate will be discussed later. The main question not answered by the study is the extent to which this increase in the return has been excessive or consistent with a normal return for these assets.

28. Ramamurti (1996) is a notable exception because he documents improvements in quality in transportation and telecommunications as a result of Latin American reforms.

29. For a survey of the improvements in efficiency, see Estache, Guasch, and Trujillo (2003).

30. To be more precise, they are distributed from the government, politicians, and the managers of the public enterprises to a new combination that now includes the government, politicians, the private managers, and the shareholders of the privatized regulated services. Consumers, as a group, only get a share of the cost savings in the form of tariff reductions if the regulators are good and fair.

31. In many instances, the request for renegotiations are consistent with the terms of the contracts or with the regulatory regime, but these are legalistic considerations the users and the opinion makers do not often get into, partly because the details of the contractual arrangements are not public or partly because they react strongly to their exclusion from the implementation of the reform process.

32. See Martimort and Straub (2006) for interesting insights.

REFERENCES

Alonso, J. A., J. Benavides, I. Yaker, and C. J. Rodriguez. 2001. "Participation Privada de Infraestructura y Determinantes de los Esquemas Contractuales Adoptados: El Caso Colombinao." IDB Latin American Research Network Working Paper R412. Washington, DC: Inter-American Development Bank.

Andres, L., V. Foster, and J. L. Guasch. 2005. *The Impact of Privatization in Firms in the Infrastructure Sector in Latin American Countries.* Washington, DC: World Bank.

Barja, G. and M. Urquiola. 2003. "Capitalization, Regulation and the Poor: Access to Basic Services in Bolivia." In *Utility Privatization and Regulation: A Fair Deal for Consumers?* ed. C. Ugaz and C. Waddams Price, 203–233. Northampton, MA: Edward Elgar.

Benitez, D., O. Chisari, and A. Estache. 2003. "Can the Gains from Argentina's Utilities Reform Offset Credit Shocks?" In *Utility Privatization and Regulation: A Fair Deal for Consumers?* ed. C. Ugaz and C. Waddams Price, 175–202. Northampton, MA: Edward Elgar.

Benitez, D. and A. Estache. 2005. "How Concentrated Are Global Infrastructure Markets?" *The Review of Network Economics* 4(3): 220–242.

Boix, C. 2005. "Privatization and Public Discontent in Latin America." Background paper commissioned for the Inter-American Development Bank.

Bonnet, C., P. Dubois, D. Martimort, and S. Straub. 2006. "Empirical Evidence on Satisfaction with Privatization in Latin America." Institut d'Economie Industrielle, mimeo.

Brune, N. and G. Barlett. 2000. "The Diffusion of Privatisation in the Developing World." Yale University, mimeo.

Campos, J., A. Estache, N. Martín, and L. Trujillo. 2003. "Macroeconomic Effects of Private Sector Participation in Infrastructure." In *The Limits of Stabilisation*, ed. W. Easterly and L. Serven, 139–170. Stanford, CA: Stanford University Press.

Checchi, D., M. Florio, and J. Carrera. 2005. "Privatization Discontent and Its Determinants: Evidence from Latin America." IZA Discussion Paper 1587. Bonn: Institute for the Study of Labor.

Chisari, O., A. Estache, and C. Romero. 1999. "Winners and Losers from the Privatization and Regulation of Utilities: Lessons from a General Equilibrium Model of Argentina." *World Bank Economic Review* 13(2): 357–378.

Chong, A. and F. López-de-Silanes. 2004. "The Truth About Privatization in Latin America." *Economía* 4: 37–111.

Combo, C. and M. Ramirez. 2002. "Privatization in Colombia: A Plant Performance Analysis." IDB Latin American Research Network Working Paper R458. Washington, DC: Inter-American Development Bank.

Delfino, J. and A. Casarin. 2003. "The Reform of the Utilities Sector in Argentina." In *Utility Privatization and Regulation: A Fair Deal for Consumers?* ed. C. Ugaz and C. Waddams Price, 149–174. Northampton, MA: Edward Elgar.

Estache, A. 2004. "Argentina Privatization: A Cure or a Disease?" In *Trends in Infrastructure Regulation and Financing: International Experience and Case Studies from Germany*, ed. C. Hirschhausen, T. Beckers, and K. Mitusch. Northampton, MA: Edward Elgar.

———. 2005. "On Latin America's Infrastructure Experience: Policy Gaps and the Poor." In *Reality Check: The Distributional Impact of Privatization in Developing Countries*, ed. J. Nellis and N. Birdsall, 281–296. Washington DC: Center for Global Development.

Estache, A., V. Foster, and Q. Wodon. 2002. *Accounting for Poverty in Infrastructure Reform*. Washington, DC: World Bank Institute of Development Studies.

Estache, A., J. Guasch, and L. Trujillo. 2003. "Price Caps, Efficiency Pay-Offs and Infrastructure Contract Renegotiation in Latin America." In *The UK Model of Utility Regulation: A 20th Anniversary Collection to Mark the "Littlechild Report": Retrospect and Prospect*, ed. I. Bartle, 173–198. CRI Proceedings 31. London: Center for Regulated Industries.

Estache, A. and L. Trujillo. 2004. "Las Privatizaciones en América Latina." *Revista Asturiana de Economia* 31: 37–59.

Fay, M. and M. Morrison. 2005. *Infrastructure in Latin America and the Caribbean: Recent Developments and Key Challenges*. Washington, DC: World Bank.

Fisher, R., R. Gutierrez, and P. Serra. 2003. "The Effects of Privatization on Firms and on Social Welfare: The Chilean Case." IDB Latin American Research

Network Working Paper R456. Washington, DC: Inter-American Development Bank.

Freije, S. and L. Rivas. 2002. "Privatization, Inequality and Welfare: Evidence from Nicaragua." Unpublished paper presented at the Universidad de las Americas in Puebla, Mexico, May.

Galetovic, A. and R Sanhieza. 2002. "Regulación de servicios públicos. ¿Hacia dónde debemos ir?" *Estudios Públicos* 85: 101–136.

Graham, C. and A. Felton. 2005. "Does Inequality Matter to Individual Welfare? An Initial Exploration Based on Happiness Surveys from Latin America." CSED Working Paper 38. Washington, DC: Brookings Institution.

Guasch, J. 2004. *Granting and Renegotiating Infrastructure Concessions: Doing It Right*. Washington, DC: World Bank.

Hachette, D. and R. Luders. 1993. *Privatization in Chile: An Economic Appraisal*. San Francisco: ICS Press.

Inter-American Development Bank. 2002. "The Privatization Paradox." *Latin American Economic Policies* 18: 8.

La Porta, R. and F. López-de-Silanes. 1999. "The Benefits of Privatization: Evidence from Mexico." *Quarterly Journal of Economics* 114(4): 1193–1242.

Lopez-Calva, L. F. and J. Rosellon. 2002. "Privatization and Inequality in Mexico." Unpublished paper presented at the Universidad de las Americas in Puebla, Mexico, May.

Lora, E. 2001. "Structural Reforms in Latin America: What Has Been Reformed and How to Measure It." IADB Working Paper 466. Washington, DC: Inter-American Development Bank.

Luders, R. 1991. "Massive Divestiture and Privatization: Lessons from Chile." *Contemporary Policy Issues* 9: 1–19.

Macedo, R. 2000. "Privatization and the Distribution of Assets and Income in Brazil." Carnegie Endowment for International Peace Working Paper 14. Washington, DC: Carnegie Endowment for International Peace.

Manzetti, L. 1999. *Privatization South America Style*. Oxford: Oxford University Press.

Martimort, D. and S. Straub. 2006. "Privatization and Changes in Corruption Patterns: The Roots of Public Discontent." Institut d'Economie Industrielle, mimeo.

McKenzie, D. and D. Mookherjee. 2003. "Distributive Impact of Privatization in Latin America: An Overview of Evidence from Four Countries." *Economia* 3(2): 161–218.

Meseguer, C. 2003. "The Diffusion of Privatization in Industrial and Latin America Countries: What Role for Learning?" Paper presented at the workshop on the Internationalization of Regulatory Reforms, Center for the Study of Law and Society, University of California, Berkeley, April 25–26.

Panizza, U. and E. Lora. 2002. "Structural Reforms in Latin America Under Scrutiny." IADB Working Paper 1012. Washington, DC: Inter-American Development Bank.

Paredes, R. 2003. "Privatization and Regulation Challenges in Jamaica." IADB Economic and Sector Study Series 4. Washington, DC: Inter-American Development Bank.

Pinheiro, A. 1996. "Impactos microeconômicos da Privatização no Brasil." *Pesquisa e Planejamento Económico* 26(3): 357–398.

Ramamurti, R. 1996. *Privatizing Monopolies: Lesson from the Telecommunications and Transport Sectors in Latin America.* Baltimore: Johns Hopkins University Press.

Ramirez, M. 1994. "Privatization and the Role of the State in the Post-ISI Mexico." In *Privatization in Latin America: New Roles for the Public and the Private Sector,* ed. W. Baer and M. Birch, 21–44. Westport, CT: Praeger Publishers.

Sirtaine, S., M. Pinglo, V. Foster, and J. Guasch. 2005. "How Profitable Are Private Infrastructure Concessions in Latin America? Empirical Evidence and Regulatory Implications." *Quarterly Review of Economics and Finance* 45: 380–402.

Torero, M. 2002. "Impacto de la privatización sobre el desempeño de las empresas en el Perú." Documentos de Trabajo 41, Grupo de Análisis para el Desarrollo (GRADE).

Torero, M. and A. Pasco-Font. 2003. "The Social Impact of Privatization and the Regulation of Utilities." In *Utility Privatization and Regulation: A Fair Deal for Consumers?* ed. C. Ugaz and C. Waddams Price, 257–288. Northampton, MA: Edward Elgar.

Ugaz, C. and C. Waddams Price, eds. 2003. *Utility Privatization and Regulation: A Fair Deal for Consumers?* Northampton, MA: Edward Elgar.

United Nations. 1999. *Privatization in Latin America in the Early 1990s.* New York: United Nations.

CHAPTER 6

Privatization in South Asia

Nandini Gupta

In the last decade, governments worldwide have raised over US$1 trillion from the sale of state-owned enterprises (SOEs) (Megginson and Netter, 2001). However, the South Asian economies of Bangladesh, India, Pakistan, and Sri Lanka have been slow to divest from government-owned firms. Revenues raised from privatization between 1991 and 1999 totaled just US$11.9 billion in South Asia (World Bank, 2001b). In contrast, Latin America raised over US$177 billion over the same period (World Bank, 2001b). In this chapter we discuss the privatization process in South Asia with a focus on India, the largest economy in the region.

State-owned enterprises in the region are extremely inefficient due to rent seeking by politicians and workers, protection from competitive forces, and the absence of market-based incentives for workers. As a result, they are a significant drain on government resources throughout the region. For example, between 1991 and 1999, the Government of India invested Rs.612 billion in SOEs and earned dividends of Rs.179 billion,[1] an average return of 3.4% (Department of Disinvestment, 2001). Almost all this investment was financed by the government by issuing debt at interest rates above 10%, which is considerably higher than the rate of return. The auditory body of the Indian government reports that between 2003 and 2004 only 156 SOEs earned profits while 116 companies suffered losses. Moreover, among the firms reporting profits, just 42 companies from the oil, power, telecommunications, coal, and steel sectors contributed 80% of the overall profits earned (Comptroller and Auditor General, 2003–2004).

Despite the inefficiency of SOEs, public support for privatization remains low. Reluctance to privatize is in part due to the historical context of state ownership, which we describe in the first section.

State-ownership was originally justified in industries requiring large investments, such as iron and steel. Given sparse private sources of capital in the immediate postcolonial era, these economies used public money in order to quickly develop an industrial base. It was believed that a dominant public sector would reduce the inequality of income and wealth and advance the general prosperity of the nation. However, in subsequent decades, the focus on heavy and strategic industries shifted, and governments nationalized loss-making private companies in many sectors just to prevent their closure. Political factors also led to the rapid expansion of state ownership. For example, after obtaining independence from Pakistan, Bangladesh nationalized companies that were owned by Pakistan nationals.

Following a balance of payments crisis in 1991, the Indian government implemented a number of reforms intended to reduce entry barriers and encourage private enterprise, which we describe in the second section. The privatization policies framed by successive governments from 1991 until the present are also discussed. Throughout the last decade, there have been numerous shifts in India's privatization strategy. In particular, until 1999, successive Indian governments sold only minority equity stakes without transferring management control (partial privatization). Starting in 2000, the government transferred management control and sold majority equity stakes to private owners in 14 companies (strategic sales). However, the new government elected in 2004 has ruled out the privatization of profitable firms and has also stated that efforts will be made to turn around loss-making firms before they are considered for privatization. Restructuring strategies however have been almost uniformly unsuccessful in the past (Department of Disinvestment, 2001).

In the third section, we describe the progress made in privatization and the two main approaches used to privatize firms in India: partial privatization and strategic sales. While partial privatization is politically less costly because it does not involve the transfer of management control, there is a risk of continued political interference in these firms. Strategic sales, on the other hand, may generate more efficiency improvements but are politically costly to implement.

In the fourth section, we discuss evidence suggesting that political competition and patronage play a significant role in the privatization process in India. From the evidence, it appears that the government is reluctant to privatize firms located in regions where the governing party faces significant competition from opposition parties. Political patronage also appears to influence the process, as the evidence suggests that politicians are unwilling to give up control of certain firms.

We discuss evidence that partial privatization has led to an improvement in the operating performance of Indian firms in the fifth section. According to agency theory, state-owned firms have difficulty monitoring managers because there is neither an individual owner with strong incentives to monitor managers nor a public share price to provide information on manager actions as judged by stock market participants. Results from Gupta (2005) suggest that selling minority equity stakes without the transfer of management control leads to a significant increase in the level and growth rates of profitability, labor productivity, and investment spending. Investment spending on research and development and expenditures on fixed capital also rise significantly following an increase in private ownership share.

The role of competition is an important factor in the privatization process as it may help improve the performance of SOEs. In the sixth section, we discuss evidence suggesting that competitive forces and private ownership have a complementary impact on firm performance. We also discuss evidence suggesting that the presence of SOEs in a sector may in fact inhibit competition in that sector. In particular, the government is much less likely to remove barriers to foreign investment in industries with profitable and capital intensive SOEs.

In the seventh section, we describe the privatization process in other South Asian economies. Some of these economies have made more progress than India. For example, the Government of Pakistan has privatized several financial institutions, a key infrastructure sector. We discuss strong evidence from the privatization of Bangladeshi jute mills that SOEs are used by politicians to dole out jobs. In particular, there is more surplus employment of white-collar workers than of low-wage workers in these firms.

In the eighth section, we discuss evidence suggesting that privatization has not led to massive layoffs in India. Moreover, the number of workers employed by Indian federal government-owned enterprises who may be affected by privatization amounts to less than 1% of India's total workforce (Department of Disinvestment, 2001). However, SOE employee unions have a lot of political clout. For example, voluntary retirement programs appear to have significantly overcompensated workers throughout the region. Evidence also suggests that SOE workers may have successfully delayed privatization in India. The chapter concludes with a discussion about privatization in infrastructure. In India, infrastructure investment is a tenth of China's annual investment. One way in which investment can be increased is by picking up the pace of privatization and using the revenues to invest in these sectors. However, past experience suggests that prior to privatization the government will need to design a regulatory framework in certain infrastructure sectors such as electricity.

INSTITUTIONAL BACKGROUND

GOVERNMENT OWNERSHIP AND STATE-LED INDUSTRIALIZATION

Prior to independence from the United Kingdom, South Asian economies were overwhelmingly agrarian with little or no investment in industry. In 1913, for example, 76% of British India's exports were foodstuffs and raw materials, while manufactured goods accounted for 79% of imports (Chandra, 1992). Although a small manufacturing sector developed in the early 1900s, it did not compensate for the collapse of the traditional handicrafts industries following the Industrial Revolution in Britain in the nineteenth century. At the time of independence, between 2% and 3% of the labor force was employed in nonagricultural sectors, and manufacturing primarily consisted of labor-intensive industries. The financial sector was similarly underdeveloped, with one bank per 1.7 million inhabitants in 1914 (Chandra, 1992). The partition of British India into India, West Pakistan, and East Pakistan (which became Bangladesh in 1971) created further imbalances in the industrial structure of these economies. Most industry was located in modern India, while raw materials were produced in Pakistan and Bangladesh. For instance, in 1947 just 5% of the large-scale industrial facilities in British India were located in what is now Pakistan.

Following independence, these countries focused on an inward-oriented development strategy that emphasized import-substituting industrialization and gave the state a dominant role in implementing this strategy. This is not surprising because the leaders of the time identified the colonial regime with laissez-faire capitalism and viewed its liberal trade policies as a means of ensuring access for manufactured goods. South Asian economies relied on their governments to operate virtually all infrastructure and financial services and many industrial units. Public sector-led industrialization was intended to make up for inadequate supply of capital in the private sector and to pursue redistributive policies. Srinivasan (2003) argues that an entrepreneurial class did exist at the time of independence, but distrust of markets and foreign trade led the government to adopt a dominant role. In subsequent decades, many of these economies significantly expanded the scope of the public sector by nationalizing many privately owned companies. Following its own independence from West Pakistan in 1971, the government of Bangladesh seized the plants formerly owned by West Pakistanis. These represented nearly 90% of industrial assets in the new nation (Bhaskar and Khan, 1995).

In the aftermath of independence, the Industrial Policy Resolution of 1948 outlined India's industrialization strategy by categorizing industries by end use (capital, intermediate, and consumer goods), ownership (public, private, cooperative, or joint), and size (organized, small scale, cottage, and village) (Srinivasan, 2003). What set the stage for the next 50 years was the reservation of particular industrial sectors exclusively for government-owned firms. These included not just infrastructure sectors such as electricity, railways, and telecommunications, but also industries producing key capital goods and raw materials such as steel, petroleum, and heavy machinery. The motivating idea was that by controlling key raw materials, the government could direct industrial development. However, there were other objectives as well. Revenues from the surplus generated by SOEs were supposed to provide an alternative to taxation revenues to finance government programs. These revenues were to be generated through fixed pricing schemes for their products. State-owned enterprises were also intended to promote economic development in backward areas and to set an example of worker welfare that the private sector could emulate.

The scope of the government expanded well beyond infrastructure and heavy industries. For example, the Indian government owns luxury hotels and bakeries. The Indian public sector consists of departmental enterprises that are run directly by government ministries, such as the railways, the postal service, telecommunications, irrigation, and power, as well as enterprises that have separate boards of directors.

The First and Second Five-Year Plans outlined the development strategy pursued in India until the last decade. These plans emphasized investment in heavy industries, import substitution, and a large expansion in the public sector. Moreover, government interference was not just restricted to particular sectors of the economy. In order to finance the investments proposed in the Second Five-Year Plan, elaborate restrictions on investment and production across all industrial sectors were necessary.

These included industrial licensing, where one needed government permission regarding the scale, location, and technology of any investment project, and exchange controls, where exporters had to remit all foreign exchange earnings to the central bank at the fixed exchange rate; the earnings were redistributed in turn through import licensing. In addition, there were restrictions on issuing capital in domestic markets, price controls on both consumption goods and raw materials, extensive trade barriers, and agricultural subsidies and price controls. Further, most nationalized banks were required to lend more than 50% of their loanable funds to the government (and SOEs) through various reserve requirements (Srinivasan, 2003).

This development strategy did not produce spectacular economic performance. From the 1950s until the 1980s, real GDP growth in India averaged about 3.75% (Srinivasan, 2003). Table 6.1 provides GDP, stock market capitalization, and industrial growth rates in recent decades for all the economies in the region.

As in the rest of the developing world, SOEs in this region are characterized by huge losses, surplus employment, overcapacity, and underutilization of assets, and are subject to political interference. More than half of the firms owned by the Indian federal government were loss-making in the 1990s. According to the government of India's own numbers, between 1990 and 1998 the average ratio of profit after tax to sales was −4.4%, and the average ratio of wages to sales was 18.9% among manufacturing SOEs (Department of Disinvestment, 2001). In contrast, among private manufacturing firms the return on sales averaged 6.7%, while the average wages to sales ratio was only half as high as that of SOEs over the same period (Department of Disinvestment, 2001). Moreover, SOEs moreover account for a large share of investment. In 1993, the public sector in India absorbed 42% of gross fixed capital formation while producing 29% of GDP (Joshi and Little, 1996).

THE ECONOMIC REFORMS AND PRIVATIZATION POLICY

ECONOMIC REFORMS (1991–2004)

Limited liberalization and fiscal expansion in the 1980s led to higher growth rates in India, which were accompanied by large fiscal and current account deficits financed by internal and external borrowing at nonconcessional rates. In 1991, the current account deficit was about US$10

TABLE 6.1 Key Economic Characteristics of South Asia

Country	Year*	Federal Government Debt (% of GDP)	GDP Growth (annual %)	GDP Per Capita (constant 1995 US$)	Industry, Value Added (annual % growth)	Market Capitalization (% of GDP)
Bangladesh	1991–1994	0	4.5957748	291.5607	6.8962422	1.47996964
	1995–1999	8.019602	5.006274	336.59334	7.1744196	4.5155396
	2000–2003	N/A	5.23999625	391.4013	6.8499135	2.6435775
India	1991–1994	51.15583	4.864195	335.73754	5.30943462	26.43449
	1995–1999	49.973048	6.5269376	415.7512	6.305769	33.13592
	2000–2003	56.67633	5.4220345	490.158325	5.4962175	31.90472
Pakistan	1991–1994	61.89656	4.5442434	472.35544	5.489095	17.1769306
	1995–1999	15.816938	3.4067906	504.24332	3.9284193	14.0026306
	2000–2003	90.00384	3.86855075	523.646975	3.64099	15.12906225
Sri Lanka	1991–1994	96.415152	5.58	665.43572	7.254278	19.307054
	1995–1999	91.480482	4.940877	808.67358	6.2718838	12.686304
	2000–2003	99.993005	3.47721675	903.371475	2.983635	9.9455465

*N/A = not available. The variables are averaged over the years indicated.
Source: World Bank, *World Development Indicators*, various years.

billion, or 3% of GDP; the budget deficit was at 10% of GDP; the inflation rate was between 12% and 13%; and foreign exchange reserves had fallen to US$1 billion, enough to finance about two weeks of imports (Joshi and Little, 1996). The 1991 crisis was a result of these macroeconomic factors, which along with political uncertainty and rising oil prices following the first Gulf War led to a sharp downgrade in India's credit rating and put a stop to foreign private lending. The time was ripe for India to institute changes in its development strategy. In particular, the fall of the Soviet Union and the increasingly visible success of China's economic reforms had led to a gradual recognition of the failure of the central planning model. The crisis allowed the reformers to step in.

In 1991, India instituted an economic reforms package, which involved a dismantling of the licensing system, stock market liberalization, entry liberalization in industries previously reserved for the public sector, decrease in restrictions on foreign direct investment, and trade liberalization. The Industrial Policy Resolution of 1991 argued for a shift in the state-led industrialization and import substitution policies of the past and stated that SOEs "have become a burden rather than being an asset to the government" (paragraph 31). The policy resolution further stated that the government should withdraw from sectors that are inefficient and non-strategic, and in which the private sector has developed expertise. It also argued for partial divestiture in SOEs "in order to provide further market discipline to the performance of public enterprises" (paragraph 34).

However, successive governments between 1991 and 1999 did not make much progress in privatization. The Committee on Disinvestment of Shares in Public Sector Units was created in 1992 to provide recommendations regarding the method of sale, the percentage of equity to be sold in particular companies, and the valuation procedure. This committee recommended that, rather than having annual targets set out in the budget, the government should have a longer-term plan, and it also recommended that a regulatory commission be set up to oversee the sales, that employees be given stock options, and that part of the proceeds be reinvested in the enterprises. None of the major recommendations of this committee were implemented by the government. The absence of a coherent policy led to allegations of inaccurate valuation of companies and also limited the participation of foreign investors.

In 1996, the government set up the Disinvestment Commission, which was to oversee the entire privatization process and revive the languishing privatization program. While the commission published 13 reports, it lacked the political clout to undertake this mission, which would involve challenging the politicians and bureaucrats in charge of the companies. This fact was finally recognized by the Bharatiya Janata Party–led government elected in 1999, which led to the creation of a separate Department of Disinvestment and a cabinet-level position for the minister of disinvestment in 1999.

Since 1991, nearly every government's annual budget has declared that the privatization goal is to reduce government ownership to 26% of equity, the minimum equity holding necessary for certain voting powers, in all state-owned firms not in the defense, atomic energy, and railway sectors. However, until 2000 the government sold only minority equity stakes, sometimes as little as 0.1%, without transferring management control. Euphemistically referred to as "disinvestment," privatization proved to be very difficult to implement.

One of the frequent refrains in the media about the privatization program is the existence of multiple, confounding objectives. The official reasons for privatizing SOEs in India have been stated as improving governance and efficiency, freeing up resources for social programs, and developing financial markets (Department of Disinvestment, 2001). Between 1991 and 2000, successive governments sold minority stakes without transferring management control because doing so proved to be a lucrative source of revenues without the accompanying political controversy of transferring control of state-owned assets to private owners. A number of different coalition governments were formed between 1996 and 1999, none of which stayed in power for long, and the political uncertainty of this period was probably the main reason why a coherent policy on privatization did not emerge.

After the elections of 1999, the new government continued the practice of minority equity sales on financial markets, but it also sold majority stakes and transferred management control in 14 firms between 2000 and 2004. While this represents a major shift in policy from previous governments, progress was still slow. Until 2004, the government retained ownership of an average of 82% of equity in all SOEs (Gupta, 2005).

PRIVATIZATION POLICY (2004–PRESENT)

Following the elections of 2004, the new government has outlined its privatization policy under the National Common Minimum Programme. The policy can be summarized as follows: (1) Profitable enterprises will not be privatized. (2) Loss-making firms will be restructured or shut down. (3) Sales of minority equity stakes in financial markets will continue. (4) A National Investment Fund will be set up for the revenues from privatization to be used for investments in health, education, and employment, and for capital investments in ailing SOEs.

Profitable SOEs include companies in the oil and gas sectors, financial services, telecommunications, and energy. For example, the Life Insurance Corporation of India is the country's largest life insurance company, and Bharat Sanchar Nigam is the country's largest telecommunications company. The main issue is whether keeping these companies under government control will erode their competitiveness. Given that many of these companies are in key infrastructure sectors, the decision to keep them state-owned has implications for the global competitiveness of the entire economy.

The policy of restructuring loss-making companies is a goal that has also been embraced by previous governments, but without much success. In fact, the literature suggests that the adverse selection associated with certain types of labor restructuring in SOEs, such as voluntary retirement, may not be beneficial and can even reduce the sale price of the firm (Haltiwanger and Singh, 1999; López-de-Silanes and Chong, 2002). However, setting up a separate fund for privatization revenues, if actually implemented, will be an improvement over the previous system, where the revenues were used to reduce government budget deficits rather than being earmarked for a specific purpose. The transparent use of privatization revenues would help in building political support for privatization.

PROGRESS IN PRIVATIZATION

According to the *Global Development Finance Report* (World Bank, 2001a), the total privatization revenues raised in South Asia in 1999 were US$11.9 billion, the second lowest amount raised among six developing/transition economy regions, and just above sub-Saharan Africa. India has been the slowest reformer in the region; however, the region as a whole lags behind most of the developing world in privatization. From 1991 to 2004, the total amount collected through privatization is Rs.476.5 billion over 14 years—an annual average of 0.2% of GDP. Table 6.2 provides an annual breakdown of the number of companies sold, the method of sale, and the revenues raised from privatization between 1991 and 2004.

TABLE 6.2   Progress in Privatization in India, 1991–2004

Year	Number of Transactions in Which Equity Sold	Target Receipts (million Rupees)	Actual Receipts (million Rupees)
1991–1992	47	25,000	30,377
1992–1993	29	25,000	19,120
1993–1994	0	35,000	0
1994–1995	17	4,000	48,431
1995–1996	5	70,000	1,685
1996–1997	1	50,000	3,797
1997–1998	1	48,000	9,100
1998–1999	5	5,000	53,711
1999–2000	5	100,000	18,601
2000–2001	5	10,000	1,871
2001–2002	8	120,000	56,323
2002–2003	8	12,000	3,348
2003–2004	2	145,000	155,474
2004–2005	3	4,000	2,765
Total		968,000	476,464

Source: Department of Disinvestment, Government of India.

While enterprises owned by the federal government of India account for about 85% of the asset base of state-owned firms, there are also 1,036 firms owned by individual state governments. The total investment in these 1,036 regional-government-owned companies was estimated at Rs.2.5 billion in 2003; of these 209 are not operational, while over half of them are loss-making (Department of Disinvestment, "Disinvestment in States"). Until 2004, 36 of these firms had been privatized and another 111 shut down, with the state of Andhra Pradesh leading the way. In table 6.3 we list the progress made in each state.

PARTIAL PRIVATIZATION

Between 1991 and 1999, successive Indian governments sold minority equity stakes through a variety of methods, including auctions and public offerings in domestic markets, and through global depository receipts in international markets. The majority of these partial privatizations were undertaken by the government led by the Congress Party between 1991 and 1996. Until 1999, the government had sold an average of 19.2% of equity in 41 industrial, financial, and service sector firms (Gupta, 2005). Starting in 2000, the government led by the Bharatiya Janata Party has sold majority stakes and transferred management control in 14 SOEs. Although the privatization program seems to have stalled since the elections of 2004, the new government's policies state that the

TABLE 6.3 Privatization in Indian States

Name of the State	Number of State Government–Owned Firms	Investment (million Rupees)	Net Accumulated Loss (million Rupees)	Number of Loss-Making Firms	Number of Non-working Firms	Number of Privatized Firms
Andhra Pradesh	128	487,940	29,190	62	9	13
Arunachal Pradesh	7	140	140	3	2	0
Assam	42	37,320	28,850	36	10	0
Bihar	54	81,690	50,600	12	28	0
Delhi	15	109,640	69,950	3	N/A	1
Gujarat	50	257,580	67,740	24	10	3
Haryana	45	4,430	3,840	10	4	1
Himachal Pradesh	21	47,310	6,050	13	2	3
Jammu and Kashmir	20	19,480	5,870	16	1	0
Karnataka	85	278,130	18,880	30	7	2
Kerala	111	164,290	35,100	52	13	0
Madhya Pradesh	26	79,230	6,000	8	15	1
Maharashtra	66	208,550	17,750	44	18	0
Manipur	14	810	N/A	10	N/A	0
Mizoram	5	620	150	4	N/A	0
Orissa	72	72,970	23,720	22	24	9
Punjab	53	133,840	14,350	25	28	1
Rajasthan	28	115,760	3,150	11	8	1
Sikkim	12	1,210	290	6	3	0
Tamil Nadu	59	61,920	N/A	33	N/A	0
Uttar Pradesh	41	177,730	53,270	21	19	1
West Bengal	82	181,830	70,620	62	8	0
Total	1,036	2,522,420	505,510	507	209	36

N/A = not available.
Source: Department of Disinvestment, Government of India.

practice of selling minority equity stakes without transferring control will continue.

In the first group of privatizations undertaken in 1991, the government sold bundles of shares combining shares from higher- and lower-value firms. This may have lowered the average price across company shares. In the first such sales between 1991 and 1992, the average price received per share was about Rs.34.83. In subsequent privatizations between 1992 and 1997, the average share price was Rs.109.61 (Chandrashekhar and Ghosh, 1999). The practice of bundling shares was only used once; subsequent partial privatizations involved the sale of shares of individual companies.

Partial privatization, where the government retains majority ownership and management control, has on average led to an improvement in the operating performance of SOEs in India (Gupta, 2005). However, this method of privatization can pose some risks for minority shareholders. In recent years, the government has sometimes undertaken actions that may be detrimental to the interests of minority shareholders. As an example, consider the case of the profitable partially privatized oil company the Oil and Natural Gas Corporation (ONGC). In 2002, the government proposed that ONGC should make a special dividend payment that would benefit the government to the tune of Rs.50 billion. The company had posted unusually high profits in the previous quarter due to an increase in world oil prices. Unfortunately, the company had also planned capital expenditures of Rs.47 billion, which it would not be able to undertake if it made the dividend payment. The government's actions in this instance were interpreted in the media as inconsistent with that of shareholder value maximization (Vaidya Nathan, 2002). In 2003, the strategic sales of two other oil companies was stalled because the government was unwilling to reduce gas subsidies prior to the elections. These subsidies on cooking gas and kerosene, the primary energy sources in India's rural areas, amounted to about US$2.53 billion in additional costs for the companies.

From the policy statements issued by the new government, it appears that it intends to continue with minority equity sales on domestic and foreign stock markets. Given the risk to investors of government expropriation, the companies may have to significantly underprice their offerings in order to be attractive to investors, which in turn would reduce the revenues received from privatization. However, underpricing is common in privatizations around the world, as documented by Jones et al. (1999).

Evidence suggests that privatizations through share issues promote the development of financial markets. Privatized firms are the most valuable companies in the stock markets of both developed and developing countries, and the largest share offerings in history have been privatizations (Megginson and Netter, 2001). This appears to be the case in India as well. Among the top 10 companies with the highest market capitalization on the Bombay Stock Exchange in 2005, five are partially privatized companies, and the company with the highest market capitalization is a partially privatized oil company.

Using an auction framework, Gupta and Harbaugh (2001) show that partial privatization may increase sale revenues. In the case of most privatizing economies, before a firm is privatized there is limited public information about the firm's likely profitability, implying that buyers will have differing opinions about the value of the firm. Because competition between buyers is reduced, the winning bidder will pay less than the expected value of the firm on average. This is consistent with the evidence of underpricing of shares in privatization that occurred in India and elsewhere (Jones et al., 1999). Once the firm is under new management, the market will have a much clearer idea of the firm's future profitability. For instance, post-privatization share prices may be a more accurate signal of the firm's long-term profitability compared to pre-privatization earnings statements. This more accurate public information about profitability will lower buyers' information rents on average, increasing revenues from selling the firm. Given this information problem, the state faces a dilemma. Only by selling the firm will information about future profitability be revealed, but only by holding on to the firm can the state avoid giving away information rents to buyers. Gupta and Harbaugh (2001) show that partial privatization and gradual privatization are appealing compromises that trade off the advantages to revealing information and to recapturing the rents from information revelation. When selling one firm, the government's optimal strategy will always be to sell a fraction of the firm first. In the case of several firms, the government's optimal strategy will be to sell a few firms completely and others partially or not at all.

STRATEGIC SALES AND TRANSFER OF MAJORITY CONTROL

Starting in 2000, the Indian government undertook strategic sales whereby majority stakes were sold and management control in 14 companies was transferred to private owners. Privatization revenues from strategic sales were about Rs.103 billion, which is less than the amount raised through partial privatizations since 1991 (Department of Disinvestment, "Disinvestment till Now").

In the strategic sale process, the government hired investment banks to value the companies, bids were invited, and the highest bidder won. The valuation of the assets and earnings potential of SOEs has been the most contentious aspect of this process. While firms that are listed on stock exchange can be assessed based on share price, most SOEs are not listed. Also, current earnings may not reflect the future earnings potential of these companies because they are subject to government interference and may not be maximizing profit.

One difficulty that has arisen is in the valuation of nonindustrial assets such as real estate and utilities owned by these firms. For example, a Morgan Stanley study from 2005 estimates the total market value of government companies at between US$150 and US$175 billion (Ahya and Sheth, 2005). These estimates are based on secondary market prices and do not include assets in the form of infrastructure facilities and other operations that are not corporatized, such as real estate. Another issue is that of bad market timing, where the government has sold firms during market downturns. For example, the sale of the mining company Hindustan Zinc to the Indian business group Sterlite Industries may have coincided with a slump in world zinc prices and the stock market. The government sold 26% of equity at a per share price of Rs.40.50 in November 2002, when data from the Bombay Stock Exchange indicates that the stock was trading at an average price of Rs.16 per share (the exchange rate was Rs.48.36 to US$1 in November 2002). In a year's time, the company's stock was trading at Rs.84.99 per share, a 110% appreciation in the value of the shares over the purchase price, and an increase of 440% in the traded price at the time of the sale the previous year. The price of Hindustan Zinc averaged about Rs.135 per share in 2004. This increase in the market value of the company may reflect market factors as well as actions taken by the new owners, but it has led to persistent allegations of underpricing of state-owned company shares.

However, underpricing in privatization may be politically beneficial for the government. For example, Biais and Perotti (2002) argue that underpricing shares of SOEs encourages public participation in privatization, thereby building support for the reform.

Underpricing may also be beneficial from a revenue maximization perspective. The sharply increasing market price of Hindustan Zinc described above also benefits the government because it retains a considerable equity stake in the company and will presumably be able to get a better price for the company in subsequent equity sales. Perotti (1995) argues that by retaining an ownership stake in the firm, the government can signal to investors that it will not implement policies that are detrimental to the finances of the firm. While this may have been a factor in the gradual approach to privatization, a more likely explanation for the government's reluctance to privatize is political opposition from organized labor unions and from opposition parties. Institutional barriers, particularly in financial markets, may have also played a role. Below we discuss political economy factors that may have played a role in delaying privatization.

THE POLITICAL ECONOMY OF PRIVATIZATION

One of the institutional barriers to rapid privatization is the relatively underdeveloped financial sector. In particular, capital markets may not be able to absorb share issue privatizations of large SOEs. For example, between 1987 and 1991, the ratio of stock market capitalization to GDP in the high-income OECD economies averaged about 61% (World Bank, *World Development Indicators*). In contrast, the ratio of market capitalization to GDP in India over the same period averaged about 12%. However, privatizations through public offerings in domestic capital markets can help develop these markets (Megginson and Netter, 2001). In 2003, the ratio of market capitalization to GDP in India was about 47% (World Bank, *World Development Indicators*).

Privatization has been one of the mostly politically contested reforms. It is opposed by labor unions, state governments that do not want a company located in their state privatized, bureaucrats who run the companies, political parties, and government ministers who do not want to lose control of the firms. Addressing the feasibility of implementing politically contentious reforms before elections, Prime Minister Atal Behari Vajpayee (1999–2004) said: "Well, if political effects are there, we will not reform. We'll not reform if there [is] a political cost to pay" (Mohan, 2003).

There is now a growing literature on the role of political and economic institutions in privatization. Biais and Perotti (2002) offer an explanation for why conservative governments are more likely to privatize: to induce median class voters to buy enough shares to shift political preferences away from left-wing parties. This may be relevant for India. A prominent political commentator said about the sale of minority shares in 2004 by the right-wing Bharatiya Janata Party government, "So, the disinvestment has little economic significance. Mainly, it is a political ploy to sell shares cheaply to a large number of voters, hoping to reap electoral dividends" (Swaminathan and Aiyar, 2004). Bortolotti and Pinotti (2003) find evidence in support of Biais and Perotti (2002) and show that right-wing governments are more likely to use privatization methods that maximize share ownership among the electorate.

While the potential benefits from privatization, such as capital market development and lower budget deficits, are dispersed across the population, the costs tend to be concentrated among a small group, those who obtain private benefits from SOEs. Using a unique firm-level data set from India, Dinc and Gupta (2006) study the role of political patronage and electoral competition in the decision to privatize. They investigate one particular determinant of political patronage: the location of a firm. Retaining control over a firm may be a greater priority for a politician if the firm is located in the politician's home state. For example, politicians may use SOEs to provide jobs for political supporters, which may affect their ability to win a seat. Dinc and Gupta (2006) identify the cabinet minister in charge of every firm in each year and match the home state of the minister with the state in which the main operations of the firm are located. They find that none of the firms located in the same state as the politician in charge are privatized.

The potentially adverse effects of privatization, such as layoffs, are likely to be concentrated in the region where the firm is located. As a result, the ruling party may lose support in that region if labor unions and political opponents organize in opposition. This consideration may influence the government's decision to privatize in regions where the ruling party faces strong opposition from other political parties and is therefore vulnerable to the effects of voter backlash. Dinc and Gupta (2006) find evidence in support of this hypothesis. Specifically, they find that the rate of privatization is significantly faster if a firm is located in a state where the ruling party and its allies won a large proportion of the seats in the elections to the federal parliament. Privatization is significantly delayed if a firm is located in a state where the ruling and opposition parties are in a close and competitive race. For example, their results suggest that the pace of privatization is likely to be more than four times higher for a firm located in the state of Tamil Nadu, where the ruling party won 100% of the seats to the federal parliament, compared to a firm located in the state of Himachal Pradesh, where the ruling and opposition parties each won 50% of the seats.

Dinc and Gupta's (2006) results also suggest that labor has played a role in the privatization decision. In India, the largest labor unions have opposed privatization and have organized massive protests and strikes. Quoting from a BBC News article from May 2003 ("Millions Strike Against Privatization"):

> The strike was called by trade unions including the All India Trade Union Congress (AITUC), Centre for Indian Trade Unions (CITU) and the Hind Mazdoor Sabha, who claimed about 40 million workers were participating in the walk-out. They are calling for a halt to the government's ongoing privatisation and plans to change labour laws.

The authors find that privatization is significantly delayed if a firm has a large workforce and a high wage bill. Taken together, the results from this study provide evidence of the role played by entrenched interests, such as the politicians in charge of SOEs and organized labor, in delaying the privatization process in India.

EFFICIENCY EFFECTS OF PRIVATIZATION

In comparison to the large literature on privatization in the transition economies, there have been relatively few studies of the effects of privatization in India and other South Asian economies. The findings of existing studies suggest that privatization has improved the performance and efficiency of SOEs. Below we discuss a study by Gupta (2005), which suggests that the most commonly used privatization method in India, partial privatization, has had a positive impact on the operating performance of firms.

PARTIAL PRIVATIZATION

Across the world, most governments have adopted a partial privatization approach where they sell small equity stakes in SOEs on domestic and international stock markets. For example, Boubakri, Cosset, and Guedhami (2005) show that the government remains the controlling shareholder in about 40% of their cross-country sample of 209 firms immediately after privatization. Similarly, La Porta, López-de-Silanes, and Shleifer (2002) show that despite the wave of bank privatizations in the 1980s, the average share of banking assets controlled by the government remained at 48% in banks from 92 countries.

Partial privatization is also of theoretical interest because of the insight it offers into the long-standing debate over why state-owned firms perform poorly. The political view argues that governments pursue objectives in addition to and in conflict with profit maximization and that this political interference can distort the objectives and constraints faced by managers. Hence, only the transfer of management control to private owners is likely to address inefficiency in SOEs. The managerial view, based on agency theory, is that state-owned firms have difficulty monitoring managers because there is neither an individual owner with strong incentives to monitor managers nor a public share price to provide information on manager actions as judged by stock market participants.

Between 1991 and 1999, India sold minority equity stakes in 41 state-owned companies in domestic and international stock markets. Because management control was not transferred to private owners, it is widely contended that partial privatization has had little impact on the behavior of these firms. Using data on Indian SOEs, Gupta (2005) finds that partial privatization has a positive and highly significant impact on firm sales, profits, labor productivity, and investment. This is the first study to document the impact of partial privatization on the performance of firms.

Under partial privatization, the shares of Indian firms were traded on the stock market while the firms remained under government control and subject to political interference. Thus, Gupta (2005) uses data on partial privatization in India to test the managerial view that inadequate information on manager actions is an important factor in the inefficiency of state-owned firms.

The data in this study consist of accounting information on the population of nonfinancial firms owned by the federal (central) government of India, as well as some manufacturing and nonfinancial service sector firms owned by regional governments. All the partial privatizations undertaken by the federal government until 1999 are observed. The data include pre- and post-privatization performance of 41 firms partially privatized by the federal government up to 1999. These firms only sold noncontrolling shares to financial institutions, foreign institutional investors, and the public through open auctions, public offerings, and global depository receipts in domestic and international stock markets.

The paper uses several approaches to address the potential endogeneity of privatization including fixed effects and instrumental variable estimations. The estimations also control for reforms in competition policy. The results suggest that both the level and the growth rates of profitability, labor productivity, and investment spending improve significantly following partial privatization. In the firm fixed effects regression, a 10 percentage point decrease in government ownership increases annual (log) sales and profit by 13% and 10% respectively, and the average product of labor and returns to labor by 8% and 5% respectively. Investment spending on research and development and expenditures on fixed capital also rise significantly following an increase in the private ownership share of a firm's equity. Hence, these results are consistent with the hypothesis that stock price information and its effect on managerial incentives will improve with the liquidity of the stock.

Evidence suggests that the effect of privatization on firm performance is due in part to the role of new human capital. To further decompose the effect of partial privatization on managerial incentives, the paper uses data on turnover in senior management from 1990 to 2000 for all SOEs privatized through 2002. Results from the instrumental variable regressions suggest that by improving the information environment, partial privatization may improve managerial incentives and facilitate the selection of better managers.

PRIVATIZATION AND COMPETITION

There is a debate in the privatization literature on the relative importance of competition policy versus ownership change. Vickers and Yarrow (1991) have argued that competition can shape managerial incentives better because it reduces the market share of inefficient firms and facilitates performance comparisons. On the other hand, Shleifer and Vishny (1994) have argued that so long as politicians are in control, state-owned firms will be characterized by political interference. Evidence from India suggests that both privatization and competition matter for the operating performance of SOEs (Gupta, 2005).

The Industrial Policy Resolution of 1991, which outlined the economic reforms, argued for a major policy shift to encourage private entry in more industrial sectors. In the last decade, the government has deregulated the economy considerably by removing draconian licensing requirements that forced companies to obtain government approval for all investments, allowing foreign entry in some sectors without prior government approval, and opening up sectors that were previously reserved for SOEs to all investors. In India, these changes in competition policy appear to have reduced the market share and employment levels of SOEs on average (Gupta, 2005).

However, the evidence also suggests that the presence of SOEs may inhibit competition-enhancing reforms. Using a firm-level dataset from India, Chari and Gupta (2006) investigate the role of incumbent firms in the government's decision to remove entry barriers to foreign investment in some industries and not others. Their results suggest that the government was significantly less likely to deregulate foreign entry in concentrated industries and in industries with SOEs. In particular, the government appears to be protecting industries with profitable and capital-intensive SOEs. Furthermore, these are not just industries that can be classified as natural monopolies or of strategic national interest. In contrast to the protection offered to SOEs, Indian business groups do not appear to have had much influence on this deregulation measure.

The recent shift in policy where the government has ruled out privatizations of large, profitable firms in infrastructure sectors raises questions about the future of private investment in these sectors. One implication of Chari and Gupta's (2006) results is that the presence of profitable SOEs may inhibit private entry in these sectors.

PRIVATIZATION IN OTHER SOUTH ASIAN ECONOMIES

Data from "Global Development Finance 2001" (World Bank, 2001b) for the years 1990–1999 and from the World Bank Privatization Database, which notes transactions undertaken since 2000, indicate that the region as a whole raised nearly US$24 billion from privatization sales between the years 1990 and 2005. Of this amount, Bangladesh contributed US$123 million, Sri Lanka US$878 million, and Pakistan accounted for US$7.4 billion in privatization sales. In contrast, the Latin America and Caribbean region raised over US$197 billion from privatization sales during the same period (World Bank, 2001b; World Bank Privatization Database).

While progress has been slow, there have been some important developments in recent years. Recognizing the political barriers to the sale of SOEs, Pakistan, Bangladesh, and Sri Lanka have all created government agencies to implement privatization transactions. While previously these agencies had only advisory capacity, they now have greater discretion to implement privatization. Pakistan has passed a privatization law to ensure transparency in the transactions, while India has created a cabinet-level ministerial position to oversee privatizations. This has helped speed up the process considerably.

Second, while these countries started by selling minor manufacturing firms in the early 1990s, the focus has shifted to infrastructure with the sale of banking, energy, and telecommunications firms in Pakistan and other nations in the region. Between 1989 and 1999, Pakistan privatized six banking/financial sector firms—nearly 80% of its privatization revenues are from the sale of firms in banking, capital markets, energy, and telecommunications sectors (Privatisation Commision, Government of Pakistan). Sri Lanka has also made considerable progress in implementing privatization. It has sold majority stakes of SOEs in infrastructure, manufacturing, and agribusiness sectors, with several sales to foreign buyers.

There is not much evidence on the effects of privatization in these economies. Below we describe the main results of two studies on privatization in Bangladesh.

PRIVATIZATION IN BANGLADESH

Bhaskar and Khan (1995) make an interesting contribution to the literature by investigating the patterns of overemployment and the effect of privatization on the performance of state-owned jute mills in Bangladesh. Jute is the principal export industry in Bangladesh, and in 1982 the government privatized 31 of 62 state-owned mills. Bhaskar and Khan argue that mills were not chosen for privatization on the basis of financial performance, but instead mills that were owned by West Pakistanis prior to their nationalization were privatized. Jute mills that had been owned by Bangladeshi owners before they were nationalized were restituted to their former owners. Thus, they treat privatization as exogenous to firm performance in their data. The control group in their data consists of the mills that remained under government ownership.

Bhaskar and Khan (1995) observe managerial, clerical, and manual employment at the mill level for the years 1983–1988 and annual output for 1981–1982 and 1984–1985. Data on the types of workers allow them to differentiate between two theories on surplus employment in the public sector. Welfarist criteria would dictate that in an economy with high unemployment, the shadow price of labor is less than the wage rate; hence a welfare-maximizing firm would hire beyond the point where marginal revenue equals marginal cost. The clientelist argument is that public sector firms are used by politicians to dole out jobs. The difference between the two should arise in the pattern of surplus employment. While the welfare-maximizing firm would prefer to increase the number of manual workers because the marginal cost is lower and their opportunities are more limited, a clientelist firm is more likely to generate greater employment of white-collar workers because the middle class is likely to have more political clout. Similar differences may arise in the relative employment of permanent versus temporary manual workers. Political reasons may not provide the only explanation for overemployment of managerial staff. Public sector managers may be complicit in creating more white-collar jobs to cater to their socioeconomic class.

Bhaskar and Khan (1995) find compelling evidence in favor of the clientelist argument that excess employment in the public sector is far greater in the white-collar category. Results from difference-in-difference estimations suggest that privatization has a negative impact on white-collar employment (clerical and managerial) and on the employment of permanent manual workers. Manual worker employment does not decrease significantly overall because of a shift toward temporary manual workers. Pooled regression estimates show that white-collar positions decline by 32%, permanent manual by 7%, while temporary manual undergoes a 24% increase.

In a related study, Bhaskar, Gupta, and Khan (2002) use the example of jute privatization to investigate yardstick competition, or the effect of privatization of some mills on the remaining SOEs. They observe aggregate employment data in public and private jute mills for the same categories of workers as in Bhaskar and Khan (1995). Univariate tests suggest that white-collar employment in state-owned mills followed that of the privatized mills with a lag but did not decline as much as output. Manual employment decreased in the same proportion as output. Thus, some excess employment in white-collar categories remained, but less than before. The authors suggest that public sector jute mills are gradually converging in their employment patterns to the privatized mills, indicating that yardstick competition may be useful in reducing public sector inefficiency.

IMPACT OF PRIVATIZATION ON EMPLOYMENT

State-owned enterprises were expected to fulfill a multitude of social objectives both for their workers by providing health care, education, and
shelter and for the economy at large with price regulation. While the conventional wisdom is that privatization will lead to massive layoffs, the evidence does not appear to support this view in South Asia. This is possibly
due to highly restrictive labor laws that govern layoffs and compensation.
The social role of SOEs, at least in India, may be exaggerated given that
the total number of workers employed by federal government-owned firms
is about 1.7 million, or 0.56% of the total workforce (Department of Disinvestment, 2001). According to some estimates, 90% of India's manufacturing workforce is employed in the unorganized sector and not even
represented by unions. Hence, potential layoffs are not likely to affect a
large proportion of the workforce.

The adverse impact of layoffs may be reduced through compensation
and training programs. A recent survey suggests, however, that retrenchment programs for SOE workers have had mixed success in terms of economic benefits. In South Asian economies, separation pay for workers
appears to be overly generous and may not yield a net economic benefit.
Moreover, economies in this region overwhelmingly favor voluntary separations rather than involuntary layoffs, which may give rise to adverse selection problems. The terms of these retrenchment programs clearly reflect
the political clout of SOE labor unions, but they may be the only way to
overcome opposition from this influential group.

Haltiwanger and Singh (1999) survey and compile data on the costs
and benefits of SOE employment retrenchment programs in 37 developing and transition economies. In particular, they describe the factors leading to retrenchment, the type and amount of retrenchment, and the
methods used. The survey yields several interesting variations in the retrenchment methods and costs across countries. For example, in the 1990s
Eastern European SOEs reduced workforce size by 2.85 million workers,
while Asian SOEs reduced employment by just 233,111 workers. Further,
while 31% of the retrenchment in Europe was through involuntary layoffs, none of the retrenchment in the Asian economies was involuntary.
The authors estimate that the total worldwide cost of retrenchment programs exceeded US$12 billion, of which US$1.4 billion was accounted for
by the Asian economies. The compensation included a mix of severance
payments, higher pensions, and retraining and job assistance. While the

transition economies in Eastern Europe spent much more on pensions and worker assistance, 92% of retrenchment costs in Asian economies were accounted for by severance payments.

Following the balance of payments crisis in 1991, a program to reduce SOE employment for chronically loss-making enterprises in India was put in place. A voluntary retrenchment program in loss-making textile firms led to a reduction in the workforce by 70,000 workers between 1993 and 1994. Haltiwanger and Singh (1999) estimate that the average cost per worker of this program was about US$17,000. The compensation formula was 30 days of wages for each year worked compared to the legally required amount of 15 days of wages for each year of permanent service. While this program cost US$1.8 billion, the amount saved in wages was US$83 million (Haltiwanger and Singh, 1999).

Investigating the privatization of jute mills in Bangladesh, Bhaskar and Khan (1995) and Bhaskar, Gupta, and Khan (2002) show that retrenchment of workers is likely to impact the managerial class more than the manual workers because the former is characterized by greater surplus employment. However, their results also suggest that white-collar workers have more influence on the government and authority within the firm. Haltiwanger and Singh (1999) describe a program for Bangladesh jute workers that reduced workforce size by 22,250 workers, of which 1,000 were involuntary separations. The program cost US$56 million while saving US$18 million in wages. Under a program undertaken between 1991 and 1993, Pakistan SOEs retrenched 7,495 workers, all through voluntary separations. This program cost US$25 million but saved the government US$350 million because of the value of the real estate released by departing workers.

In the last decade, the Indian government has reduced barriers to entry in most industrial sectors. These measures have contributed to the rapid increase in private investment and to significantly higher rates of economic growth. Other economies in the region have also made significant progress in privatization. However, SOEs remain a significant drain on public finances throughout the region. Privatizing SOEs could attract foreign investment, increase domestic investment, develop financial markets, and release scarce public funds for other uses, such as investment in infrastructure. But these benefits are dispersed across the population, whereas the costs are concentrated among an influential group of politicians, bureaucrats, and workers. Along with political factors, other constraints such as underdeveloped financial markets, which have led to problems associated with asset valuation and methods of sale, have also contributed to the slow pace of privatization.

Looking forward, one of the major remaining issues is the privatization of infrastructure industries. The key infrastructure sectors are electricity, telecommunications, and transportation. A Morgan Stanley report estimates that in 2003 India's infrastructure spending was US$35 billion compared with US$325 billion for China (Ahya and Sheth, 2005). This report argues for an increase in annual investment of at least US$10–$15 billion.

In India, most of the power generation and distribution companies are owned by regional state governments. The Government of Orissa was the first to privatize its electricity generation and distribution facilities through a strategic asset sale. The state government sold 49% of Orissa Power Generation Corporation to the AES Corporation of the United States in 1998, and 51% of equity shares of its four distribution companies to private companies between 1999 and 2000. Recognizing the need for power sector reform, seven other states have initiated reforms, and the state of Delhi has also privatized its electricity distribution facilities. As in Orissa, most of these states have adopted the approach of unbundling the generation, transmission, and distribution facilities. However, none of the electricity distribution companies in Orissa have posted a profit in the years since privatization. The main reason for this has to do with the regulatory framework. In Orissa, a separate regulatory body sets electricity prices, which the distribution companies claim are not high enough to cover their transmission and distribution costs. The government has been unwilling to raise prices because that would be politically costly. The government has also not been willing to subsidize the newly privatized companies in the transition period. Clearly, the main challenge facing other states seeking to attract private investment is to design a proper regulatory framework.

In the telecommunications sector, the Indian government has followed a two-pronged approach. First, it allowed private entry into telecommunications, ending the monopoly of SOEs. Second, it privatized the nation's international long-distance provider. Prior to the reforms undertaken by the government, the telecommunications sector was restricted to two state-run monopolies. In contrast to power, the telecommunications sector has experienced significant growth. For example, while in 2002 the percentage of the population with access to a telephone was 0.6% (*The Economic Times*, 2002), this number had increased to about 9.5% by 2005 (India Infoline, 2005), primarily due to the growth of mobile telephone services. The experience with this sector indicates that privatization is necessary to encourage further private investments in infrastructure.

In summary, privatization of infrastructure sectors remains the key challenge confronting the economies of South Asia. Infrastructure privatization is likely to differ from that of manufacturing because of the need for regulatory oversight. The evidence also suggests that to increase private participation, the government needs to pursue both privatization and competition policy reforms in these sectors.

NOTE

1. Between 1991 and 1999, the average rupee-to-dollar exchange rate was 32 to 1, ranging from Rs.18 to US$1 in 1991 to Rs.42 to US$1 in 1999.

REFERENCES

Ahya, C. and M. Sheth. 2005. "India: Privatization Policy—Missing the Big Picture?" Global Economic Forum 2005, Morgan Stanley.

Bhaskar, V., B. Gupta, and M. Khan. 2002. "Partial Privatization and Yardstick Competition: Evidence from Employment Dynamics in Bangladesh." Unpublished manuscript.

Bhaskar, V. and M. Khan. 1995. "Privatization and Employment: A Study of the Jute Industry in Bangladesh." *American Economic Review* 85(1): 267–273.

Biais, B. and E. Perotti. 2002. "Machiavellian Privatization." *American Economic Review* 92(1): 240–258.

Bortolotti, B. and P. Pinotti. 2003. "The Political Economy of Privatization." Working Paper 2003.45, Fondazione Eni Enrico Mattei.

Boubakri, N., J-C. Cosset, and O. Guedhami. 2005. "Postprivatization Corporate Governance: The Role of Ownership Structure and Investor Protection." *Journal of Financial Economics* 76: 369–399.

Chandra, B. 1992. "The Colonial Legacy." In *The Indian Economy*, ed. B. Jalan. New Delhi: Penguin Books.

Chandrashekhar, C. and J. Ghosh. 1999. "Disinvestment at What Price?" Macroscan Policy Watch, December 28. http://www.macroscan.com/pol/dec99/pol281299Disinvestment_1.htm.

Chari, A. and N. Gupta. 2006. "Incumbents and Protectionism: The Political Economy of Foreign Entry Liberalization." Working paper.

Comptroller and Auditor General of India. 2003–2004. *Union Audit Reports*. New Delhi: Government of India.

Department of Disinvestment, Government of India. 2001. *Annual Report*. New Delhi: Government of India.

——. "Disinvestment in States." http://divest.nic.in.

——. "Disinvestment till Now." http://divest.nic.in.

Dinc, S. and N. Gupta. 2006. "The Decision to Privatize: Finance, Politics, and Patronage." Working paper.

The Economic Times. 2002. "India 8 Years Behind World in Teledensity." June 24.

Government of India. 1991. *Industrial Policy Resolution.* New Delhi: Government of India.

Goyal, S. K. 2000. "Privatization in India." In *Privatization in South Asia: Minimizing Negative Social Effects Through Restructuring,* ed. G. Joshi. New Delhi: International Labour Organization.

Gupta, N. 2005. "Partial Privatization and Firm Performance." *Journal of Finance* 60(2): 987–1015.

Gupta, N. and R. Harbaugh. 2001. "Recapturing Information Rents Through Partial and Gradual Privatization." Working paper.

Haltiwanger, J. and M. Singh. 1999. "Cross-Country Evidence on Public Sector Retrenchment." *World Bank Economic Review* 13(1): 23–66.

India Infoline. 2005. "Telecom Sector Update—May 2005." www.indiainfoline .com.

Jones, S., W. Megginson, R. Nash, and J. Netter. 1999. "Share Issue Privatizations as Financial Means to Political and Economic Ends." *Journal of Financial Economics* 53: 217–253.

Joshi, V. and I. M. D. Little. 1996. *India's Economic Reforms 1991–2001.* Oxford: Clarendon Press.

La Porta, R., F. López-de-Silanes, and A. Shleifer. 2002. "Government Ownership of Banks." *Journal of Finance* 57: 265–301.

López-de-Silanes, F. and A. Chong. 2002. "Privatization and Labor Force Restructuring Around the World." Policy Research Working Paper Series 2884. Washington, DC: World Bank.

Megginson, W. and J. Netter. 2001. "From State to Market: A Survey of Empirical Studies on Privatization." *Journal of Economic Literature* 39: 321–389.

Mohan, C. 2003. "Politics of Economic Liberalization in India." *Harvard Asia Quarterly* (September).

Perotti, E. 1995. "Credible Privatization." *American Economic Review* 85(4): 847–859.

Privatisation Commission, Government of Pakistan. http://www.privatisation. gov.pk/.

Shleifer, A. and R. W. Vishny. 1994. "Politicians and Firms." *Quarterly Journal of Economics* 109: 995–1025.

Srinivasan, T. 2003. "Privatization, Regulation, and Competition in South Asia." Center for Research on Economic Development and Policy Reform Working Paper 172. Stanford, CA: Center for Research on Economic Development and Policy Reform.

Swaminathan, S. and A. Aiyar. 2004. "Disinvestment as Soap Opera." *The Times of India,* February 29.

Vaidya Nathan, S. 2002. "PSU Stocks—Bizarre Are the Ways of Govt." *The Hindu Business Line,* November 17.

Vickers, J. and G. Yarrow. 1991. "Economic Perspectives on Privatization." *Journal of Economic Perspectives* 5: 111–132.

World Bank. 2001a. *Global Development Finance Report*. Appendix 4. Washington, DC: World Bank.

——. 2001b. "Global Development Finance 2001: Building Coalitions for Effective Development Finance." Washington, DC: World Bank.

——. Various years. *World Development Indicators*. Washington, DC: World Bank.

World Bank Privatization Database. http://rru.worldbank.org/Privatization/.

CHAPTER 7

A Critical Review of the Evolving Privatization Debate

Jomo K. S.

The impetus for privatization emerged in the 1980s under the aegis of the Thatcher government in the United Kingdom, which made privatization a core component of its economic reforms. Privatization in the United Kingdom gained momentum through politically popular projects such as the privatization of public housing. Thousands of families living in public housing became homeowners through government sales of such units. This project, while not wholly successful due to various factors (Vickers and Yarrow, 1991), was popular among segments of the working class.

Privatization soon became a central tenet of the Washington Consensus package of economic reforms associated with the neoliberal agenda (Bayliss and Cramer, 2001). The primary argument for privatization has been belief in the ability of private ownership to rectify weaknesses in state or public provision of goods and services; privatization would bring private investment and efficiency gains through overcoming principal-agent problems by giving incentives to owners.

The privatization policies promoted in recent decades have been based on some dubious theoretical bases. Privatization presumes that private ownership will generate desirable incentives to improve enterprise management (Bouin, 1992), but there is no reason to assume such an outcome unless the owners also run the enterprises, thus overcoming the principal-agent problem of public ownership. This helps explain the success of "land to the tiller" land reforms and management buyouts of small enterprises, but little else. Privatization advocates criticize the "self-serving bureaucrat" of state-owned enterprises (SOEs), but seem to ignore the likelihood of "self-serving managers" in large private enterprises as well as the distortive consequences on incentives of various efforts to address principal-agent problems in the private sector.

Yet, the British wave of privatization in the 1980s did not lead to across-the-board improvements in enterprise performance or to healthy, robust competition. The few undisputed successes (e.g., National Freight) involved employee buyouts and improving incentives, thus generating higher productivity. In the 1990s, the former Soviet Union and many Eastern European transition economies rapidly transferred state assets through "voucher privatization" programs that sought political support for privatizing assets by distributing them for free or at nominal cost to all citizens. Ultimately, many such vouchers were resold for modest gains to a handful of buyers, leading to the creation of oligarch-controlled private monopolies (Nellis, 2002). Again, the most successful privatizations, e.g., of retail shops in Hungary, were limited to the privatization of small enterprises where incentives were improved by manager or employee buyouts (Earle et al., 1994).

Despite its limited success, privatization in the United Kingdom became the model for emulation by developing country reformers. In the 1980s and 1990s, many governments in the south voluntarily climbed on the privatization bandwagon, enthusiastically led by the international financial institutions, particularly the World Bank. Elites saw the opportunities for profiteering from the policy at the expense of the state and the public.

Many developing countries adopted privatization only to deliver mixed outcomes while experiencing declining public support from citizenries, who are often initially keen for alternatives to state inefficiencies, abuses, and monopolies. Recognizing the growing popular resentment of privatization since the 1980s, privatization advocates have recently been forced to acknowledge this checkered track record, and instead now insist on improving the "preconditions" needed for privatization. The real lessons to be learned from the experiences, the need to improve and align incentives and competitive processes with the public interest, remain obscured by the property rights or ownership fetish (Bayliss and Fine, 1998). Indeed, the ideological faith in the virtues of private ownership continues to inspire privatization proponents despite its record and the lessons thereof.

PRIVATIZATION: CONCEPTUAL FOUNDATIONS

Generally, privatization has been defined in terms of the transfer of enterprise ownership from the public to the private sector. More generally, privatization, or "denationalization," refers to changing the status of a business, service, or industry from state, government, or public to private ownership or control. The term sometimes also refers to the use of private contractors to provide services previously delivered by the public sector. Privatization can be strictly defined to include only cases of the sale of 100% or at least a majority share of a public enterprise, or its assets, to private owners. Full or complete privatization would therefore mean the complete transfer of ownership and control of a government enterprise or asset to the private sector.

For many, however, the term *privatization* is often understood to include cases where less than half of the assets or shares of public enterprises are sold to private shareholders. In fact, privatization is usually understood to also include cases of partial divestiture where less than half of the assets or shares of public enterprises are sold to private shareholders, with the government retaining control through majority ownership. The definition of *privatization* in some contexts is so broad that it includes cases where private enterprises are allowed to participate in activities previously the exclusive preserve of the public sector.

By the 1980s, the generally lackluster performance of the public sector, including many public enterprises, required a policy response. Various reasons have been advanced to explain the poor performance of many public enterprises. In many instances, SOEs have been hampered by unclear or contradictory objectives. Similarly, performance criteria have been ambiguous. So-called social, but actually political (and sometimes also welfare) objectives have often been invoked to circumvent profit, efficiency, or other cost-effective criteria. Coordination problems have also been serious, especially with the different levels of government (federal, state, municipal, regional authorities, etc.) as well as inter-ministry and other intra-governmental rivalries. With the proliferation of such enterprises, many were assigned or developed similar, often redundant, functions. Monitoring and evaluation of public enterprise performance were often weak and superficial, if not absent. As larger enterprises developed in size and clout, they often became less answerable to external monitoring, let alone supervision. Off-budget agencies have proved particularly problematic, especially as they were not subject to normal federal and state budgetary constraints. And, even when public enterprises were subject to such constraints, administrative limitations and political circumstances often meant that they were only subject to "soft" budget constraints.

A key question here is whether such inefficiencies are necessarily characteristic of public or state ownership, and hence cannot be overcome except through privatization. If instead, the performance record of public enterprises is primarily due to the nature, interests, and abilities of those in charge (management) rather than to the inevitable consequences of public ownership per se (Chang and Singh, 1997), then privatization, in itself, cannot and will not overcome the root problems. Also, while privatization may improve enterprise profitability for the private owners concerned, such changes may not necessarily benefit the public or consumers, or only some at the expense of others.

Because many SOE activities are public monopolies, privatization is likely to pass monopoly powers to private interests who are likely to use this market power to maximize profits. The privatization of public services tends to burden the public, especially if charges are raised or if services provided are reduced. Obviously, private interests are only interested in profitable or potentially profitable activities and enterprises. This may mean that the government will be left with unprofitable and less profitable activities, which, consequently, will worsen overall public sector performance (Vernon-Wortzel and Wortzel, 1989). Public sector inefficiencies and other problems need to be overcome, but privatization in many developing and transition economies has primarily enriched the few with strong political connections who secure most, if not all, of these profitable opportunities, while the public interest is sacrificed and vulnerable to the powers of private business interests.

Thus, while the experiences of privatization have been shaped by their political economy contexts, its proponents claim the moral high ground in assuming that private ownership will necessarily eliminate the abuse and corruption associated with public ownership. Privatization advocates tend to conflate private property with the market, and often presume that privatization will necessarily engender competition, eliminating rents and rent-seeking behavior. Such presumptions and claims have been misguided. Privatization advocates have also neglected to consider alternative prescriptions for mitigating corrupt behavior, e.g., by focusing on rent management for development by structuring rents to create incentives for desired behavior instead of simply seeking the avoidance or elimination of rents.

OLD ARGUMENTS

It is worthwhile to critically review some of the major arguments made for adopting privatization policies. First, privatization is supposed to reduce the financial and administrative burdens of the government, particularly in providing and maintaining services and infrastructure. Second, it is expected to promote competition, improve efficiency, and increase productivity in the delivery of these services. Third, privatization is expected to stimulate private entrepreneurship and investment, and thus accelerate economic growth. Fourth, it is expected to help reduce the presence and size of the public sector, with its monopolistic tendencies and bureaucratic support. To put it differently, then, privatization is supposed to accelerate growth, improve efficiency and productivity, shrink the public sector, and reduce the government's financial and administrative roles and responsibilities. These arguments in favor of privatization have been refuted on the following grounds:

1. The public sector can be more efficiently run, as has been demonstrated in many countries. Also, privatization is not going to provide a miracle cure for all the problems (especially the inefficiencies) associated with the public sector, nor can private enterprise guarantee that the public interest is most effectively served by private interests taking over public sector activities. Also, by diverting private sector capital from new productive investments to buying existing public sector assets, economic growth would be retarded, rather than accelerated.

2. Greater public accountability and a more transparent public sector would ensure greater efficiency in achieving the public and national interest while limiting public sector waste and borrowing.

3. The government would be able to privatize only profitable or potentially profitable enterprises and activities because the private sector would only be interested in these.

4. Privatization may postpone a fiscal crisis by temporarily reducing fiscal deficits, but it could also exacerbate it in the medium term because the public sector would lose income from the more profitable public sector activities and would be stuck with financing the unprofitable ones, which would undermine the potential for cross-subsidization within the public sector.

5. Privatization tends to adversely affect the interests of public sector employees and the public, especially of poorer consumers, which the public sector is usually more sensitive to.

6. Privatization would give priority to profit maximization at the expense of social welfare and the public interest, except on the rare occasions when the two coincide; hence, for example, only profitable new

services would be introduced, rather than services needed by the public, especially the poor and politically uninfluential, or for development.

7. Public pressure to ensure equitable distribution of share ownership may inadvertently undermine pressures to improve corporate performance, because each shareholder would then only have a small equity stake and would therefore be unlikely to incur the high costs of monitoring management and corporate performance.

According to several criteria, privatization in many countries has been making good progress. Privatization has been credited with enhancing economic growth, and resources are said to have been released through efficiency gains for corporate expansion, although no strong evidence of this has been produced (United Nations, 1995). Growth is also said to have been generated by allowing private entrepreneurship in sectors previously monopolized by the government. While this seems plausible, the examples of build-operate-transfer projects and licensed activities are less than convincing (Augenblick and Custer, 1990) because they merely involve the private sector substituting for what the public sector would otherwise have undertaken, typically at lower cost to users.

The privatization debate has since shifted with its current acknowledgment of the difficulties of implementation. The new privatization advocacy recognizes many of the privatization failures of the 1980s and 1990s and blames them on unfavorable conditions. The revised advocacy view puts greater emphasis on the need to prepare more favorable conditions for privatization to succeed, i.e., on creating the preconditions for successful privatization.

Privatization advocates now include several lessons in the privatization prescription. Emphasizing practical problems of implementation, they suggest that (1) governments must create more favorable preconditions (e.g., by providing better regulatory and institutional frameworks) and (2) reforms should be tailor-made and should not utilize a one-size-fits-all approach (i.e., strategies for privatization must adapt to local conditions) as well as ensure a level playing field in promoting transparent and competitive bidding processes (Kikeri and Nellis, 2004; Kikeri and Kolo, 2005).

The agenda today accepts that change of ownership alone is not sufficient for success. Privatization reforms now need to pay more attention to the regulatory environment, pricing policies, and context specificities to facilitate and encourage private sector participation. Advocates now recognize that the state has a larger role to play in supporting competitive markets and nurturing private sector growth; SOEs cannot simply be replaced by private firms, with capital accumulation, growth, technological progress, healthy competition, and the public interest ensured.

The more sophisticated privatization advocates today accept that, in the past, privatizations were often premature, but now insist that with the appropriate preconditions established, the privatization strategy still remains almost universally desirable. The government's role then is primarily to help private enterprise ensure a smooth transition from state to private ownership. The state is now expected to crowd in, not crowd out, private investments by investing considerable public revenue to improve conditions that cause SOEs to perform poorly to ensure the greater profitability of privatized SOEs.

PRIVATIZATION VERSUS STATE REFORM

It is often overlooked that likely gains actually achieved are generally due to improvements in incentives—improvements that could mostly be made to publicly owned organizations through less obtrusive policies than a complete change of ownership. While the distribution of welfare consequences necessarily changes as a result of partial divestiture, firm behavior need not. Hence, partial divestiture may be merely cosmetic, e.g., giving the appearance of privatization without changing firm conduct. Advocates of partial divestiture claim, however, that the resulting mixed (public-private) enterprises ensure the best of both worlds by introducing (private) pressures for greater efficiency while ensuring (public) accountability and interests. Critics emphasize that the result is the worst of both worlds, with the private pursuit of profits augmented by government privileges (regulation, licensing, credit, etc.).

The key question is whether the ostensible efficiency and welfare gains from partial divestiture could have been achieved without such divestiture. For example, could such gains have been made through other means of ensuring greater autonomy, flexibility, or managerial reform, such as through competition, corporatization, and commercialization? After all, the presence of private shareholders may only give the government the excuse it needs to do what it wanted to do before. However, this does not negate the fact that the welfare gains claimed cannot be attributed to partial divestiture, or that there are viable policy alternatives to partial divestiture that should be seriously considered by the authorities concerned. The most compelling argument for partial divestiture is that the presence of private shareholders reduces the probability of reversal of efficiency-enhancing public enterprise reforms, e.g., with the change of government.

In many cases, supposed privatization has actually involved only partial divestiture, with majority ownership, and hence ultimate control, still in the hands of the government, which usually remains the majority or largest shareholder. Even when the government share should decline to less than half, in preparing some enterprises for privatization, governments create preferential or golden share arrangements, allowing them to retain control even with considerably diminished minority ownership. Such partial divestiture cannot really be considered privatization because the government's power to determine firm behavior is virtually unchanged, though, of course, firm behavior may change in response to the presence of the other minority owners.

Privatization has generally reduced the size of government bureaucracy in personnel terms. While most affected public sector employees used to feel threatened by privatization, many others—fed up with the waste, inefficiency, and corruption usually associated with the public sector—have been indifferent to, if not supportive of, the policy. Some other more ideological proponents identify state intervention with socialism and support privatization as a measure to restore capitalist hegemony. While statist capitalism is not socialism, undermining the public sector, especially public services, through privatization has important adverse welfare implications for the public, especially public sector employees, consumers, and the poor.

Governments have had to legislate many changes to existing laws to facilitate privatization. The primary concern has been with overcoming legal obstacles and disincentives to privatization. Little attention has gone to ensuring greater competition or public or consumer accountability, matters of considerable public concern, as many privatized entities remain virtual monopolies. Because there is not much scope for increasing competition with natural monopolies, proponents promise appropriate regulatory frameworks to protect consumer interests, particularly in terms of price, quality, and availability of services, as well as commercial freedom for private monopolies. Implicit in this formulation is the acknowledgment that such regulation does not yet exist and, if introduced, is unlikely to threaten enterprise autonomy.

Efforts to encourage competition remain well behind those of privatization. While there has been a great deal of rhetoric about deregulation accompanying privatization, such efforts have been quite limited and mainly oriented to inducing foreign investments. Golden share agreements, discussed earlier, guarantee ultimate control over the privatized enterprise, ostensibly to exercise veto powers over decisions of strategic and public significance. Such powers suggest only limited loosening of public sector control through privatization. Privatization, in itself, then involves only the transfer of property rights, and in many instances (e.g., the privatization of major public utilities and management buyouts), management personnel have not even been significantly changed.

Improvements in management generally reflect managerial initiatives encouraged by increased enterprise and administrative autonomy as well as new incentive systems, i.e., changes that do not require privatization as a prerequisite but can alternatively be achieved by greater decentralization, devolution, or administrative authority, long advocated by trade unions and others in the public sector in many societies. If one accepts the view that competition and enterprise reorganization—rather than mere changes in ownership status—are more likely to induce greater enterprise efficiency, then it becomes difficult to conclude that economic efficiency has been improved because of privatization. Some of the often exaggerated efficiency gains attributed to privatization have been brought about by greater employee and managerial motivation with new incentive systems and greater scope for managerial initiatives with administrative autonomy, i.e., enterprise reform.

While privatization undoubtedly reduces the role of the public sector in the economy, it is not clear whether shrinking the state-owned sector is an end in itself or merely the means to an end. If it is the former, then the policy is often essentially intended to aggrandize its politically influential beneficiaries, or is clearly ideological in inspiration, or else is meant to please ideologically motivated governments and the powerful international economic institutions (such as the World Bank and regional development banks) that developing country governments seek to find favor with.

Claims that privatization will reduce the government's financial and administrative burdens are therefore misleading and flawed. While there undoubtedly have been one-off revenue gains for governments from the sale of public assets, the retention of such assets could have been in the government's and the public's medium- and long-term interest for the variety of reasons mentioned earlier. Perhaps most importantly, the considerable evidence of heavy discounting in public asset prices for sale or lease in conjunction with privatization suggests otherwise. Also, the sale of the government's most valuable assets, while it is obliged to retain less profitable activities and assets of little interest to the profit-seeking private sector, contributes to the self-fulfilling prophecy of the unprofitability of public sector economic activities. The shrinking of the public sector also reduces the scope for government intervention, e.g., for equity reasons or in support of industrial policy.

There should instead be a comprehensive critical review of the public sector, including statutory bodies and other public enterprises, to enhance efficiency and cost-effectiveness as well as dynamic, equitable, balanced, and sustainable national economic development. After all, many public enterprises were set up precisely because the private sector was unable or unwilling to provide the services and goods concerned. Such arguments may still be relevant in some cases, no longer relevant in other cases, and perhaps never even true or relevant in yet other cases. And regardless of the validity of the rationale for their establishment in the first place, many public enterprises have turned out to be problematic, often inefficient, frequently even failing to achieve their own original declared objectives or abused by those who control them for their own ends, and draining scarce public resources due to their soft budget constraints and the very inertia associated with their existence.

But privatization is certainly not a universal panacea for the myriad problems of the public sector, as is often touted. Privatization may be no more of a solution to the problems of public enterprises than public enterprises have been a solution to the problems they were ostensibly set up to overcome. In many instances, the problem of public enterprise is not a problem of ownership per se, but rather due to the absence of explicit, feasible, or achievable objectives, or even to the existence of too many, often contradictory goals. In other cases, the absence of managerial and organizational systems (e.g., flexibility, autonomy) and cultures that support and encourage fulfillment of these goals and objectives may be the key problem (Vernon-Wortzel and Wortzel, 1989). Privatization may seem to facilitate the achievement of such organizational goals or objectives due to the changes following privatization, but this does not necessarily mean that such improvements are due to privatization per se. In such cases, managerial and organizational reforms may well achieve the same objectives and goals, or even do better. However, the better option cannot be determined a priori, but should instead follow from careful analysis of the roots of an organization's malaise.

Such a critical review to consider reform should consider the variety of modes of privatization, marketization, and other reform measures as options in dealing with the public sector. Thus, privatization becomes one of several options available to the government for dealing with the undoubted malaise of many public sectors. This flexible approach seems superior to the current narrow and dogmatic approach, which presumes privatization to be the only or best solution to a complex variety of problems faced by public enterprises. The approach also neglects the persistent problems faced by the rest of the public sector not targeted for privatization, which may in fact require more urgent attention. Ironically, their problems are often the most serious, and hence in greater need of remedy, which usually explains the lack of private sector interest in privatizing them. Furthermore, if privatization succeeds in selling off the sector's most profitable enterprises and activities, the public sector will be left with uneconomic, unprofitable, and unattractive enterprises and activities, thus only confirming prejudices and charges of public sector incompetence and inefficiency, besides worsening the public sector deficit and reducing possibilities for cross-subsidization.

In contrast to privatization, which essentially involves only property rights, the broader concept of marketization—sometimes termed "commercialization" or, even more ambiguously, "economic liberalization"—is understood not only to entail denationalization, but also market liberalization, involving greater competition. Privatization is widely expected to be accompanied by the relaxation or abolition of monopolistic practices, including statutory monopoly powers, such as those usually conferred on and enjoyed by public utilities. Privatized entities are thus expected to find themselves in competitive markets or environments. Competition generally encourages more efficient behavior among private—as well as public—entities or companies in order to achieve both productive and allocative efficiencies.

Enhanced efficiency is therefore conceived of as the result of the interaction between private ownership and the competitive environment. Hence, a privatization exercise that merely involves selling a portion, even a majority, of the shares of a public enterprise to the public, but is not accompanied by greater exposure to market forces, may not bring about desired efficiency improvements. Conversely, efficiency gains may be achieved through other changes, like management reforms, without any changes in ownership. Even improvements in capital resource allocation may be achieved by eliminating soft budget constraints (typically identified with, but not a necessary characteristic of, public sectors) as well as strengthening management accountability, e.g., through greater organizational transparency.

Frequently, desired improvements in efficiency may not be achieved through privatization, because there has been mixed evidence of increased competition associated with privatization. Some of the selected enterprises already privatized or expected to be privatized are natural monopolies. Thus, if privatization merely involves transforming a public monopoly into a private monopoly, consumer welfare may well be adversely affected. In such circumstances, even greater enterprise efficiency may not necessarily enhance consumer welfare; rather, only the monopoly profits accruing to the privatized enterprise. To evaluate the impact of privatization on the economic performance of an enterprise is not easy. There is uneven evidence suggesting improvements in various aspects of some firm performances following privatization. The problem is that such improved performance may be wrongly attributed to changes in ownership per se, without any conclusive evidence of such causation. Efficiency gains, for instance, may well be due to other changes coinciding with, but not caused by, the change in ownership considered to be privatization.

The failures, other problems, and unpopularity of privatization have forced the World Bank and other earlier advocates of privatization to pause and revise their analysis and advocacy of privatization. They now implicitly recognize that privatization per se has little to do with marketization and liberalization, and greater emphasis is now sometimes given to the latter in line with the broader thrust for economic liberalization associated with them. Relatedly, it is difficult for them to justify strengthening intellectual property rights—and the exclusive monopoly rights associated with them—in relation to the broader economic liberalization agenda.

In order to be able to credibly continue advocacy of privatization in the face of its track record of failures, abuses, and inequity, privatization advocates now put much more emphasis on correct sequencing and establishing the preconditions for privatization before actually undertaking it. Hence, much more attention is now placed on prior legal development, ensuring a well functioning capital market as well as protection of consumer and employee concerns, if not rights. This more nuanced approach has caused some anti-privatization campaigners to claim victory, although such claims are premature. The existence of a growing body of research underscoring such problems, including work done by agencies that have been advocating privatization, has also been misinterpreted as suggesting a U-turn by these institutions. Such agencies have long tolerated varying degrees of self-critical research, and it would be misleading to prematurely conclude that such critical research has profoundly affected operations, including the advocacy of privatization by country teams providing policy advice or imposing policy conditionalities on borrowing governments.

It is also important to acknowledge that there are significant constituencies favoring or even advocating privatization in the countries concerned. These are not simply the corporate interests who hope to acquire and operate lucrative business opportunities arising from privatization. Many financial institutions also recognize the opportunities available to them from such privatizations. But perhaps more important from a political point of view in democratic polities is the popular resentment of the abuses and inefficiencies often widely associated with the state-owned sector. The transnational advocacy of privatization has successfully mobilized media and public support for their cause by drawing on such popular frustrations. Until there is a credible and popular effort at reform of the SOEs to minimize such abuses and inefficiencies, it will be difficult for the embattled anti-privatization advocates to succeed in their efforts.

NOTE

Acknowledgments: I am grateful to Sheila Chanani of the Initiative for Policy Dialogue, Columbia University, for helping me prepare this at short notice. I also want to thank Noelle Rodriguez and Suzette Limchoc for additional help.

REFERENCES

Augenblick, M. and B. S. Custer Jr. 1990. "The Build, Operate and Transfer (BOT) Approach to Infrastructure Projects in Developing Countries." Working Paper 498. Washington, DC: World Bank.

Bayliss, K. and C. Cramer. 2001. "Privatisation and the Post-Washington Consensus: Between the Lab and the Real World?" In *Development Policy in the Twenty-First Century*, ed. B. Fine, C. Lapavitsas, and J. Pincus, 52–79. London: Routledge.

Bayliss, K. and B. Fine. 1998. "Beyond 'Bureaucrats in Business': A Critical Review of the World Bank Approach to Privatisation and Public Sector Reform." *Journal of International Development* 10: 841–855.

——, eds. 2007. *Privatization and Alternative Public Sector Reform in Sub-Saharan Africa: Delivering Electricity and Water.* London: Palgrave Macmillan.

Bouin, O. 1992. "Privatisation in Developing Countries: Reflections on a Panacea." Policy Brief 3. Paris: OECD Development Centre.

Chang, H-J. and A. Singh. 1997. "Can Large Firms Be Run Efficiently Without Being Bureaucratic?" *Journal of International Development* 9(6): 865–875.

Earle, J., R. Frydman, A. Rapaczynski, and J. Turkewitz. 1994. *Small Privatization: Transformation of Retail Trade and Service Sectors in Poland, Hungary and the Czech Republic.* New York: Central European University Press.

Kikeri, S. and A. F. Kolo. 2005. "Privatization: Trends and Recent Development." Policy Research Working Paper 3765. Washington, DC: World Bank.

Kikeri, S. and J. Nellis. 2004. "An Assessment of Privatization." *The World Bank Research Observer* 19(1): 87–118.

Nellis, J. 1986. "Public Enterprises in Sub-Saharan Africa." Discussion Paper 1. Washington, DC: World Bank.

———. 2002. "The World Bank, Privatization and Enterprise Reform in Transition Economies: A Retrospective Analysis." Washington, DC: Operations Evaluation Department, World Bank.

Singh, A. and A. Zammit. 2006. "Corporate Governance, Crony Capitalism and Economic Crises: Should the US Business Model Replace the Asian Way of 'Doing Business'?" *Corporate Governance: An International Review* 14(4): 220–233.

United Nations. 1995. *Comparative Experiences with Privatization: Policy Insights and Lessons Learned.* Geneva: United Nations Conference on Trade and Development.

Vernon-Wortzel, H. and L. Wortzel. 1989. "Privatization: Not the Only Answer." *World Development* 17(5): 633–641.

Vickers, J. and G. Yarrow. 1991. "Economic Perspectives on Privatization." *Journal of Economic Perspectives* 5(2): 111–132.

World Bank. 2004. *Operational Guidance for World Bank Group Staff: Public and Private Sector Roles in the Supply of Electricity Services.* Washington, DC: Energy and Mining Sector Board, World Bank Group.

Bernardo Bortolotti is an associate professor of economics at the University of Turin and executive director of Fondazione Eni Enrico Mattei. He received his Ph.D. in economics from the Université Catholique de Louvain. His research interests are in privatization, regulation, and corporate governance. Bortolotti has served as a consultant for the World Bank and as secretary of the Italian Global Advisory Committee on Privatization. He is the founder and scientific coordinator of Privatization Barometer (www.privatizationbarometer.net).

Antonio Estache is a professor at the European Centre for Advanced Research in Economics and Statistics (ECARES) of the Universite Libre de Bruxelles. Prior to his position at ECARES, Dr. Estache worked for 25 years at the World Bank, where he advised governments on various types of public sector reforms, including tax reform, infrastructure privatization, and regulation. In addition, he has taught regulation at universities in Africa, Asia, Europe, Latin America, and North America.

Nandini Gupta is an assistant professor of finance at Indiana University's Kelley School of Business. She obtained her doctorate from the University of Pittsburgh. Prior to Indiana University, she was at the William Davidson Institute at the University of Michigan. Her research focuses on reforms that facilitate the development of financial markets, with a particular emphasis on privatization. She has looked at the design of these reforms, the political economy of the decision to adopt them, and their impact on firms and industries. Gupta serves as a consultant to the World Bank, and her work has been published in leading economics and finance journals.

Gupta's work has been published in the *Journal of Finance, Journal of Financial Economics, RAND Journal of Economics,* and *European Economic Review.*

Jan Hanousek is Citigroup Professor of Economics at the Center for Economic Research and Graduate Education of Charles University and the Economics Institute of the Academy of Sciences of the Czech Republic (CERGE-EI), whose research interests include applied economics and econometrics, international money and finance, and European integration. He is former director of CERGE-EI, Prague, and he has been a research fellow at the Centre for Economic Policy Research (CEPR), London, the William Davidson Institute, University of Michigan, and affiliated faculty at the Center for Organizational Dynamics, University of Pennsylvania. Prior to joining CERGE-EI, Hanousek received a scholarship at Banach Center, Warsawand, and was a visiting research fellow at Carleton University, Ottawa; the Free University, Amsterdam; Princeton University; and the University of Pennsylvania.

Hanousek's principal fields of specialization are econometrics, applied finance, and development economics. His work covers various theoretical and applied econometric problems in both micro and macro areas. During his professional career, Hanousek has written more than 30 articles and book chapters that have appeared in numerous professional publications.

Jomo Kwame Sundaram is Assistant Secretary General for Economic Development in the United Nations Department of Economic and Social Affairs. Previously he was a professor of applied economics at the University of Malasiya. His other teaching experience includes Harvard University, Yale University, the National University of Malaysia, the Science University of Malaysia, Cambridge University, Cornell University, and the National University of Singapore. Jomo studied at Yale and Harvard, where he received his Ph.D. He has authored over 35 monographs, edited over 50 books, and translated 12 volumes, besides writing many academic papers and articles for the media. He is on the editorial boards of several academic journals and was founder chair of International Development Economics Associates. His books include *Privatizing Malaysia: Rents, Rhetoric, Realities* (1995).

Evžen Kočenda received a Ph.D. in economics from the University of Houston, following his early education at the Prague School of Economics and the University of Toledo in Ohio. He is currently a professor of economics at CERGE-EI. In addition to his teaching commitments, Kočenda is a member of the editorial board of the *Czech Journal of Finance and Economics,* a research affiliate of CEPR, and a research fellow of the William Davidson Institute. He has taught widely as a visiting scholar and continues to hold leading and advisory roles on numerous economic and scientific boards and committees.

Valentina Milella is a senior researcher in the Privatization, Regulation and Corporate Governance research program at Fondazione Eni Enrico Mattei in Milan. She is an economics graduate of the University of Turin, Italy. Milella has written several papers on privatization and is currently working as a researcher for the Understanding Privatization Policies Project funded by the European Commission. She is also senior analyst at Privatization Barometer (www.privatizationbarometer.net).

John Nellis is a nonresident senior fellow at the Center for Global Development in Washington, D.C., and principal of the consulting/research firm International Analytics. From 1984 to 2000 he worked at the World Bank, managing privatization assistance to client countries in Eastern Europe, Latin America, and Africa. Before joining the World Bank, Nellis was a university professor in Kenya, Canada, and the United States and an official of the Ford Foundation in North Africa. Recent publications include a volume coedited with Nancy Birdsall, *Reality Check: The Distributional Impact of Privatization in Developing Countries* (2005); "Privatization: A Summary Assessment" (*SAIS Review of International Affairs* 27(2), Fall 2007); and "Leaps of Faith: Launching the Privatization Process in Transition" in *Privatization in Transition Economies* (forthcoming in 2008).

Gérard Roland joined the faculty at the University of California, Berkeley, in 2001. He received his Ph.D. from Universite Libre de Bruxelles in 1988 and taught there from 1988 to 2001. Roland is also a CEPR research fellow, where he was program director between 1995 and 2006. He serves as editor of the *Journal of Comparative Economics* and was an associate editor of several other journals.

Roland has been one of the leading researchers in the field of transition economics and wrote the only existing graduate textbook on the subject. He has made important and widely cited contributions not only on privatization but also on the political economy of transition, enterprise restructuring, financial reform, and the macroeconomics of transition. Roland has also made important contributions in political economy. His contributions span from the optimal speed and sequencing of reforms to the breakup of nations and federalism to the separation of powers in democracies and comparative analysis of parliamentary and presidential systems.

Among Roland's awards and honors are recipient of the Medal of the University of Helsinki, Officier de l'Ordre de Leopold II, and entries in *Who's Who in the World, Who's Who in America,* and *Who's Who in Economics since 1776.* He was a fellow at the Center for Advanced Studies in Behavioral Sciences in Stanford during 1998–1999. He was program chair of the Fifth Nobel Symposium in Economics devoted to the economics of transition in 1999. He was named Jean Monnet Professor at Universite Libre de Bruxelles in 2001 and received an honorary professorship at Renmin University of China in 2002.

Joseph E. Stiglitz is University Professor at Columbia University, copresident of the Initiative for Policy Dialogue, and chair of Columbia's Committee on Global Thought. He holds a part-time appointment at the Brooks World Poverty Institute of the University of Manchester, England. In 2001 he was awarded the Nobel Prize in economics for his analysis of the role of information asymmetry in market failure. He served as chair of the Council of Economic Advisers during the Clinton administration and then as Chief Economist and Senior Vice-President of the World Bank from 1997 to 2000. His most recent book, *Globalization and Its Discontents* (2001), is an international bestseller translated into 28 languages.

Jan Svejnar is the Everett E. Berg Professor of Business Administration, director of the International Policy Center, and a professor of economics and public policy at the University of Michigan. His areas of interest include economic development and transition, labor economics, and behavior of the firm. Svejnar's research focuses on the determinants and effects of government policies on firms and labor and capital markets, corporate and national governance and performance, and entrepreneurship. He has published widely and serves as an adviser to governments and firms in advanced and emerging market economies.

Lourdes Trujillo is a professor at the University of Las Palmas de Gran Canaria, where she teaches microeconomics. She has served as an adviser on infrastructure reform to various Spanish authorities and Latin American governments as well as to global agencies, including the European Union, the Organisation for Economic Co-operation and Development, and the World Bank.

INDEX

Note: Page numbers followed by *f* or *t* indicate figures or tables.